The Story of Knighton

The Story of Knighton

by

Keith Parker

LOGASTON PRESS

LOGASTON PRESS
Little Logaston Woonton Almeley
Herefordshire HR3 6QH
logastonpress.co.uk

First published by Logaston Press 2012
Copyright © Keith Parker 2012

ISBN 978 1 906663 64 3

Typeset by Logaston Press
and printed and bound in printed in Spain
by Graphy Cems

For Steve, Sue and Jeremy

Contents

Acknowledgements

In writing this book I have incurred many obligations, not least to the historians of both the past and present from whom I have gained many insights into the development of Knighton. My thanks are also due to the staff of many record offices and libraries, who dealt with my many queries with unfailing patience and courtesy. In this respect I should especially mention Catherine Richards and the staff of Powys County Archives Office. My thanks are also due to Edward Harley, who most kindly gave me access to his family archives at Brampton Bryan; to Neil King, the town clerk of Knighton, who made the Town Council Minutes for 1974-2000 available for me to study; and lastly to Paul Woodfield and the Radnorshire Society who have allowed me to reproduce a map of medieval Knighton from the Society's *Transactions* of 1973. My interest in the history of Knighton was first aroused by conversations with the late Mary Cadwallader back in the 1980s, and my knowledge of its history in recent decades has been greatly enhanced by more recent conversations with Roger Bright, Roy Edwards and Neil King.

My thanks are also due to those who have kindly allowed me to reproduce documents, paintings and photographs as illustrations: Roger Bright (plates 1, 17, 18, 22, 27, 28, 31, 35, 36, 39 and 42-55); the late Mary Cadwallader (plates 15 and 16); Edward Harley (plates 5, 6 and 7); Tony Hobbs (plate 19); Judge's Lodgings (plates 11, 30, 32 and 33); Logaston Press (plate 8, courtesy of Edward Harley); National Library of Wales (plates 37 and 38); Joan Parker (plates 2, 3, 4, 9, 14, 21, 23, 29, 34, 40, 41 and 56); Jonathan Coltman Rogers (plate 12) and Wooden Books Ltd (plates 10, 13, 20, 24, 25 and 26).

I am also indebted to Andy and Karen Johnson of Logaston Press, who have nudged me into providing greater detail and precision in the text and also 'eased' my very formal academic written style, and transformed my ill-drawn sketch maps into models of clarity. Lastly, and by no means least, I must thank my wife Joan, who acted as my photographer and taxi driver and has shown, as ever, considerable patience and forbearance in tolerating my sometimes unreasonable preoccupation with matters historical.

Foreword

Although this book covers the history of Knighton from early times until almost the present day, it is mainly concerned with the period from the 1770s to the 1970s and seeks to explain the way in which the present townscape and local economy have evolved. An attempt has been made to provide a personal dimension to the story of the town by highlighting the contribution made to the town by outstanding individuals whose achievements may have been all but forgotten.

During the 60 years or so since the publication of William Hatfield's history of Knighton, perspectives have changed substantially, while the sources available to the historian have not only increased greatly, they have also become more accessible, thanks to detailed cataloguing and the advent of the internet. As a result our understanding of the history of the town has been greatly enhanced, not least by the publications of Frank Noble, the town's eminent recent historian, but also by other articles published in the *Transactions* of the Radnorshire Society and other journals. Our knowledge of the town during the last century or so has also gained considerably from the publication of reminiscences of several old inhabitants, most notably that by the late Mary Cadwallader, which includes a large selection of photographs of old Knighton.

However such memoirs, like learned journals, are not always readily accessible to the general reader, while not all the relevant articles, books and theses have the history of Knighton as their central theme. An important task has therefore been one of synthesis, to update William Hatfield's conclusions of 1947 in light of recent research. Thus to some extent the book relies upon the scholarship and hard work of many others, particularly so in respect of the pre-17th century sections, though the responsibility for the conclusions arrived at, and for any errors, rests solely with myself.

One of the more unusual features of this book is the reliance on newspapers which have been the major source for the chapters on 19th- and 20th-century Knighton. Such reliance is not without its dangers, but it should be noted that since the Hereford newspapers of the 19th century and the Radnorshire newspapers of the early 20th centuries represented either the Conservative or Liberal standpoint, any marked departure from factual accuracy on the part of one newspaper was quickly shown up by its contemporary rival.

A full bibliography has been provided to assist anyone who wishes to research an aspect of the town's history in greater depth. For the same reason, detailed notes on the sources have been provided for each chapter at the end of the book.

Map showing Knighton in relation to other settlements mentioned in the text on either side of the English/Welsh border

Introduction

Knighton is the classic border town. It lies on the west bank of the River Teme which, for the most part, marks the boundary between Wales and England in the locality. The town also lies immediately to the east of Offa's Dyke, long regarded as the traditional boundary between the two countries, Knighton's Welsh name, *Tref-y-Clawdd,* 'the town on the Dyke', serves to emphasise its border status.

Lying at the point where the hitherto narrow valley of the Teme begins to broaden out, Knighton is situated at the junction of two contrasting physical regions with complementary rural economies: the Welsh uplands ready to trade dairy products and store cattle and later, store sheep, and the more fertile rolling countryside of south Shropshire and north-western Herefordshire producing cereals, fatstock, hops and cider. It is not surprising that Knighton developed into the major market town of Radnorshire with a hinterland that included most of the north-east and north-central regions of the county as well as the adjacent areas of Shropshire and Herefordshire. In addition to its role as a market, Knighton also processed much of the agricultural produce of its hinterland and provided the goods and services which the surrounding countryside could not provide for itself.

Until the advent of the railway in the mid-17th century Knighton's links with Wales beyond its own hinterland were difficult, and the town's commercial links were with its English neighbours: Ludlow, Leominster and Shrewsbury. English influences were thus always strong. The local farming pattern, the local accent and the town's vernacular architecture have much more in common with north-west Herefordshire and south Shropshire than with the Radnorshire heartland, characteristics which should remind us that the town was considered to be in England until 1536, when the county of Radnorshire was created and it was placed unambiguously in Wales by the Acts of Union. Even then, until 1921 Knighton lay in the English diocese of Hereford, rather than in the Welsh diocese of St David's, which included all but a few of the other Radnorshire parishes.

However, countervailing Welsh influences have been much stronger than has been the case with Knighton's near neighbour, Presteigne. Thanks to the weekly market and the busy livestock auction markets which continued to flourish into the second half of the 20th century, Knighton has always maintained strong commercial and personal links with the sparsely populated Radnorshire heartland, where Welsh cultural influences have remained stronger than on the south-eastern fringes of the county. Again, continuous migration from the Welsh uplands, encapsulated in the old Radnorshire tradition of going 'up country for a wife and down country for a farm', has also served to keep Knighton much more Welsh in outlook than initial impressions might suggest.

Like most small market towns, Knighton has never found it easy to flourish, given its small customer base. Even so, Knighton has shown a capacity to survive and to adjust to economic changes, notably the development of industrial mass production in the late 19th century which destroyed many of the old trades and crafts. The town's prosperity was probably at its height between 1850 and 1970, since when changes in the structure of agriculture, increased mobility and changes in consumers' shopping patterns, have meant that Knighton can no longer rely solely upon its function as a market town for its prosperity.

ORIGINS

In the wider Knighton area there have been considerably more Neolithic and Bronze Age finds than in the Presteigne area. These include significant numbers of arrowheads, scrapers and small flints, particularly in the Heyope valley and the Racecourse, Knucklas; hammer axes at Stanage and Bryndraenog; a palstave at Llanfairwaterdine; and the Bronze Age tumulus dating from *c.*1500 BC discovered during road widening at Jackets Well in 1935. This more intensive occupation may have been because glaciation produced a landscape more conducive to human occupation than had been the case in the marshy Lugg valley bottom. Another factor was the important prehistoric route that passed through the Knighton area, running from Rhayader, via Abbey Cwmhir and Llanbister, through the gap between Beacon Hill and Radnor Forest to the head of the Heyope valley, to then either link up with the Clun ridgeway, or continue on down the Teme valley.[1] The area also contains two Iron Age forts, Caer Caradoc, 4½ miles to the north-east of the town, and Coxall Knoll, 5 miles to the east, near Bucknell, both associated by local tradition, now discredited, with Caratacus and the last stages of his resistance to the Romans.

Plate 1: The Iron Age hillfort now known as Caer Caradoc

The town's Welsh name, *Tref-y-Clawdd*, dating from 840 and usually rendered as 'the town on the Dyke', would seem to provide an obvious clue as to its origins. Thus Sir Cyril Fox in his survey of Offa's Dyke published in 1955, sees Knighton as initially an Anglo-Saxon town, occupying a well defended position on the Dyke which had been constructed by Offa of Mercia (757-796) between 780 and 790 to mark the negotiated boundary between his kingdom and the Welsh principalities or kingdoms of Powys, Gwynedd and Gwent.

Knighton's 'top of the town' above The Narrows certainly occupies a strong position on a promontory of high ground extending out from Garth Hill. It was defended to the west by a well defined section of the Dyke, to the north by a steep slope down to the Teme and to the south by a still steeper slope down to the Wylcwm Brook. The only access was by a climb up a steep hogsback slope, now occupied by Broad Street and High Street. However Frank Noble contests Fox's view, pointing out that, except the Dyke itself, no archaeological evidence has been found of such a settlement. Noble argues that the first element of the Welsh name of the town, *tref* meaning 'town', 'township' or even 'household', suggests a civilian rather than a military origin. He suggests that if the settlement had primarily a defensive function, its Welsh name would probably contain an element such as *caer* or *din*, meaning 'fort' or 'stronghold'.[2] In this instance *tref* would most likely refer to a township, the settlement probably consisting of no more than six or seven dwellings. Noble also takes issue with the suggestion of the Radnorshire historian Jonathan Williams, accepted by William Hatfield, that Knighton may have been a pre-Offan settlement, arguing that in spite of its strong natural defences, there was no archaeological evidence to support the contention.[3]

In order to understand Noble's views as to Knighton's origins it is necessary to consider the various views as to the origins and purpose of Offa's Dyke, bearing in mind that in the absence of documentary evidence as to the making of the Dyke, 'nothing is possible beyond speculation and intelligent guesswork'. The attribution of the Dyke to Offa in Asser's *Life of King Alfred*, together with a folk memory that gave the name of *Offedich* to the central part of the earthwork, was known in the Middle Ages.[3]

Following eight years of fieldwork between 1925 and 1932 along the line of the Dyke, initially reported in *Archaeologia Cambrensis* between 1926 and 1934, Sir Cyril Fox published his considered conclusions in his *Offa's Dyke* in 1955. He saw the Dyke as a negotiated boundary rather than a military barrier between Mercia and the Welsh principalities or kingdoms, stretching 149 miles from the coast at Prestatyn in the north to Sedbury Cliffs on the Severn Estuary in the south. He was prepared however to concede that the Dyke had a defensive purpose, in that it channelled traffic through controlled crossing points.[4] He identified some 81 miles of constructed earthwork, fairly continuous in the central uplands but intermittent elsewhere, while stretches of the rivers Severn and Wye served as the boundary in some areas. He considered that in some parts of Herefordshire dense impenetrable woodland made any marked boundary both unnecessary and impracticable.

Frank Noble, a local teacher who researched, lectured and wrote upon the historical geography of the area, was fascinated by the Dyke and spent many years walking and researching it. It also provided the theme for his M. Phil. thesis in 1978, a section of which, dealing with the southern two-thirds of the Dyke, was published in 1983 under the title *Offa's Dyke Reviewed*. One objection to Fox's view of the Dyke as a boundary between Mercia and the Welsh is that it leaves a number of early Anglo-Saxon settlements in the Radnor valley (Downton, Walton, Womaston, Harpton and Kinnerton), the Arrow valley (Burlinjobb), the Lugg Valley (Cascob, Weston and Pilleth) and the Teme valley (Llanfairwaterdine) on the Welsh side of the Dyke, along with others in the Severn valley in Montgomeryshire. Noble thought it highly unlikely that a powerful king such as Offa would have agreed to a boundary leaving Mercian settlements and valuable agricultural land under Welsh control. Nor do township or parish boundaries follow the Dyke in the Radnor valley (Burfa, Barland and Evenjobb townships in Old Radnor parish), the Lugg valley (Discoed township in Presteigne parish) or the Teme valley (the eastern boundary of Llanfairwaterdine parish), which suggests that the Dyke was superimposed upon pre-Offan arrangement of parish and township boundaries.[5]

Noble sees Offa's Dyke as a control line with supervised crossing points, to the east of the Mercian-Welsh border, where the western limits of Mercian expansion may have been protected by a number of short dykes across valley floors or across ridges of upland, such as Ditch Bank to the north-west of New Radnor and the Llanlluest Dyke along the western boundaries of Bleddfa and Llangunllo parishes. He suggests that the people to the west and possibly those immediately to the east of the Dyke were responsible for the maintenance and prevention of unauthorised crossings and the defence of this buffer zone or March, which had its own law, distinct from the Welsh and Mercian codes, with the Dyke serving as a fall back line of defence in the face of a Welsh attack. Noble points out that the Domesday Book described manors in the Radnor valley and the upper Lugg valley as being 'In the March of Wales' in 1086, well before the emergence of the Marcher lordships. He sees the clue to the origins of Knighton in its Domesday name of *Chenistetune*, 'the town of the knights', and suggests that the settlement grew up around a camp of 'riding men', mounted and armed retainers, charged with the task of patrolling the control line represented by the Dyke.[6]

Within the immediate Knighton area Noble, following Fox, traces the Dyke, in the form of a hedge bank, from the summit of Ffrydd Hill to the south of the town, through Ffrydd Wood to above Ffrydd Road where it is lost in old quarries and spoil heaps (see the outline traced in Figure 1, p.8). It reappears to the north of the road briefly as a massive bank but there is little sign of the Dyke on the slopes each side of the Wylcwm Brook where it takes the form of a low bank. There is little sign of the Dyke on the steep slope on the other side of the brook. The stretch to the west of the later castle was strongly built, but 'survives poorly and ignominiously' according to Noble, at the rear of the Laurels Meadow housing estate. At the junction of Penybont Road and Market Street the alignment of the Dyke changes and is obscured by the bungalows on the east side of Offa's Road, the road itself running along the Dyke's western ditch to the junction with the Knucklas road. Across the road, the Dyke runs between the site of the old clothing factory and the houses to its west as a boundary bank, and thence down to Pinner's Hole, from where it continues as a steep bank with a ditch to its west as far as the terrace above the Teme. Thereafter the line followed by the Dyke is far from clear until the summit of Panpunton Hill. To the north of the Teme, Noble identifies a shadow line starting opposite Pinner's Hole and running diagonally from the west of Kinsley Wood to the summit of Panpunton Hill as the probable line of the Dyke and suggests that here the Dyke was represented by a palisade of some type.[7]

Knighton is the only settlement on the Dyke along its whole length, but Noble gives little indication as to possible crossing points within the town itself, beyond suggesting that there may have been one on or near Ffryd Road. His reluctance may well have stemmed from the disturbances caused over the centuries by building as the town has developed. Paul Woodfield, however, suggests that within the town, the most likely crossing point may have been at a gap in the Dyke at the west end of Market Street.[8]

Noble's explanation of the town's origins as a base for patrolling the Dyke stems from his views as to the Dyke's own origins and purposes based upon his detailed fieldwork and 'intelligent guesswork', rather than from incontrovertible archaeological or documentary evidence. However, his explanation does not depend upon the validity of his views as to the origins of the Dyke; even if this represented a negotiated boundary, crossing points on the Dyke would still require supervision.

Plate 2: Offa's Dyke at Pinner's Hole

❧ 2 ❧

MEDIEVAL KNIGHTON

At the outset it should be stressed that there is little material evidence as to the town's development in this period. Writing in 1975, C.J. Delaney and I.N. Soulsby stressed

> ... the almost total lack of research and evidence concerning the material aspects of the town's development. No excavations have been undertaken [beyond those relating to the Dyke] and no significant stray finds are recorded.

Clwyd and Powys Archaeological Trust provide a similar *caveat* in their *Historic Settlements Survey: Radnorshire*.[1] Those writing of the history of the medieval town have to base their conclusions upon observation and the relatively sparse documentary evidence.

The Domesday Book of 1086 gives a very concise description of 11th-century Knighton which then lay in the Leintwardine Hundred of Shropshire:

> Hugh the Donkey holds Knighton (*Chenistetune*) from the King. Leofled held it before 1066. 5 hides. Land for 12 ploughs. It was and is waste. A large wood.

Despite its brevity, this account gives a valuable insight into the locality's history.[2] It shows that Knighton was a manor of about 600 acres of cultivable land – a hide was about 120 acres of average quality land – surrounded by extensive woodland. It had clearly suffered severely as a result of the raids of the Welsh led by Gruffydd ap Llewelyn, particularly that of 1052, from which it had not recovered some 30 years later. The situation was aggravated by Eadric the Wild's rebellion of 1068-69 in north Herefordshire and south Shropshire. However, 'waste' should not be taken to imply wholesale devastation and depopulation, but rather that the local economy was functioning some way below its maximum and that the manorial organisation was not operating effectively enough, even in 1086, to enable an estimate of its potential worth.

The Domesday Book also provides an insight into the administrative structure of the area in the second half of the 11th century. During the reign of Edward the Confessor (1042-66), Knighton and its neighbour Norton were held by an Anglo-Saxon woman, Leofled, who also held a further 11 manors in neighbouring Herefordshire. After the Norman Conquest, Knighton and Norton passed into the hands of Hugh the Donkey, as did another manor later to be included in Radnorshire, 'Bernaldeston' or Barland. Hugh also held a further 20 manors in Herefordshire, including many of those formerly held by Leofled. Hugh, whose soubriquet reflected his stubbornness rather than stupidity, probably came to England with William FitzOsbern (d.1071), the first post-Conquest earl of Hereford, and served under him defending the English borderland from Welsh attacks, retaining his lands after Earl William's son, Roger, rose in an abortive rebellion in 1075.

Knighton and the Mortimers [3]
On the death of Hugh the Donkey, Knighton and Norton passed to his kinsmen, the Chandos family of Snodhill, Herefordshire, who as a result lost them when Roger rebelled against Henry II in the early 1180s. By 1191 the two manors and their castles had passed to William Braose, who held them until 1207 when they were seized by King John who granted them to Thomas Erdington, sheriff of Shropshire. The conflict between King John and William Braose continued intermittently until 1210 when Braose was forced to flee the country. However in 1215 Llewelyn ap Iorwerth (Llewelyn the Great) destroyed the castles and took both manors, holding them until 1230.

At the time of the Domesday Book the Mortimers held land in 12 English counties, mainly in Herefordshire and Shropshire, together with a few manors such as Pilleth in the March of Wales, with Wigmore Castle as the family seat. By the early 1090s they had conquered Gwerthrynion and another part of the later Radnorshire, Maelienydd, adjacent to Mortimer lands in Herefordshire and Shropshire, only to lose them later to Llewelyn. Knighton and Norton were obvious targets for Mortimer expansion and Roger Mortimer II (d.1214) briefly held them in 1207 but was unable to recover them before his death. His son Hugh Mortimer III (d.1227) sought unsuccessfully to recover the two manors by legal means and it was left to his brother and heir, Ralph Mortimer II (d.1246), to secure them by means of his marriage in 1230 to Gwladus Ddu, the daughter of Llewelyn the Great, who granted Knighton and Norton to the couple as a dowry. Following the death of Llewelyn in 1240 Ralph succeeded in bringing Gwerthrynion and Maelienydd back under Mortimer control. The marriage of Ralph's son and heir Roger Mortimer III (d.1282) to Maud de Braose in 1247 brought the lordship of Radnor to the Mortimers, making the family a dominant power in the Middle March.

As a Mortimer possession one might expect that Knighton would have enjoyed greater security than if it had been held by a lesser lord, but this was not always so, since it became at risk in any conflict stemming from the rivalry for dominance in Wales between the Mortimers, their rival Marcher lords, the Welsh, and the English Crown. Thus Knighton was sacked by the Welsh in 1260 and by Llewelyn ap Gruffydd in 1262.

Nor was Knighton always under the direct control of the Mortimers of Wigmore, sometimes passing to a Mortimer widow to hold for life as her dowry. Thus between 1282 and 1301 Knighton was held by Maud de Braose, the widow of Roger Mortimer III, and between 1304 and 1334 it formed part of the dower of the widow of Edmund Mortimer I, Margaret de Fiennes. On other occasions, when the heir was a minor, the Mortimer estates passed to a nominee of the Crown. Thus, between 1334 and 1341 when Roger Mortimer V regained it, Knighton, along with other Mortimer possessions, was administered by William de Bohun, his step-father. Again, when Roger Mortimer VI died in 1398 he was succeeded by his 6-year-old son Edmund Mortimer IV and the estates passed into the hands of King Henry IV, to be restored to Edmund by Henry V in 1413.

Knighton's castles

Knighton has two castles, not much more than 500 yards apart; one on Castle Hill above The Narrows, called Castle Bank or Castle Mount, and the other to the south-west, at Bryn-y-Castell. Little remains of the castle above The Narrows, which was of the motte and bailey type, with the keep, circular or polygonal, linked to a detached bailey on the south side. The flat summit of the mound has a diameter

Plate 3: The motte at Bryn-y-Castell

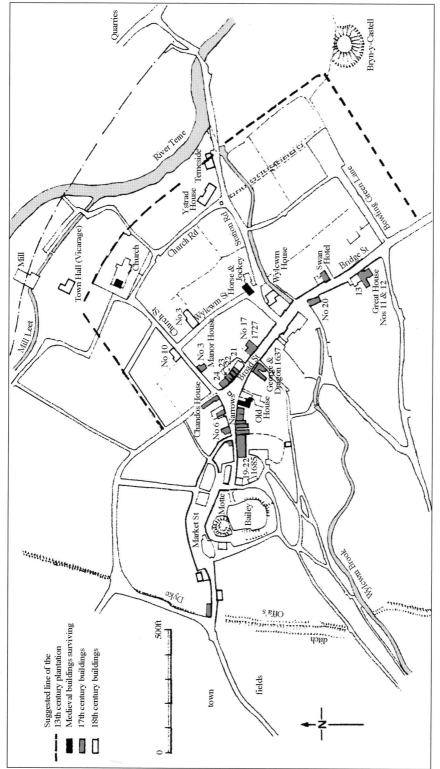

Legend (map key):

Suggested line of the
13th century plantation
Medieval buildings surviving
17th century buildings
18th century buildings

Map labels:

Quarries
River Teme
Mill
Mill Leet
Town Hall (Vicarage)
Church
Church Rd
Ystrad House
Termeside
Station Rd
Wylcwm St
Horse & Jockey
Wylcwm House
Swan Hotel
Bridge St
Bowling Green Lane
Bryn-y-Castell
Church St
No 3
No 3
No 10
No 3
Manor House
No 17 1727
24 23
21
Broad St
George & Dragon 1637
Great House
Nos 11 & 12
13
No 20
Chandos House
No 6
Narrow St
Old House
19-22 1685
Market St
Motte
Bailey
Dyke
Olfa's
ditch
Wylcwm Brook
town
fields
N
500ft
0

Figure 1: The suggested Knighton plantation settlement (by kind permission of Paul Woodfield)

8

of rather more than 50 feet and slight traces of the ditch remain, though in later periods houses were built in it and against the mound.[4]

The castle at Bryn-y-Castell occupies a dominant position overlooking the town on the edge of a plateau sloping down steeply to the Teme. It may have been of the motte and bailey type, but if a bailey ever existed it has been obliterated by cultivation and a levelling of the ground when a cricket pitch was laid out in the 19th century. Paul Remfry suggests that the mound itself, 20 feet high and 50 feet in diameter and surrounded, except to the east, with a deep ditch 15 feet wide, may have carried a shell keep.[5]

Historians have differed widely in their views as to the dates of construction and the relationship, if any, between the two castles. Perhaps the most straightforward explanation is that of William Hatfield, who sees Bryn-y-Castell as no more than an outpost of the castle at Castle Bank. Paul Woodfield, W.H. Howse and Ian Soulsby see the Bryn-y-Castell fortification as the earlier structure, superseded in the late 12th century by the castle on Castle Bank at the top of the town, though only Paul Woodfield goes into any detail. He sees the castle as a timber structure built before 1135 by the Normans some distance away from a hostile native Welsh settlement, and abandoned in favour of the castle 'at the top of the town' when its timbers decayed.[6]

Paul Remfry and Frank Noble see the Bryn-y-Castell fortification as postdating the castle at Castle Bank. Noble sees it as built at some time in the Anarchy (1135-54) when Stephen and Matilda and her son Henry, later Henry II, were disputing the throne, during an unrecorded siege of Knighton by Henry. Paul Remfry dates its construction to the period after 1215 when Llewelyn the Great had seized Knighton, possibly by Brian Brampton of Brampton Bryan to block a Welsh advance further down the Teme valley.[7]

Paul Remfry sees the castle at Castle Bank as initially built by Hugh the Donkey at some time before 1086, presumably a timber structure, at least initially, while Frank Noble also sees a castle at this site as predating that at Bryn-y-Castell. The town's other historians see the castle as dating from 1182, when Ralph de Poer was paid for castle building at Knighton and/or 1191-93 when William de Braose received payment amounting to 20 marks (a mark = 13 shillings and 4 pence or 66½p) for his work on the castle.

Whatever its earlier history, the castle at Castle Bank was destroyed by Llewelyn the Great in 1215, to be rebuilt at least partly in masonry by Ralph Mortimer II or possibly by his son Roger Mortimer III. It was however to have only a brief further history, for it was at least partly destroyed by the Welsh in 1260, their work being completed by Llewelyn ap Gruffydd in 1262. The devastation was such that the population was dispersed, and for almost two decades Knucklas served as the local Mortimer power base.[8]

The medieval town

We know relatively little of medieval Knighton, beyond that it received a charter in 1230 granting it the right to hold a market on the eve of St Matthew's feast, 20 September by the modern calendar, and that in 1260 and 1277 it received grants of murage, the right to levy dues to finance the construction of town defences. Beyond these details the town's historians have nevertheless been able to construct credible, if differing, narratives of the town's development.

Maurice Beresford suggested that Knighton was a new plantation town of the 12th century to establish English settlers in a location inhabited by a native Welsh population whose loyalty to the Mortimers and the English Crown was unreliable. Noble and Woodfield see the plantation as an extension of an existing settlement, though they differ as to the date of foundation. Noble suggests that the plantation dates from the reign of Henry I (1100-1135) but Woodfield, while accepting that it might date to before 1160, suggests that its foundation is more likely in the period of 1180-1190, with settlement encouraged by the protection offered by the newly constructed (or reconstructed) castle. Soulsby, pointing to the large proportion of the town's taxpayers in 1292 – 60% – who were Welsh, concurs with the view of Knighton as a Welsh settlement extended by plantation.[9]

Woodfield, on the basis that the street pattern to the east of West Street, Broad Street and Bridge Street between Victoria Road and Bowling Green Lane has some semblance to a grid pattern, sees that plantation as occupying a rectangle. To the north the boundary ran along the present Victoria Road and then the eastern edge of the old cemetery, while to the south the boundary ran along the present Bowling Green Lane and then along the boundary of the car park and Bryn-y-Castell. To the west the boundary ran along Broad Street and Bridge Street, while to the east the Teme provided a natural boundary.

The plantation provided burgage plots not only for the new settlers, but also for those displaced by the rebuilding of the castle at the 'top of the town' and the need to provide its garrison with a clear field of fire. The rectangle together with the area immediately to the west of Broad Street and Bridge Street would, Woodfield calculates, provide sufficient ground for the 162½ burgage plots recorded in 1304, each giving sufficient land for a dwelling, outbuildings and garden for a family. However, Noble maintains that the area around the castle was not cleared in the 12th century but retained poor quality housing up to at least the 17th century. Certainly much of the open space to be found at the 'top of the town' was cleared in the last half of the 19th century and the first half of the 20th century. Delaney and Soulsby maintain that the 162½ burgages could easily be accommodated in Market Street, High Street, Plough Road, Broad Street and Bridge Street.[10]

The parish church lies within the hypothetical plantation, although Woodfield acknowledges that it 'does not tie in happily with the street grid', possibly because of the need to align the building on an east-west axis. Today's structure largely dates from the rebuilds of 1876-77 and 1896-97, and the date of the original building is uncertain. Hatfield and Howse have no doubt that it was Norman, on the evidence afforded by the lower storeys of the existing tower and its massive scale. However, Woodfield maintains that there is no architectural evidence of a Norman date and sees the church as of the late 12th century, possibly built to replace an earlier church destroyed in the construction of the castle, while Soulsby suggests it may be even later in origin. However one should not entirely discount the possibility of a church of an earlier date than Norman on the site, possibly with an alternative dedication, despite the distance between the site and the original settlement at the 'top of the town', since the Celtic tradition favoured a clear distinction between the secular and spiritual elements of any settlement. The unknown author of *The South West Borderland of Shropshire*, published in 1938, claimed that the church was built in 990, but gives no source for this assertion. Again, the original church may have been built on this site because it was considered as sacred in pre-Christian times.[11]

Of Knighton's medieval church, possibly dedicated to St Michael, we know little, for with the exception of the tower it was demolished in the 1750s to make way for a new church on the same site. However, the mid-18th-century description of the medieval church's ruinous state mentions that it had two chancels, which suggests that it may have had a chantry chapel running parallel to the chancel, a similar arrangement to that of St Andrew's in Presteigne, where the Lady Chapel stands alongside the chancel.[12]

The location of the open fields on which the townspeople grew their grain is not known, and does not appear to have been considered by the town's historians apart from Woodfield. However, the land purchased by the Urban District Council from Colonel Price's estate in 1911 for use as allotments was known as the Town Field. It lay below the Garth, adjoining the land allocated by the enclosure commissioners in 1855 as field gardens and already in use as allotments in 1905. Given the terrain and the proximity to both the old settlement around the castle and the area of the plantation town suggested by Woodfield, this area may well have been the location of the town's open fields.

If the murage grants of 1269 and 1277 were utilised to build town defences, probably in the form of a timber palisade built on an earthen bank, no signs of them remain, beyond a slight change in the level of the land on the north-east side of the car park off Bowling Green Lane. There is, however, one reference to the walls of Knighton in a source, as yet untraced, used by Hatfield in his account of the battle of Pilleth. On the other hand, the town's natural defences, the Teme and Wylcwm Brook, together with the strong section of Offa's Dyke to the north, might be considered sufficient to render any further extensive fortification unnecessary.[13]

Chancery and Exchequer records of the late 13th and 14th century provide indications of the size of the town's population, its composition and its wealth. Thus the assessment for the tax called the Fifteenth – nominally one fifteenth of the taxpayer's movable wealth – to be collected in 1293 gives the names of 71 taxpayers in Knighton and the sum due from each of them. For the first time we are introduced to inhabitants of the town such as Cadogan ap Lewelin, assessed at 16 pence, Howel ap Meredit (18 pence), Howel ap Meredith (3 shillings and 6 pence), Adam de Lentwordin (4 shillings and 4 pence), Willielmus de Nortone (4 shillings and 6 pence), Philippus de Lyngeyne (2 shillings and 4 pence) and Yuor de Bultibroc (2 shillings).[14]

From this assessment Michael Faraday has calculated the average wealth of the manors of Radnor, Presteigne, Norton, Stapleton and Knighton in 1293 and, on the basis of the names of the taxpayers, the proportion of the population in each manor who were Welsh. Thus Knighton was one of the poorer manors with an average tax charge of 28 pence, compared with a charge of 34 pence in Stapleton and Radnor, 31 pence in Presteigne, 29 pence in Norton but only 17 pence in Bleddfa. On the basis of the names given, clearly a very rough approximation, Bleddfa was 100% Welsh, Knighton 66%, Norton 53%, Radnor 47%, Stapleton 25% and Presteigne 9%.[15]

The 1293 assessments cannot be used to provide an estimate of the population of the town since not all householders would possess sufficient means to be liable to pay the Fifteenth. However, Chancery records for 1304 show that 126 burgesses held more than 160 plots in the town, and if this figure is multiplied by 5, the conventional multiplier, the records suggest that the population may have been 630, far in excess of Presteigne's estimated population of 350. However this figure for Knighton is probably too high since even a population of 400 for the town in the mid-16th century has been considered excessive in comparison with other towns, given the sparsely populated hinterland, and the population of the town by 1670 has been estimated at no more than 495.[16]

Decline and adjustment

In the second half of the 14th century Knighton faced considerable difficulties. In part this stemmed from the deterioration in climatic conditions from the optimum of *c.*1300, which led to the height above sea level at which cereal production could viably be undertaken falling by as much as 200 feet by 1350 or so. This was bound to have a harmful impact upon towns such as Knighton whose economy was almost wholly dependent upon its hinterland.

Another factor may have been the series of plague epidemics of the second half of the century, not just the initial outbreak of 1349-50, the 'Black Death', which may have killed some 25-35% of the population of England and Wales (some areas suffering more than others), but also further outbreaks in 1360-62, 1368-69, 1373-75, 1382 and 1390. There is no direct evidence as to the effect of such epidemics upon Knighton itself, though inferences may be drawn from Hereford diocesan records and those of other Mortimer manors.

The diocese of Hereford was hit hard by the 1349-50 outbreak, the episcopal register recording that 'it swept away half the population, land was untilled and the supply of clergy was lamentably reduced'. Although after 1349-50 there were heavy arrears of rent and some leasing of demesne (land directly farmed by the lord) along the central Marches, the Radnor-Presteigne-Knighton area seems to have been harder hit by the plague outbreak of 1368-69. Thus in 1372 the demesne at Pilleth was let, which suggests that the customary labour – labour supplied by tenants as a form of rent – used by the lord to work it was no longer available in sufficient quantity.[17]

One of the results of climate change and the heavy mortality of the plague epidemics, which had led to a labour shortage, was an expansion in sheep farming, which was less labour intensive. Thus in 1392, 300 sheep were bought at Knighton to stock the manor of Clifford. This relatively large transaction may indicate that Knighton and its hinterland may have adjusted to the changed situation rather earlier than places further south on the Herefordshire border, and had already become an important centre in the sheep trade. Another result was a growth in labour mobility since the villeins and landless labourers were no longer tied so firmly to the manor where they were born and could move elsewhere – on the payment of a yearly fine – the *chevage* or *capitagium*. Thus the Ministers' Accounts – the financial records of various royal officials – for 1424 record that William Phillips paid 3 shillings and 4 pence *capitagium* in order that he could remain outside the manor of Leintwardine at Knighton.[18]

However, adjustment to the changed economic situation was almost certainly delayed by the devastation which resulted from the campaigns of Owain Glyndwr, which saw Knighton and Norton ravaged and Sir Edmund Mortimer defeated at Pilleth in 1402.

The Battle of Pilleth 1402

At the outset it should be acknowledged that the chronology of the events connected with the campaigns of Glyndwr in the Knighton and Radnor areas is confused. While it is almost certain that Glyndwr was in what is now Radnorshire in both 1401 and 1402, it is not entirely clear in which year he laid Knighton waste. At this time Mortimer lands were in the hands of the Lancastrian Henry IV, since Edmund Mortimer IV was not only a minor, but also the Yorkist claimant to the

English throne through his descent from Lionel, duke of Clarence, the younger son of Edward III, and therefore a potential threat. The *de facto* head of the Mortimer family was Sir Edmund Mortimer, the uncle of Edmund Mortimer IV.

When Glyndwr led his forces into mid Wales in June 1402, Sir Edmund Mortimer gathered a force of Herefordshire men at Ludlow, later joined by a force from Maelienydd, and advanced to meet him. According to Hatfield, citing a source which has yet to be identified:

> The Welsh crossed the hills from Llanidloes and were marching towards Knighton, burning and slaying on all sides. Sir Edward [*sic*] Mortimer sent 400 men to Knighton and found all the males under arms; they had sent their women and children in wagons towards Ludlow, but as the town had strong walls the men were determined on making a stout defence. A party advanced five miles beyond the town, and found a village on fire and attacked the Welsh, who were repulsed and the party returned to Knighton.[19]

The battle of Pilleth itself took place on the feast of St Alban, 22 June. Glyndwr's forces, with Rhys ap Gethin in command, were drawn up on Bryn Glas Hill and as Mortimer advanced to give battle, many of his Welsh troops deserted him and joined Glyndwr. Even so, the battle was fierce and the casualties heavy according to chroniclers of the time, Adam of Usk and Thomas Walsingham, and ended with the capture of Mortimer and the flight of his troops. According to the partisan chronicler Walsingham, after the battle Welsh women mutilated the corpses and refused to allow the bodies to be buried until they had received a payment.[20]

Knighton and Norton were laid waste by Glyndwr either shortly before the battle or, more likely, in its aftermath. Nor were they the only local victims, for archaeological evidence suggests that Bleddfa and Pilleth churches were destroyed at that time, while the village mentioned as burned in the extract above was either Knucklas or Llangunllo. It would seem that Glyndwr was deliberately targeting the Mortimer lordships in his campaign prior to Sir Edmund Mortimer switching sides and entering into an alliance with Glyndwr. As Remfry recounts, by 1406 both Knighton and Norton were 'so burned and wasted by the rebels that no profit could issue to the king without their better custody'. Moreover, the locality suffered further devastation as the Crown regained it from the rebels between 1406 and 1409.[21]

Knighton in the later 15th century

By the middle of the 15th century Knighton's economy seems to have recovered, largely as a result of the expansion of the Flanders wool trade, as a result of which even the coarse wool of the Welsh uplands found a market. Knighton by now had

Plate 4: The Old House, High Street

the beginnings of a cloth manufacturing industry of its own, marked by its fulling mill. Another factor may well have been its apparent immunity from the plague epidemics which affected the kingdom every decade or so in the second half of the 15th century; the town was probably protected by its relative isolation. Certainly Knighton does not feature as one of the parishes in the diocese of Hereford with a high mortality rate in the period 1442-1500.

Two buildings survive in the town from this period, the Horse and Jockey and the Old House, the narrow layout of the latter suggesting that the commercial demand for frontage in medieval Knighton was greater than one might expect.[22]

The Wars of the Roses

Knighton's direct link with the Mortimers was broken in 1425 with the death of Edmund Mortimer V from the plague. His lands passed to his sister, Ann Mortimer, to her husband, the earl of Cambridge and then to his son, Richard, duke of York. On the defeat of the Yorkists in 1459 the former Mortimer lands passed into the hands of Henry VI. Richard was killed at the battle of Wakefield in 1460 but after his victory at Mortimer's Cross in Herefordshire in 1461 his son, Edward, earl of March, ascended the throne as Edward IV and in 1477 he bestowed the former Mortimer estates on his son, Edward, Prince of Wales, the future Edward V.

After the battle of Bosworth in 1485, these estates, including Knighton, passed into the hands of Henry Tudor as Henry VII and he, in 1493, granted the lordship of Maelienydd in the locality to his son Prince Arthur. For administrative purposes all the lands granted to Arthur in 1493 were grouped into the Lordship of Cantref Maelienydd. Although all the other manors in the lordship were sold in the 1820s, the manors and boroughs of Knighton, Knucklas, Presteigne and Rhayader have remained in the hands of the Crown.[23]

∽ 3 ∾

TUDOR AND STUART KNIGHTON

The political stability of the Tudor and Stuart periods, especially after the Acts of Union of 1536 and 1542, combined with the town's apparent immunity from major epidemics, meant that external factors, apart from those to do with climate such as drought or floods, had little influence upon Knighton's development. In conjunction with its hinterland, the town became relatively self-sufficient.

The Formation of Radnorshire

The Acts of Union abolished the hundreds of petty lordships in the Welsh Marches outside the control of the Crown and integrated Wales into the English system of government and justice. The creation of Radnorshire and the introduction of the English structure of local government gave the local gentry such as the Price family of Monaughty, Pilleth and Knighton, huge opportunities of advancement, both by way of appointment to public offices such as sheriff and justice of the peace, and by election to Parliament as MP representing either the county or the Radnor Boroughs.

The Acts also advanced the status of Knighton itself in that along with Cefnllys, Knucklas, Radnor and Rhayader it became one of the five boroughs whose burgesses elected the MP for Radnor Boroughs. It also headed one of the six Hundreds into which the county was divided for purposes of administration and justice. Knighton Hundred consisted of 18 parishes and townships in east and north-central Radnorshire covering

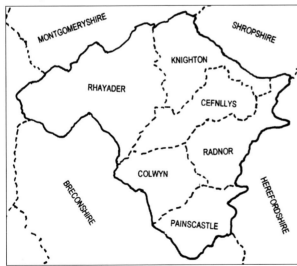

Figure 2: The Radnorshire Hundreds

some 61,841 acres. Knighton was the venue for the court of petty sessions which dealt with petty crime in the Hundred.

Borough Government[1]

Knighton had enjoyed borough status since at least the 13th century, although it had never been granted a charter of incorporation and was thus a borough 'by prescription', that is by long-standing custom and usage. Though it had some powers to regulate its own affairs it remained in the control of the lord of the manor and borough, from 1461 the Crown, which exercised its authority through

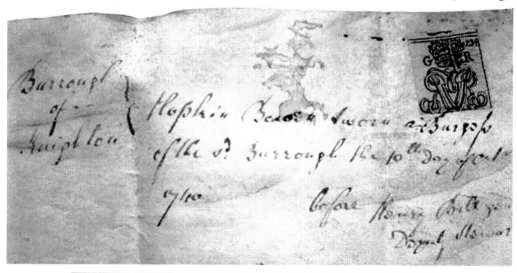

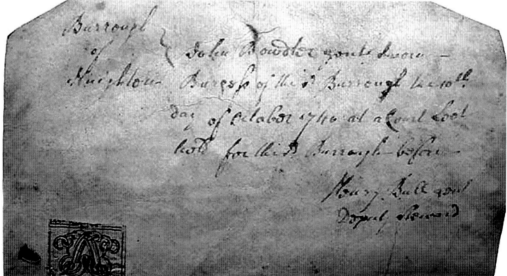

Plate 5: Certificates declaring Hoskin Beddoe and John Bowdler
to be burgesses of Knighton

18

the steward. There is some evidence to suggest that at the beginning of the 17th century the leading townsmen had ambitions of becoming a self-governing borough along the lines of New Radnor with a corporation in control of the town. Thus, in an Exchequer case of 1603 the lessees of the market tolls alleged that 25 leading burgesses of the town were seeking to transform themselves into a corporation, although the town had 'no liberty, franchise or freedom other than other inhabitants of the lordship of Melenith [sic]'.[2]

The affairs of the town were in the hands of the bailiff and the burgesses, who met at court leets held half-yearly at Easter and Michaelmas, and courts baron, which met every three weeks. The Easter court leet dealt with the payment of chief rents – residual rents paid by freeholders annually to the Crown – and the swearing of allegiance to the Crown, while the Michaelmas sitting dealt with the selection of the bailiff and the appointment of constables. The court baron dealt mainly with property matters – cases of trespass, strays, encroachment on the common and the surrender and re-granting of leases. These courts sat at the town hall, which also served as the market hall, and which stood on the site now occupied by the town clock. The hall also housed the town lock-up and was occasionally used for holding the quarter sessions.

The bailiff was chosen each year by the steward from three men nominated by the incumbent bailiff or, should the burgesses disagree with the bailiff's choice, three men nominated by themselves. The bailiff was assisted by four constables selected from the burgesses, two of them appointed by the bailiff and two by the steward. The bailiff also appointed a sergeant to deliver summonses.

Burgesses were elected by general consent of their fellows and did not have to be resident in the town, but if any two burgesses objected to a nomination then that person could not be admitted. In Knighton, unlike the other boroughs in the Lordship of Maelienydd, the oldest son of a dead burgess was admitted as a burgess by right on the payment of a penny. Burgesses had the sole right to cut wood from Garth Wood and were also exempt from market tolls. The burgess was, however, liable to pay to the Crown a chief rent on his dwelling and on his death an heriot of 2s 6d was payable by the heir before entering into the inheritance.

To meet the costs of administering the borough, the bailiff and burgesses received the rents of all the standings at the market hall and the tolls on corn and grain sold on market days and fair days. In addition the bailiff received the profits from weighing wool, the fees for sealing leather with the town seal (which provided a guarantee of origin and quality) and half the profits from the stalls (other than those at the market hall) on market days and fair days.

Lordship of the borough was expected to produce revenue for the Crown: thus in 1649 it was calculated that the quit rents and chief rents from burgages, together with fees and fines levied by the manorial courts and heriots, produced an income of

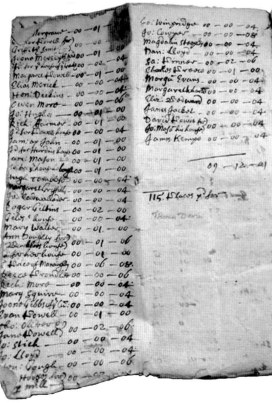

£14 10s 2d per annum. In addition the Crown had also leased out for three lives (usually estimated at 60 years) the tolls on livestock levied at the weekly markets and the two fairs of 6 May and 20 September, estimated to be worth £20 a year. The Crown also owned 189 acres of land in the borough valued at £36 17s 8d which had been let to a courtier named Edmond Sawyer for £2 13s 8d per annum. He had sub-let the land which, apart from Whitterleys (70 acres), Ffrydd Wood (70 acres) and Cwmgilla (18 acres), consisted of plots of an acre or so, to local people at market rates.[3]

The number of Crown tenants in Knighton in the 16th and earlier 17th centuries is not known, but in 1671 there were 115. Of these only four, including Thomas Harley and Richard Crowther, were paying more than 10 shillings, while 65 were paying no more than a few pence in chief rent. Most tenants were very proud of renting directly from the Crown, and when Charles I sold the Lordship of Maelienydd (including Knighton) and the manors of Gladestry and Presteigne to property speculators in August 1633, the response of the tenants was to raise £741 12s. Then, rather than retaining the property for themselves, rather quixotically they returned it to Charles I, with the

Plate 6: Tenants of the Crown in Knighton in 1671

request that 'they ... might continue as tenants of the King of England as they formerly had been.'[4] As tenants of the Crown they would have a measure of protection from powerful neighbours, and moreover, to hold land directly from the Crown was considered a mark of distinction – it put the humblest Radnorshire tenant on the same footing as the great magnates of the realm.

This gesture has been seen as a sign of a special relationship between the Radnorshire tenants and the Crown, but it is more likely to have been calculated self-interest. The tenants realised that the steward of Maelienydd was more likely to be interested in patronage than in maximising the Crown's rental revenue, whereas the speculators were only interested in a quick return. This was certainly the case with Charles Price of Pilleth who, as deputy steward of the Lordship of Maelienydd in the 1620s, was mainly interested in furthering his family's political interests by creating voters in the boroughs who were ready to return a Price nominee in a parliamentary election.

The Price family of Knighton

The third son of Ieuan ap Rhys, Edward Price (d.1587) and his son Thomas were the dominant figures in the Knighton of the second half of the 16th and the early 17th century. Ieuan ap Rhys, originally of Weston Hall, Llangunllo, and the constable of Clun Castle, had become the major landowner in the eastern borderland of Radnor, having first leased and then purchased the grange of Monaughty Poeth from the monastery of Abbey Cwmhir, and later purchased Crown lands in Knucklas. At his death, Ieuan's three older sons, James Price of Monaughty, Stephen Price of Pilleth and – to a lesser extent – Edward, exercised considerable influence in the county, where they and the Lewis family of Harpton dominated both local government and parliamentary representation in Radnorshire. Price family influence stemmed partly from the extent of their lands, but also through their connections, for over a few generations they had married into the Croft family, the Lewis family of Harpton, the Vaughan family of Clyro and the Bradshaw family of Presteigne.[5]

Edward Price of Knighton served as sheriff of Radnorshire in 1550, 1565, 1571 and 1586, dying in office in early 1587. However, this appointment was not enough for him; he had parliamentary ambitions and thought that in the election of 1571 his opportunity had come. Unfortunately for him, the Monaughty branch of the family had a candidate of their own, Walter Price, Edward's nephew, who was duly elected, and in revenge, in the election of 1572 Edward secured the return of Roger Vaughan at the expense of Thomas Lewis, favoured by the senior branches of the Price family.

Edward owned substantial property in Knighton and the surrounding area, including the Lower Mill – the site of the 19th-century Silurian cloth works – which he connected to the Teme by an eight foot channel, along with The Great Close near Discoed which was granted him by the Crown. Edward married Ann Hoel by whom he had three children: his heir, Thomas, another son, Richard, and Maud.

Thomas, who served as sheriff of Radnorshire in 1591, clearly enjoyed high status in Knighton and was named second in the list of burgesses accused at the Exchequer Court in 1603 of seeking to form a corporation in Knighton to govern the town at the expense of the other burgesses. Thomas married a Margaret Barker by whom he had nine children, and the need to provide for his sons and to give his daughters dowries appropriate to their status probably crippled him financially, contributing to the eclipse of the Price family of Knighton for the better part of a century.[6]

The economy

Far more than is the case today, the economies of Knighton and its hinterland were closely interdependent. The countryside depended upon Knighton to process and sell its products and provide it with those goods and services which it could not provide for itself, while Knighton depended upon its hinterland to provide it with a living. In the 16th and 17th centuries Knighton seems to have got the better bargain, for between 1545-1560 and 1670 the town's population grew by 25%, whereas that of Knighton Hundred grew by only 10%.

The prosperity of the town depended essentially upon the trade done at the weekly market on a Thursday, and at its fairs, initially that held on 21 September and later the fair held on 6 May which, on the change in calendar in 1752, became the fair of 17 May. The scale of Knighton's livestock trade can be seen in an Exchequer case of 1603 when the lessees of the market tolls, Thomas Purcell and Thomas Meysey, alleged that two drovers, Gruffith ap David and Rees ap Meredith, refused to pay market tolls on the livestock purchased at Knighton market over the past few years. It was claimed that ap David had bought 400 oxen, 200 cattle, 400 horses and 6,000 sheep in that time, and ap Meredith 300 beasts, 1,000 sheep, 40 horses and 200 swine. As buyer and seller were each expected to pay a toll of 1d on cattle, 4d per horse 4d for every 20 sheep and ½d per pig, the drovers had evaded paying some £13 in all, a substantial sum by 17th-century standards.[8] Since a number of drovers' roads passed through the town, the transactions of these two drovers would make up only a small proportion of Knighton's livestock trade. The building of a new market hall in 1649 may indicate a steady growth in the town's trade in spite of the inevitable dislocation caused by the civil war.

The town was also a market centre for wool, skins and leather and also wheat, barley and oats, while farmers' wives would attend the market with poultry, eggs, butter, cheese, and rabbits to sell to the townspeople, and also to buy a few essentials that could not be produced at home, together, maybe, with a few small luxuries from the town's shops. In the more distant parts of the hinterland, where travel was difficult, higglers would visit the farms buying dairy produce and poultry at the farm door and also offering ribbons, scarves and cheap jewellery for sale.

The farmers would occasionally also have business to do in town: with solicitors to draw up a will or a contract, or deeds needed to buy or sell a piece of land, or with a wheelwright, a cartwright or a smith about some farm equipment. Such visits would be few and far between, but even so the town's inns and beer houses would be busy providing food and drink, as market was always a thirsty business. Nor did the townspeople always bother themselves with such niceties as licences. Thus in 1665, 15 townspeople, some with familiar Knighton surnames such as Child, Watkins, Cadwallader and Bright, were outlawed for supplying drovers with ale without a licence.[9]

While there is no evidence that the fulling mill of the medieval period continued to function, the town remained an important centre for the dressing and stapling of wool, and woollen cloth may have been manufactured in the town on a greater scale than that needed to satisfy any local need. In the second half of the 17th century, in addition to sources naming weavers, there are also references to mercers – large scale dealers in good quality cloth – with businesses in the town.[10]

Knighton and the Civil War: the siege of Brampton Bryan, 1643-44

Knighton, like the rest of Radnorshire, was broadly sympathetic to Charles I at the outbreak of the Civil War in the autumn of 1642, and for much of the time between then and mid-1645 a small Royalist garrison of about 30 soldiers was stationed in the town. However the Knighton area was only directly involved in the conflict on three occasions.

The first came in 1643-44 with the two sieges of Brampton Bryan Castle, the home of Sir Robert and Lady Brilliana Harley. Sir Robert was one of the MPs for Herefordshire and a leading member of the Opposition in the House of Commons which sought to limit the powers of the Crown and to make the Church of England more puritan. Such an attack on the status quo was greatly resented by most people in the area surrounding Brampton Bryan, and it became almost routine for those travelling from Ludlow to Knighton market on Thursdays to roundly abuse any of the Brampton Bryan household whom they happened to see.[11] With her husband in London and fearful of an attack by a Royalist mob, Brilliana

Plate 7: Lady Brilliana Harley

built up stocks of arms and ammunition and established a small garrison in the castle.

Once hostilities had begun, Brampton Bryan Castle was an obvious target for local Royalists since it posed a potential threat to their lines of communication along the March, served as a rallying point and a place of refuge for the Parliamentarian minority in the area, and also acted as an intelligence gathering centre. As far as Brilliana Harley was concerned, she was doing no more than defend her family home and Sir Robert's estate.

There was no immediate attack on Brampton Bryan, partly because the local Royalists were reluctant to breach the local social fabric irreparably, and partly because such an attack had a low priority in the eyes of the Royalist leadership whose main objective in the southern borders of Wales was the capture of Gloucester. By the summer of 1643, however, Royalist forces in the region had been reorganised and a professional soldier, Sir William Vavasour, placed in command of an army of 1,400 foot and horse with Henry Lingen in charge of the local troops amounting to 700 foot soldiers and the Radnor county troop of 60 horse. Before advancing on Gloucester, Vavasour decided to move against Brampton Bryan to boost local Royalist morale and to encourage the payment of contributions to fund the main campaign. To defend the castle Lady Harley had a garrison of 50 troops, assisted by the men amongst the 50 or so civilians in the castle.[12]

As one would expect of a professional soldier, Vavasour conducted the siege of Brampton Bryan Castle, which began on 26 July 1643, with rigour. A blind man who professed loyalty to King and Parliament rather than to the King alone was allegedly shot in the village street, while the castle was sealed off from any

Plate 8: Brampton Bryan Castle

outside contact. The locality then had an object lesson in the destruction which civil war could bring to any community. Harley's parks and warrens were plundered by Royalist foragers, who also drove off 800 sheep, 30 cattle and 30 brood mares from the estate. The village was largely destroyed, including 20 houses, the mill, the parsonage and the church.

Early in August Vavasour drew off his forces to launch the attack on Gloucester, leaving Henry Lingen to conduct the siege from his headquarters in Knighton. The tempo of the assault slackened, and with the castle not invested as closely as it had been, the garrison began to receive a steady flow of messages. Lingen's tactics seem to have been to launch occasional artillery attacks on the castle in the hope of intimidating Lady Harley into surrendering, rather than making any direct assault. Brilliana Harley exploited Lingen's reluctance to attack by spinning out negotiations. Whereas Vavasour had agreed to one short truce, Lingen agreed to several, one lasting from 23 August until 6 September. The siege was finally lifted on 9 September, Lingen's forces being hastened on their way by an attack on Lingen's Knighton headquarters by a detachment from the castle.

It has been suggested that Lingen's reluctance to press home his attack on 'the honourable and valiant lady' may have stemmed from the fact that social niceties still carried much weight with amateur military commanders. Significantly, after the final Parliamentarian victory, Sir Robert Harley refused compensation for his losses, estimated at £12,990, from Lingen's estate, possibly a tacit recognition of Lingen's forbearance. This would also suggest that allegations that during the course of the siege Lingen poisoned the village water supply and sanctioned the use of 'poisoned bullets' were no more than Parliamentarian propaganda.

Though Sir Robert wished that Lady Harley and the children should now leave the castle, Brilliana decided to stay. By the end of September, following the failure of the Royalist attack on Gloucester, Vavasour was back in Hereford and planning another attack on Brampton Bryan. Soon Royalist forces were gathering in the vicinity – 150 foot at Leominster, 50 at Kingsland, 50 horse at Knighton, the Radnor troop at Presteigne and other troops at Aymestrey and Deerfold. For the second time Lady Harley made preparations to withstand a siege: the earlier siege works around the castle were levelled, supplies of food were seized from neighbouring Royalists, reinforcements and powder were obtained from the Gloucester garrison and a small out-garrison was established in the ruins of Wigmore Castle – only to be chased out quickly by the local Royalist gentry. Even before the end of the first siege Brilliana had been ill, and the continuing stress led her health to deteriorate further. She died on 29 October 1643 and her body, wrapped in lead, was placed in a tower of the castle to await burial.

Command of Brampton Bryan passed to Lady Harley's physician, Dr Wright, now commissioned by Parliament as a colonel. He continued to build up the castle's supplies and in mid-February established another out-garrison of 30 or so troops at Hopton Castle under the command of Samuel More. Such a situation was unacceptable to Prince Rupert, the King's nephew, now in charge of the Royalist war effort in the region, and he ordered Colonel Sir Michael Woodhouse and 500 of his battle-hardened veterans to reduce both Hopton and Brampton Bryan castles.

Woodhouse invested Hopton Castle and after three summons to surrender had been rejected, he warned More that the defenders could expect no quarter. When More eventually agreed to surrender on 13 March 1644, in the hope of receiving mercy, he and his junior officer were led away and the garrison was massacred. The junior officer was also killed later, but two maids in the castle were spared, one being told to go to Brampton Bryan and tell what she had witnessed. One soldier of the garrison, who hid in the castle cellars, also escaped with his life. The massacre of a garrison which offered more than a token resistance to a vastly superior force was technically within the rules of war. The later local tradition that 'wagon loads' of Woodhouse's troops later died of wounds from 'poisoned bullets' used by the garrison may be a survival of a Royalist attempt to justify the massacre.

Initially the massacre had an adverse impact upon the morale of the Brampton Bryan garrison; 15 deserted and a number of prisoners were able to escape. However, towards the end of March when Woodhouse invested Brampton Bryan, the massacre seems to have stiffened the remaining defenders' resolve. A raiding party from the castle chased most of Sir William Croft's regiment from the siege works, but only succeeded in killing two of them because the others were so 'swift of foot'. A woman who had taken a letter from the castle and was returning to the castle dressed as a man, when arrested, cheekily offered 'to be a soldier in Croft his [*sic*] company'.

Plate 9: Hopton Castle

After the siege had lasted nearly three weeks, Samuel More, the commander of the Hopton garrison, urged Wright to accept the proffered terms of quarter and on 17 April 1644 he surrendered on these terms. Sixty-seven prisoners were taken, not all of them combatants, together with quantities of plate, arms, powder and provisions, and the castle was slighted. The garrison was imprisoned first at Ludlow and than at Shrewsbury, while the Harley children were ultimately given safe conduct to join Sir Robert in London.

Knighton and the Civil War: Charles I in Radnorshire, August-September 1645

Knighton's next appearance in the central narrative of the Civil War came in the late summer of 1645 when, after the Royalist defeat at the battle of Naseby in June 1645 and a subsequent failure to raise substantial forces in south Wales, Charles I travelled through the Knighton area on possibly two occasions in the course of abortive attempts to link up with Scottish Royalist forces in northern England.[13]

The first occasion was in early August when, after crossing into Radnorshire at Glasbury with a force of 3,000 troops, he marched through the county in a north-easterly direction, spending the night of 6-7 August at Harpton Court, The Stones at Barland, or Bush Farm at Evenjobb, according to conflicting local traditions. On the morning of 7 August, while the main army marched via Presteigne and Wigmore to Ludlow, the Revd John Webb, a usually reliable source, suggests

Figure 3: Charles I's journeys through Herefordshire, Radnorshire and Shropshire, August and September 1645

that King Charles and a few companions took an alternative route, travelling through Knighton to Ludlow, where he arrived that night without having eaten in the day.[14]

With his route north blocked by Parliamentarian forces he turned south once more, first to Oxford, then to Hereford and on to south Wales. Having failed to raise a substantial number of recruits there, Charles revived his plan to link up with the Scots Royalists. On 18 September he travelled through Leominster, Weobley, and possibly Pembridge to Presteigne and then, on 19 or 20 September according to conflicting local traditions, he set out as if making for Kington or Leominster, before doubling back on his tracks, to cross the Lugg and join up with the main body of his troops on the march who were heading, via Willey and Norton, to the Knighton area and then on to Newtown.

Closely associated with this episode is the local tradition of the pillaging of Willey Court by Parliamentarian troops in pursuit of King Charles. With the men of the household harvesting in the fields, the house was unprotected and some of the female servants were assaulted by the soldiers. At noon, puzzled by the non-appearance of food for the labourers, the owner, Colonel William Legge, returned to the house and discovered the outrage. Gathering together his labourers, some of whom had armed themselves with pitchforks, he set out in pursuit. They caught up with the troops at Knighton and in the ensuing fight, killed one and injured several others. There are conflicting traditions as to where the fight took place: according to Hatfield it took place at or near a barn near The Cottage (a larger house than the name implies in Bridge Street), while others place it at Bryn-y-Castell, or in the vicinity of the Great House (also in Bridge Street).[15]

Knighton and the Civil War: Sir William Vaughan, 1645-46

Knighton's last appearance in the narrative of the Civil War came in the winter of 1645-46. Following a defeat in north Wales at the beginning of November, the ruthless Royalist cavalry commander, Sir William Vaughan, briefly established his quarters at Knighton, possibly, according to Noble, using the hollow known as Pinner's Hole as a horse-pound, before regrouping his forces in the Leominster, Dilwyn and Pembridge area. This was not the last Knighton heard of him however, for in January 1646 Vaughan was raiding the Knighton, Presteigne and Radnor areas before heading for Bridgnorth.[16]

Knighton personalities of the Civil War period

The major figure in Radnorshire at the outbreak of the Civil War was Charles Price of Pilleth, the 'Prince of Radnorshire' or 'Baronet Price' as he was termed by Lady Harley. He was an able and experienced soldier and dominated the county's politics in the period 1640-42. He was to play little part in Radnorshire in the conflict however, for he was captured by the Parliamentarians at Presteigne in October 1642 and after his release in March 1643 he served in Royalist forces outside the county until his death in September 1645, when Parliamentarian forces stormed Priors Hill Fort at Bristol.

Bryan Crowther of the Great House, Knighton, on the other hand, was at the centre of the Royalist war effort in Radnorshire and paid dearly for his loyalty to the Crown. The Crowthers were a large and influential family of the Radnorshire-Shropshire borders. Bryan Crowther came from the Bedstone branch of the family and his father, or possibly his godfather, also Bryan Crowther, was a successful lawyer who practised at the Court of the Marches at Ludlow and built up a substantial estate.

Bryan Crowther junior had an income of nearly £110 a year from estates in Knighton, Cwmgilla, Whitton, Norton, Harpton and Clun. He married the sister of Sir Herbert Price of The Priory, Brecon, an important figure in the royal household and a future Royalist leader. Crowther's first public office came in 1639 when he was appointed sheriff of Radnorshire. Hatfield, following Jonathan Williams, described him as 'a man of unblemished honour and many arbitration cases were referred to his decision' – possibly confusing him with Bryan Crowther the elder.[17]

Crowther was an opponent of Puritanism and when John Tombes, the puritan vicar of Leominster, visited Presteigne in 1642 to obtain signatures for a petition to the House of Commons, Crowther treated him with high-handed contempt. In August 1642, as civil war loomed, Crowther and two of his neighbours, Charles Price and John Powell of Stanage, were amongst those appointed as commissioners of array for Radnorshire and charged with securing the county trained band and stock of arms for the Crown.[18]

While Price and Powell were under arms and out of the county, Crowther's role in the Crown's cause within Radnorshire was administrative, raising men and money. He served on the committees 'for the guarding [of] the county', for raising money, for the impressments of men and for auditing the accounts, and when the county, increasingly war-weary, was drifting into neutralism in 1644 and 1645, he again served as High Sheriff.

Once Parliament had defeated Charles I, it began to levy fines on those of means who had actively supported the Royalist cause. In May 1649 Crowther paid a fine of £300 19s 8d, one-sixth of the total value of his estate, and also a further fine of £100 for not coming to terms with Parliament before 1647. In 1650 his personal estate, then valued at £20 10s, was seized and sold, though the reason for this is not clear. However, he somehow managed to escape further financial penalty when it emerged in 1650 that he had concealed his ownership of an estate in Norton from the authorities.[19]

Even before these financial penalties Crowther was in severe financial difficulties, for Parliament's investigation of his affairs showed that he had debts amounting to £1,700. It is not clear if this huge debt was the result of generous contributions to the Royalist cause or an extravagant lifestyle. Though the Crowthers remained substantial landowners on the Radnorshire-Herefordshire-Shropshire borders, they subsequently played no significant role in public life.

Another prominent Knighton Royalist was Samuel Powell of Stanage, whose family had only recently settled in the locality, though he had strong local connections since his grandfather, Walter Powell, had lived at Bucknell. Samuel's father,

John Powell 'of London and Hamburg', was a Merchant Adventurer who had made his fortunes from the Baltic trade. Samuel was born in Hamburg in 1624 and was naturalised in 1628 when the family returned to London. Early in the 1630s John Powell returned to the Welsh borderland and built up substantial estates in Radnorshire, Herefordshire and Shropshire. Initially he lived at Willey Hall, but subsequently moved to Stanage which he had purchased in 1633. His appointment as sheriff of Radnorshire in 1640 marked his acceptance into the county establishment.[20]

John Powell was a Royalist and served on the Radnorshire commission of array, but although accorded the rank of colonel, he played little part in the conflict because of his age. His son Samuel played an active role, serving on the commissions of array for Herefordshire and Shropshire in 1642 and as a colonel in Royalist forces. However, though he had an estate valued at £600 a year and livestock worth £1,500, he escaped punishment at the hands of the Parliamentarians as a result of judicious bribes and his skill in playing off the Parliamentarian committees of Herefordshire, Radnorshire and Shropshire against each other. He may also have been involved in the Second Civil War of 1648, for it was alleged that he received 'some of the raised party' at Stanage, on their way to Hampton Court near Leominster, the headquarters of an abortive rising in Herefordshire. He was closely questioned at Hereford and an inventory of his possessions was drawn up in preparation for their confiscation, but in the end he escaped with no more than a fine of £200.[21]

The aftermath of the Civil War

In Radnorshire the early enthusiasm for the Royalist cause soon faded in the face of continuous demands for men and money. Nor did the formation of a republican government improve matters, for taxation increased; in particular the range of goods upon which excise duty was levied was steadily widened. In mid-September 1652 attempts to collect excise duty produced serious rioting and when the excise men arrived at Knighton a week later trouble soon flared:

> ... the said excise officers were at Knighton to collect the excise, but were assaulted by three constables, Richard Giles, Edward Bowen and John Prosser, who having first disarmed them, bade the people fall upon them with clubs, bills, weapons and stones, and threatened them they should be served as Lt Col Jones had served them at Rhayader [where they had to flee for their lives], and that though they brought a 100 men with them to collect the excise, they should all be beaten.

The excise men, two of them wounded, were put to flight, leaving behind them their weapons and a horse.[22]

The execution of Charles I in January 1649 and the new regime's attempt to transform the political, religious and social status quo alienated the county establishment, while Knighton was no doubt incensed by the sale of the manor of Knighton to two military men, Giles Saunders and Wroth Rogers, in June 1651.[23] It was not until Cromwell came to power that figures of the Knighton elite such as Samuel Powell and Robert Curtler began to play an active role in the affairs of Radnorshire, to be joined on the eve of the Restoration by the three sons of Sir Robert Harley: Edward, Robert and Thomas.

Sir Robert Harley had opposed the execution of the king in January 1649 and thereafter he and his family were excluded from power, and in 1650 barred from living in Herefordshire for 10 years. His second son, Robert, became a serial intriguer against the regimes of the 1650s and, like his older brother Edward, played an influential role in the restoration of Charles II in 1660. After the Restoration the Harleys became major players in Radnorshire for a century or so, while in the Knighton area little happened without their at least tacit consent.

Robert Curtler, a Knighton figure of the Restoration period

Robert Curtler was a lawyer who came to local prominence in the decade or so after the defeat of Charles I, possibly gaining from the power vacuum in the town after the fall from power of Bryan Crowther, and from his post as steward of Samuel Powell's manor of Stanage.

In 1645, 1647 and 1657 he served on the Radnorshire Committee which oversaw the financial administration of the county, but it should not be assumed from this that he was an ardent supporter of either the Parliamentarian cause or the Cromwellian regime. His membership may have stemmed from professional competence rather than from any ideological commitment. He did not hold public office again until the eve of the Restoration, in March 1660 serving on the Assessment Committee which was responsible for taxation and on the prestigious Militia Committee, an appointment equivalent in status to that of a deputy lord lieutenant.[23]

Since these appointments coincided with the re-emergence of the Harley family as a major power in the Middle March, there is a possibility that he was a Harley client. However he was prepared to act independently of the Harleys, clashing in 1660 with the Harley choice of an incumbent for the Knighton living. His professional career clearly brought him wealth, for in 1666 he built his mansion at Farrington (in Knighton parish but outside the borough), while his membership of the Radnorshire elite was confirmed by his appointment as sheriff of Radnorshire. He died in 1678, and it was his son, also Robert Curtler, who served as sheriff in 1694 and whom Hatfield describes as moving to Kingsland after buying Street Court.[24]

Religious tensions in mid-17th-century Knighton

The conventional list of the Knighton incumbents of the first half of the century or so – 1615 Roger Powell, 1653 Thomas Froysell, 1662 Robert Milward – follows Anglican tradition and names only those clergymen who were ordained and instituted according to canon law. Thus the list gives no indication of the religious upheaval which followed the victory of Parliament in the Civil War. Powell did not hold the living until 1653, but was ejected from it in October 1647 in favour of a John Siddall who died in 1650. The living was than vacant until 1653 and the appointment of Thomas Froysell, who was succeeded in 1655 by a Ralph or Robert Fenton.[25]

Fenton was described by Sir Edward Harley as 'a studious man and a constant preacher', but he did not remain in Knighton for long as he was appointed to Ludlow in 1658 or 1659 and was confirmed to that living in 1661. Fenton's removal to Ludlow led to intense competition for the living, with no fewer than six candidates. The final choice was between a John Harris, possibly the Bleddfa schoolmaster of that name, who was backed by Curtler, and Robert Milward, recommended by a Cambridge friend of Thomas Harley. Since he had Harley backing, Milward's appointment was perhaps inevitable.[26]

The Harleys were puritans, more precisely they were Presbyterians who wanted a church organised on national lines, ideally controlled by the clergy and the congregations, rather than by the bishops. But even before the outbreak of civil war there were a few in Radnorshire whose religious views were more radical and who wanted each congregation to choose its clergyman and decide its own doctrines. The local leader of these Independents was Vavasor Powell of Knucklas, who served as curate to his uncle, the vicar of Clun, and was converted to puritan views in 1637. He was sheltered at first at Brampton Bryan by Sir Robert Harley, and with his help became schoolmaster at Llanfairwaterdine. Between 1640 and 1642 he embarked upon a preaching campaign, as a result of which his followers claimed that 'Radnorshire that before was a dark country, came to have so much light'.[27]

He left Radnorshire for London in 1642 and did not return until 1646 to resume his preaching campaign and purge the Church of unfit clergy. After an attempt to establish a network of puritan preachers throughout Wales had failed in 1653, he became a Fifth Monarchist, believing in the imminent second coming of Christ, and campaigned against Oliver Cromwell's seizure of power. Powell built up a following in Radnorshire, notably in the Glasbury, Glascwm and New Radnor areas, and early in 1654 there were indications that he and his more radical supporters were preparing for a call to arms, while in Knighton there were rumours of secret meetings at night of armed groups of Powell's supporters.

Powell's Fifth Monarchist stance and his opposition to Cromwell fragmented the puritan cause in Radnorshire and beyond, while a change in his religious stance did not help. In 1655 he converted to the Baptist cause, but without abandoning his Independent views completely, thus offending many in both the Baptist and Independent camps.

How much influence Vavasor Powell exercised in Knighton is difficult to measure. There is no evidence to suggest that he preached in the town, despite its proximity to Llanfairwaterdine, while the choice of Knighton in 1658 as the venue for his public debate with the Quaker Morgan Watkin, who hailed from Wigmore, was Watkin's choice rather than Powell's. Unfortunately, no records appear to remain of the debate or its outcome. Even so there is evidence of a few puritans in Knighton in the decades following the Restoration. Thus in 1663 John Colley, yeoman, his wife Margaret, Mary the wife of John Dantsey and Robert ap Prys, all of Knighton, were presented by the Grand Jury for trial at the Great Sessions of August 1663, on the charge that they had 'wilfully abstained' from attending the parish church for three months. Several years later, in 1688, the churchwardens' presentations included a husband and wife, possibly Baptists, for failing to have their children baptised, and also another husband and wife who may have been Quakers. Nonconformity in Knighton certainly persisted into the 18th century, for the presentation for the triennial visitation of the parish in 1716 reported a group of dissenters and a preacher 'of the Presbyterian persuasion'.[28]

Knighton in the later 17th century

The second half of the 17th century seems to have been a time of great prosperity for the town, which received favourable comments from travellers of the time. Leland (1540) thought it 'a pretty town after the Welsh [style of] building' as did Symonds a century or so later. The buildings were probably timber-framed, in-filled with wattle and daub, pleasant to look at but not particularly warm in winter, since the walls were usually thin.

According to Woodfield, 'buildings of the seventeenth century are common in Knighton' and he identifies the Swan and the Great House in Bridge Street; 6, 19-22, 23 and 26 High Street; the George and Dragon, 17, 21 and 24 Broad Street; and 3 Church Street (the Manor House) as having 17th-century elements (see Figure 1, p.8). He attributes the rebuilding to the prosperity which the town enjoyed, particularly in the second half of the century.[29]

The Hearth Tax returns of 1670 give us an impression of housing standards in Knighton and its level of prosperity compared to other communities. Of the hundred houses in the borough, two-thirds had only one hearth or fireplace, while the largest houses were owned by Robert Danvers (The Chandos, 24 hearths), James Beck (probably The Great House, 9 hearths) and Hugh Price, John Mason and John Woolley senior each owned a house with five hearths. The relative prosperity of an area can be estimated by dividing the number of hearths by the number of houses:

the higher the hearths/houses ratio the greater the prosperity. Knighton's ratio of 1.93 compares with Old Radnor's 1.8, Presteigne's 2.34 and Leominster's 1.8, and is much more in keeping with Herefordshire's average ration of 1.78 than with Radnorshire's average of 1.41.[30]

However, this picture of a prosperous later 17th-century Knighton needs to be treated with some caution since the bishops' transcripts – annual lists of baptisms, marriages and burials – show that between 1662 and 1700 baptisms usually exceeded burials by only a small margin, especially between 1680 and 1700, suggesting that unless there was significant in-migration, the population of the town was growing only slowly. Knighton also experienced occasional years of abnormally heavy mortality, probably caused by epidemics of some kind, possibly smallpox. Thus in 1667 burials exceeded baptisms by 71%, with younger age groups hardest hit, 25 of the 52 burials of that year being of persons described as 'son/daughter of'. In 1679 burials exceeded baptisms by more than 250%, though the number of both baptisms and burials was small – 9 and 23 respectively. Again, one should not underestimate the economic impact of the Civil War of 1642-46 in which up to 20 or 25% of the county's adult males were under arms and the vast majority of them out of the county.[31] While we have no information as to the number of men recruited in Knighton, it is clear that the loss of part of the labour force in the town on this scale would have significant repercussions. Certainly there are grounds for thinking that by the closing decades of the 17th century the town's growth rate was beginning to slow down.

❧ 4 ❧

18TH-CENTURY KNIGHTON: MARKING TIME?

As is the case with Radnorshire as a whole, documentary sources relating to Knighton in the 18th century are relatively sparse. Those documents that have survived give an impression not of decline, but of stagnation and a lack of ambition. One very significant feature of the period, however, was the renewed importance of the Price family.

The re-emergence of the Price family

The renewed dominance of the Price family in Knighton is usually attributed to the attorney John Price (d.1774) and his marriages with two heiresses. However, the process may well have begun with John Price's father, also John Price (d.1727), and described as 'of Farrington'. Probably also an attorney, he was a man of means, making at least one foray into the Norton land market in 1699-1700, which involved a bond for £600.[1] He married twice, his first wife Anne bearing him at least six children including his son and heir, John Price II, probably born in the 1690s, though his christening is not recorded in the Knighton parish register, and four daughters.

John Price I acted as a land agent, managing the Radnorshire estates of absentee landowners, possibly including the estates which William Chase, a wealthy London ironmonger, had purchased in Llanddewi Ystradenni and neighbouring parishes in 1705. He also managed some of the 15 Radnorshire manors of James Brydges, the first duke of Chandos, and when Chandos became steward of the Lordship of Maelienydd in 1722, he immediately appointed Price as his deputy and thus manager of his political interests in both Radnor constituencies. Price also acted for local gentry and in 1721, if not earlier, was steward of the manor of Norton for Thomas Harley of Kinsham.[2]

On the death of John Price I in 1727, if not before, John Price II took over his father's legal practice, including the Chase, Harley and Chandos interests. He had already married the daughter and heiress of the wealthy John Barnsley, though there seems to be some confusion over the name of his bride. Jonathan Williams gives her name as Anne, though the Knighton parish register always refers to her as Elizabeth.

By this first marriage John Price II had a daughter and four sons, but of these only one, Henry Price, 1722-95, married and produced a family. Henry married into the wealthy and influential Foley family of Shropshire, in the person of Elizabeth, the daughter of Captain Thomas Foley RN and settled in Bitterley, though retaining a close interest in Knighton matters. The oldest son of the marriage, John Price III (d.1780), after being admitted to the Inner Temple to study law, later secured an appointment in the Exchequer Office, possibly through the influence of his half-brother, Chase.[3]

On the death of his first wife in 1729, John Price II immediately married the daughter of Richard Chase, her uncle William Chase giving her a dowry of £4,000. Again there is some confusion over the name of the bride, for Jonathan Williams refers to her as Sarah, while the parish register styles her as Mrs Elizabeth Price. This second marriage produced two sons, Chase and Richard, both of whom received a legal education. After matriculating at Christ Church, Oxford, Chase studied law at the Inner Temple and was called to the Bar in 1757, while Richard became an attorney.[4]

Chandos cherished the hope that his son would be elected as Member for one of the two Radnorshire constituencies, and between 1722 and the death of Chandos in 1744, both John Price I and II in turn schemed on his behalf against Thomas Lewis, the MP for Radnor Boroughs, and Sir Humphrey Howorth, the MP for Radnorshire, but without success. In New Radnor borough, which extended

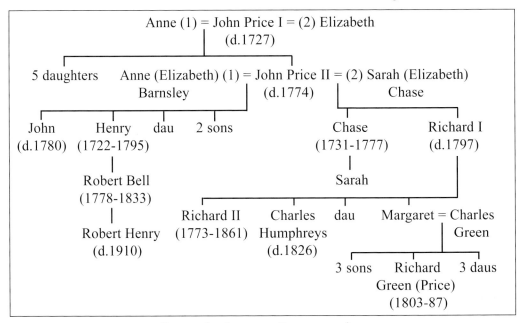

Figure 4: A concise Price genealogy
(Sources: *Burke's Peerage, Baronetage and Knightage*, 1929;
Powys Archives Office, R/D/BRA/2052/16-19 and NLW, Price of Norton Deeds)

well beyond the parish boundary, the dominance of the Lewis family and its allies was such that, despite creating 140 burgesses in the out-boroughs of Knighton, Knucklas and Rhayader, the Chandos faction, led by the John Prices, were unable to unseat Thomas Lewis.[5]

The campaign against the opponents of Chandos could get violent. Following his success in the election of May 1734, Howorth claimed that in Knighton effigies of four of his supporters had been burned by a mob led by the servants of 'Justice' Gough and the clerks of John Price II, and that the servant of James Roberts of Knighton, also a Howorth supporter, 'would have been murdered by the mob if he had not been rescued by a friend who happened to be passing through Knighton'. In consequence, in June 1734, Howorth wrote to Sir Robert Walpole asking that a company of soldiers or a troop of dragoons might be sent to Knighton to restore order. The outcome of this request is not known, but it is clear that John Price II's influence in his capacity as the agent of Chandos was such that the vast majority in the Knighton area sided with him. In the county election of 1741, only 42 of the Knighton area's voters backed Howorth, while 149 voted for his opponent. However, Price's personal standing in the Knighton area was limited, and when Chandos found it necessary to appoint a deputy lieutenant for the Knighton Hundred he chose first 'Justice' Hugh Gough of Knighton, and then Thomas Legge of Willey, rather than Price. Again, after Howorth's death in 1755, when Price's brother-in-law, Sir Richard Chase, sought to stand as the Tory candidate for Radnorshire, Price found that he could not get sufficient backing, despite having Harley support.[6]

John Price's oldest son by his second wife, Chase Price, MP for Leominster 1759-67 and for Radnorshire 1768-77, was described by a contemporary in 1777 as 'one of the most extraordinary persons who have lived in the present age'. He was a skilful political intriguer, always courting a more powerful patron who would protect him and enable him to get revenge on his real or imagined enemies, and in particular upon Thomas Lewis of Harpton, his arch-rival in Radnorshire, to whom the Harleys were bitterly opposed. Chase spent little or no time in Knighton, though he seems to have built the old Butter Cross in the town in the 1750s, and beyond his political intrigues his only claim to a measure of posthumous celebrity seems to have been his offer in 1766 to Rousseau to provide him with a refuge at Monaughty. Jean Jacques Rousseau was a Genevan-born philosopher, writer, and composer whose works are thought to have helped inspire the French Revolution. His book *The Social Contract*, published in 1762, led to widespread condemnation from both Calvinists and Catholics and he sought refuge first in Prussia and then in England. Price was prepared to let Rousseau live at Monaughty, then home to one of his tenant farmers, for a small rent. He discussed the plan with Rousseau and as a result instructed the house to be put in order for the philosopher's use, but this never seems to have been done, and when Wootton Hall in Staffordshire was made available to him, Rousseau moved there instead. Whether the supposed friendship between Price and Rousseau flourished thereafter is not known, but in any event Chase Price died suddenly the following year and Rousseau shortly afterwards.

Price was an acquaintance of James Boswell, who described him as 'one of the most celebrated and ribald wits of his time'. In his brief biographical sketch of Price in his *History of the House of Commons, 1759-90*, Sir Lewis Namier describes him as 'impetuous, resourceful and passionately persevering, he was buzzing round, gathering information and retailing it, constantly scheming and seeking patrons under who to act'.[7]

The second son of the second marriage, Richard, like his father, married a wealthy heiress, Margaret, the daughter and heiress of Dr Charles Humphreys of Penant, Montgomeryshire. Richard Price lived first at Farrington and later at Chandos House, Knighton, and gained little from his brother's political career beyond a pension of £200 a year secured for him in 1766. His major preoccupation was building up the family estate, since the family property in Knighton had been settled on the children of John Price II by his first marriage. Amongst his purchases was a large property in Norton bought in 1766, though the lordship of Norton manor was not secured until 1829.[8]

His marriage produced four children, the oldest son, Richard Price II (1773-1861), graduating at University College, Oxford in 1794. After serving as sheriff of Radnorshire in 1794 and briefly again in February to March 1799, he was elected as MP for Radnor Boroughs with the backing of the Harley family and served until 1847, by which time he was 'Father of the House'. A 'firm unbending Tory', Price was an uncompromising opponent of Parliamentary Reform and never really forgave the Duke of Wellington for accepting Catholic Emancipation – the granting of full civil rights to Roman Catholics – in 1829.

The rebuilding of the parish church

Of the old church, described in a mid-18th-century document as 'by length of time ruinous and decayed', we know very little beyond that it consisted of 'ancient buildings'.[9] The churchwardens, in their replies in the triennial visitations of 1716 and 1719, describe the fabric of the buildings as in good condition – the roof well covered, the windows well glazed, the interior walls white and clean, and the floor paved 'plain and even'. However, a church brief of 1724 issued on behalf of Knighton and 'Laintwarden' appealed to other parishes in the kingdom for financial assistance 'toward a loss by fire' amounting to £1,093. What proportion of this sum was for Knighton is not known, nor is the outcome. The issue of another brief on behalf of Knighton church in 1751 suggests that the appeal of 1724 together with funds raised locally were insufficient to make good the damage incurred in the

*Plate 10: The church of St Lawrence as it appeared in the mid 1800s,
before it was replaced by St Edward's church in 1878*

fire. The ensuing deterioration was such that the church was unsafe and had to be demolished and rebuilt, apart from the ground floor of the tower, at a cost of more than £1,456.[10]

The new church, dedicated to St Lawrence, was built in the mid-1750s – in 1752 according to Richard Haslam and in 1756 according to William Hatfield. A very plain structure, 'with no pretensions to architectural order or beauty', according to the *Hereford Journal* of 5 June 1861, it had a low ceiling only 22 feet above floor level, 10 feet lower than that of the old church. The interior of the church was not completed until 1762, when window sills were fitted, the lower sections of the interior walls boarded, and the high box pews installed, along with the three-decker pulpit erected against the central pier on the south side of the church. A gallery was built on the west side of the church in 1770 at a cost of £94, and a font was built at the west end in 1773. The north gallery was added in 1813 by the incumbent, the Revd Robert Morris.

Perhaps the most sensitive issue in the building of the new church was that of the pews which were privately owned. After six or so of the town establishment had laid claim to build pews in the new church, it was decided in 1762 that the other pew-holders in the old nave should build their own pews 'on their own ground', that is on the site of their old pews. The pews were to be 'fronted with oak in a handsome and uniform manner of ye same height and according to ye same model and form in which Mr [John] Price's seat in ye said Church is already erected'.

There were to be 27 pews on the south side of the nave and 34 on the north. However there was not sufficient room for all the old pew-holders in the nave and those who were dispossessed, along with pew-holders in the old gallery and chapel, both of which had been demolished, had to wait until the new west gallery was built before they received the right to build pews at a cost of £3 each.[11]

The ownership of the pews was attached to houses, and the right to a pew was sold with the property. Thus the advertisement of the sale of the George Inn, Knighton in the *Hereford Journal* of 22 July 1807 concluded: 'There is a large pew in the church opposite the pulpit which is an appurtenance to the above premises, and will go with the premises.'

Private ownership of the pews in the church provoked controversy periodically until the restoration of the nave in 1877, since the practice greatly reduced accommodation for the poorer inhabitants of the town.

Population trends

While the parish register and the bishop's transcripts – annual lists of baptisms, marriages and burials in the parish – are largely complete, the entries for some years prior to 1750 or so are not fully legible, meaning that the number of baptisms and burials for some years cannot be calculated with any real certainty. Any conclusions concerning population change must therefore be considered as tentative, the more so because no allowance is made for any in- or out-migration.

To minimise any margin of error, the analysis uses the difference between the average annual number of baptisms and burials over 20-year periods for 1662-1840 (a 19-year period for the period 1662-1680) as an indicator of Knighton's rate of population change. Figure 5 shows that the population of the town increased consistently between 1660 and 1800, though the rate of growth was very small prior to 1720 – and possibly even negative due to out-migration – but then grew at a faster rate, and particularly so from around 1800.

Population growth was checked from time to time by epidemics, most notably in 1742 when there were just 21 baptisms but 61 burials. The high mortality rate was probably the result of a smallpox epidemic, for against 20 of the 33 burials between April and July 'sp' has been written, presumably an abbreviation denoting a smallpox fatality. There may also have been epidemics, though on a much smaller

	Annual average number of christenings	Annual average number of burials	Difference: (christenings – burials)
1662-80	20.1	16.3	+3.8
1681-1700	15.1	13.2	+1.9
1700-20	18.4	16.8	+1.6
1721-40	24.9	19.7	+5.2
1741-60	26.3	19.1	+7.2
1761-80	28.2	21.5	+7.0
1781-1800	27.1	21.0	+6.1
1801-20	36.2	22.9	+13.3
1821-40	41.9	28.5	+13.4

Figure 5: Knighton parish: annual average baptisms and burials, 1662-1840
(Source: Parish register and bishop's transcripts)

scale, in 1671, 1674 and 1682, since in these years burials exceeded christenings by more than 50%, and again in 1731, 1752 and 1768, though in these years the excess of burials over christenings was less than 50%.

The Economy
In his introduction to his account of Knighton in 1795 Sir Frederick Eden wrote: 'Knighton is a small market town, but a place of no manufacture, it is surrounded by hills, and is in a very secluded situation.'[12]

This would seem an appropriate description of late 18th-century Knighton since, for the most part, the town appears to have been content to survive through doing no more than serving its large but thinly populated hinterland.

Information relating to the town's commerce and industries in the 18th century is very sparse. From wills and property deeds we hear of blacksmiths, coopers, millers, tanners, maltsters, wool staplers – the typical occupations one would expect to find in any small market town in the later 18th and early 19th centuries. According to Sir Richard Green Price, Chase Price had helped the town's trade in the mid-18th century by building 'a free market house at the upper part of the town' for the sale of poultry, eggs and butter. From the type of goods on offer, the building may well have been the old Butter Cross, replaced by a larger version in the mid-19th century.[13] The town still possessed a vestigial cloth industry, for at least one weaving business, first mentioned in a deed of the 1630s, was in the hands of the Woosnam family through most of the 18th century and continued in their hands until 1813.[14]

Professional men – surgeons such as David Jenkins and solicitors such as John Meredith and his two lawyer sons – made a good living in the town, as did tradesmen such as hatters, tailors, and even a dancing master and a peruke (wig) maker. Clearly

Knighton possessed a small genteel and leisured middle class who considered the services of a barber essential – hence the advertisement in the *Hereford Journal* of 9 October 1793:

> Wanted at Knighton – A barber – any clean man will have encouragement, there being but one old man of the business in the town, and he has no assistants.

A significant barrier to the development of Knighton in the 18th century was its isolated position. In 1743, when the author of *A Journey to Llandrindod Wells* inquired of a Knighton innkeeper about Llandrindod and how to reach it, the innkeeper could give him no information. The town lay on the long, roundabout routes from Presteigne to Montgomery and Newtown via Clun and Bishops Castle respectively, but the other routes into the Radnorshire uplands to villages such as Llangunllo, Llanbister or Penybont were little more than rough tracks negotiable for most of the year by pedestrians, horsemen and goods carried by panniered horses, sledges or 'wilkers' – wheelcars with wheels in the middle of the vehicle and runners at the front. Such tracks were normally impassable during the winter months, and even the relatively major route up the Teme valley was very difficult beyond Beguildy. Folk travelling into Knighton market often rode on 'double-barrelled horses'[15] with the farmer's wife riding pillion, or travelled in pairs, one riding on the horse burdened down with panniers and the other walking, the two changing places every few miles.

There was little incentive to improve these roads, which were maintained on behalf of the parish by a surveyor appointed each year by the ratepayers. Since the work was done by the parishioners or paid for by them, the surveyor was unwilling to risk the wrath of his neighbours by doing too much. Normally road maintenance meant no more than filling the ruts with stones and ploughing the worst sections level. The more important of these parochial roads were maintained to a rather better standard, but even on these, wheeled transport had difficulties, and wagons were normally pulled by teams of 8 or 16 horses.

Passengers travelling by coach needed deep pockets and considerable powers of endurance. Those who travelled on the London coach from Knighton in August 1794 left the Duke's Arms at noon on a Friday and reached the Bull and Mouth Inn in London on Sunday morning. The return coach started at the Bull and Mouth at noon on Tuesday and arrived back in Knighton at 9am on Thursday. The fare to Leominster was 6s inside and 3s 6d outside, while the fare to London was £2 2s inside and for those hardy or impecunious enough to travel on the outside seats, £1 3s.[16] One should bear in mind that in 1794 a farmworker earned 7s a week. The direct service does not seem to have been in operation long, and townspeople wishing to travel or to transport goods to and from London could normally do so only via a change at Leominster or Ludlow.

The formation in 1767 of the Radnorshire Turnpike Trust, which charged tolls on goods, stock and road users, using the proceeds to improve the roads, had little impact upon the Knighton area initially since it concentrated on improving the London to Aberystwyth road and its feeders.

The Relief of Poverty [17]

Prior to the mid-1830s the task of relieving poverty in the town lay in the hands of the churchwardens and the two overseers of the poor elected by the ratepayers, the money being raised by a rate or 'lewn' collected from property owners according to the rateable value of their property. With the town's population increasing faster than its economy was growing, the means by which the poor could be relieved effectively and economically loomed large at the vestry meetings of the Knighton ratepayers. The minutes of the vestry meeting of 28 May 1773 expressed concern that:

> Whereas there has been great sums of money collected for the poor of this parish, and yet they appear to be greatly in want.

Normally the overseers delegated the task of relieving the poor to an agent who carried it out for a small fee. At the vestry meeting of 30 April 1761 it was agreed that:

> Lloyd Griffiths shall keep the poor of ye said p[arish] for one year with sufficient meat, drink, washing and lodging from this 20th of Ap[ril] and we do further agree that the said Lloyd Griffiths shall be paid by the overseers eighteen pence a week for every person delivered to him, and if any person is impotent and not able to help themselves then for every such person two shillings a week. ... and likewise the said overseers shall send bedding and sufficient clothing for every person sent to his care.

Such an agreement was open-ended and did not make for economy, so it became more usual to allow a fixed sum with which poverty was to be relieved for the year. This might include the provision of a workhouse in which some of the poor could be accommodated, the workhouse keeper being allowed to keep any balance he could achieve by 'careful economy' from the sum he was given to run it, irrespective of the suffering this might inflict on the paupers. In Knighton, such provision was made in a house rented on an annual basis. However the quality of the workhouse keeper inspired little confidence on the part of the vestry and in 1772 the governor of the workhouse, Edward Pinner, was given two months' notice to quit. In 1795, according to Sir Frederick Eden, a pioneering investigator and writer on poverty who was gathering information for his book *The State of the Poor* which he hoped would further the debate on poor law reform, the administration of the Poor Law in Knighton left much to be desired at a time when 13 of the borough's poor were maintained in a workhouse and 12 poor families received 17s a week. The situation in the workhouse was noted as chaotic as it was:

> ... under the direction of a governess who is perfectly incompetent to enforce obedience to her orders; the poor seldom obey, and often beat her; and, even among themselves, they have continual disputes.

The Knighton overseers dismissed the 'governess' and in March 1796 advertised for a man and a woman to look after the poor of Knighton in the workhouse.[18]

Other means of keeping down the poor rates were also tried. In 1762 a poor boy aged eight was apprenticed to Widow Smith of Lower Woodhouse, who received 12 pence a week for the first year of the apprenticeship. Whilst the parish gave his some clothes at the outset, Widow Smith had to clothe him for the remaining period of his apprenticeship. Such apprentices were not sought after and were usually placed with newcomers to the district or such people as the overseers could bully into accepting a boy. Another expedient, which seems to have been rarely used in Knighton, was to build a house on the common for a pauper. Thus in 1777 the vestry meeting of 21 February ordered the overseers to pay a Richard Roberts 10 shillings for building a house on the Rhos for a widow, Mrs Pugh.

At vestry meetings the less well-to-do ratepayers, whose poor rate commitments were no more than a few pence, were less troubled than their wealthy neighbours by rising poor relief expenditure. A means of excluding poorer ratepayers from the administration of poor relief, and thus curbing a large increase in the poor rate, was to set up a select vestry of wealthier ratepayers to administer the system. This occurred in Knighton in 1779 when 'settling the poor' was entrusted to a 13 man committee or select vestry consisting of the vicar, five 'gentlemen' and seven tradesmen. Nevertheless expenditure on the poor in Knighton continued to rise. In 1776 it amounted to nearly £121, rising to an annual average of nearly £234 for the years 1783-85, though in the six years 1790-95 it dropped back to an average of nearly £190. But with food prices set to rise rapidly as a result of inflation during the Napoleonic Wars, expenditure on poor relief was to reach unprecedented levels.[19]

$$\approx 5 \approx$$

Knighton at War and Peace, 1793-1815

Any stimulus provided by the Revolutionary and Napoleonic Wars of 1793-1815 seems to have been short-lived, and the pace of development in Knighton did not substantially quicken until the 1830s and 1840s.

Knighton and the French Wars 1793-1815

Given Radnorshire's small population, its contribution to Britain's forces was bound to be insignificant. When the small part-time Royal Radnor Militia was embodied for regular service in January 1793 it totalled 120 other ranks and at no time in the war did its strength exceed 340 men. It was recruited from men between the ages of 18 and 50, physically fit and at least 5 feet 4 inches in height, drawn by lot to serve for three years. If a man was unwilling to serve he could pay a substitute to take his place. At any time the number of Knighton men serving in the Radnor Militia was small, no more than four or five, and in 1807 when a total of 109 men was needed from across the county, out of the 258 men who qualified for service in Knighton Hundred only 23 recruits were needed.[1] The regiment was deployed for the greater part of the wars on garrison duty in Kent and Cornwall, but also served in Ireland at Armagh in 1811-12. For those of an adventurous nature garrison duty was not enough, and often members of the Militia volunteered for a regiment of the line.

A more direct route to adventure and excitement was to 'take the king's shilling' when recruiting parties from regiments of the line attended one of Knighton's fairs. Perhaps the most successful of such recruiting forays was that made by Captain William Meredith, a member of Knighton's prominent legal family, on behalf of the Duke of York's Highlanders in 1795, when it was reported that he succeeded in raising 'a company' which he marched to Inverness. (Why he chose a Highland Regiment is unclear; perhaps it had one of the few commissions available for purchase at that time.) At first sight this would appear to be a wild exaggeration since a company would consist of at least 60 to 80 men.[2] However, an account of the funeral at Knighton of a veteran of that regiment, Thomas Cowdell, in the *Hereford Times* of 20 November 1847 described how he was 'carried to his last resting place by six of his old companions, followed by the sergeant of his company and old friend, Samuel Owens'. The fact that at least eight of Meredith's recruits were alive in Knighton more than 50 years after they had signed on suggests that Meredith had recruited a significant number of men in the Knighton area in 1795.

The *Journal* also gave a brief resumé of Cowdell's military career which reveals that the Duke of York's Highlanders, including its Knighton contingent, took part in most of the significant actions of the wars. Between 1795 and 1800 the regiment was involved in suppressing an Irish rebellion. In 1801 Cowdell saw action in Egypt after Nelson's victory in the Battle of the Nile, taking part in the sieges of Alexandria and Cairo, and being wounded in both actions. Between 1809 and 1812 the regiment was in action in the Peninsular War, with Cowdell taking part in the battles of Corunna in 1809, Badajoz in 1810 and Salamanca in 1812. In 1815 he fought at the battle of Waterloo and was severely wounded. If the *Journal's* account of Cowdell's military career is accurate, it would seem that a group of Knightonians played a small role in some of the most decisive actions of the Napoleonic War.

Following the French defeat and Napoleon's abdication in the spring of 1814 and his exile to Elba, the British government declared 6 July as a day of general thanksgiving. This was celebrated in style at Knighton according to the *Hereford Journal* of 13 July. An ox was roasted, tables were set out on High Street and the poor of the town sat down to a magnificent dinner 'bountifully provided by the gentlemen of the area', while Richard Price MP provided a hogshead of excellent old ale. After the dinner, the band of the Radnorshire Militia played and 'many respectable young ladies and gentlemen amused themselves and the spectators by dancing'. The day finished with the whole town brilliantly illuminated by flaming torches, while candles and lanterns lit up the windows of the town's elite.

The celebrations turned out to be premature, and Napoleon had to be decisively defeated at Waterloo in 1815 before peace was assured. A permanent reminder of Britain's victory was the naming of areas of the town after two of the heroes of the war: Nelson Square and Wellington Place.

The economic impact of the French Wars
The period of the Revolutionary and Napoleonic Wars saw a marked rise in the price of wheat, barley – which was frequently used as a substitute for wheat – and a rather smaller rise in the prices of other agricultural products. Initially the price rise stemmed from a run of poor harvests in the 1790s, made worse by the wars which disrupted overseas supplies and by Napoleon's attempt to block British trade with Europe. The annual average wheat prices in Radnorshire between 1792 and 1817, calculated from the weekly price returns from Knighton and Presteigne published in the *London Gazette*, are shown in Figure 6. The impact of such high prices may be judged from an assertion made in 1794 that a price of 8 shillings a bushel for wheat

was considered to be high in Radnorshire,[3] for in 15 of the 26 years the average annual local wheat price was well in excess of this. The use of annual average prices also tends to understate the extent of price inflation: thus during the years of 1800-01 and 1809-13, the wheat price in Knighton and Presteigne sometimes exceeded 25 shillings a bushel, and in December 1809, March-June 1810, most of 1811 and in January 1812, local wheat prices were amongst the highest in the kingdom.

Year	Average price	Year	Average price
1792	5s.4d	1805	10s.11d
1793	6s.1d	1806	10s.11d
1794	6s.9d	1807	7s.8d
1795	9s.5d	1808	9s.5d
1796	9s.11d	1809	12s.2d
1797	6s.4d	1810	15s.7d
1798	6s.0d	1811	12s.10d
1799	8s.7d	1812	14s.1d
1800	16s.2d	1813	13s.10d
1801	17s.0d	1814	9s.2d
1802	7s.6d	1815	8s.8d
1803	6s.5d	1816	10s.3d
1804	6s.8d	1817	12s.10d

Figure 6: Annual average wheat prices in Knighton and Presteigne 1792-1817
(Source: The *London Gazette* www.london-gazette.co.uk)

The reasons for this are far from clear. It may be that the local supply was relatively small, and with demand fairly stable, minor changes in that supply had a magnified impact upon the price level. Certainly the staple foodstuffs in upland Radnorshire were oatmeal and barley bread, and demand for wheat was largely confined to the lowland areas such as the lower Teme and Lugg valleys. The rural parts of such areas were largely self-sufficient in terms of wheat, and the price level for wheat at Knighton depended upon the stocks which local farmers could offer for sale at the Thursday markets. If demand exceeded supply, even a small shortfall could have led to a steep price rise. Even if this situation were to continue for a few weeks, the amounts involved were so small it would hardly be worthwhile for speculators to bring in supplies from outside the area.

The steep rise in the price of wheat in the war years hit the working people of Knighton hard, for even in the best of times the labouring poor lived at or rather below the subsistence level, spending more than 80% of their income on food. Even then they relied upon expedients such as gleaning, and gifts of flour at the farmhouse door on St Thomas's Day (3 July) to tide them over.[4] During the years of 1800-01 and 1809-13 their situation became well-nigh impossible. Labourers working on a fairly regular basis for a farmer were sometimes slightly better placed, since some farmers sold grain to their workers at below market prices and allowed them to plant a row of potatoes in one of their fields.

During the course of the war labourers' wages had risen: from 6 shillings a week in 1793 to 7 shillings in 1794, and to 8-10 shillings per week in winter and 9-12 shillings in summer in 1814.[5] However, these figures tend to overstate wage levels since most labourers were hired by the day and few could expect to be employed for six days a week throughout the year. In any event, such wage increases were not sufficient to keep up with rising food prices, and in spite of switching to cheaper bread made from barley or muncorn (a mixture of wheat and barley) instead of their customary second quality wheaten loaves, and increasingly substituting potatoes for bread, most of the labouring poor found it necessary to seek relief from the parish.

Year	£	Year	£
1800	445	1809	264
1801	454	1810	308
1802	370	1811	277
1803	234	1812	374
1804	283	1813	331
1805	282	1814	386
1806	289	1815	199
1807	317	1816	323
1808	261		

Figure 7: Expenditure on the relief of the poor in Knighton parish 1800-1816 (Source: Powys Archives Office, R/QS/S3706)

For some such a step was only necessary when work was short or at those times of the year when food prices were at their highest, but many found it necessary to supplement their earnings with relief from the parish on a regular basis. In these cases relief took the form of the payment of house rent, or a small weekly cash payment which varied according to the number of children in the family. The parish continued to maintain a workhouse during this period in which the 'impotent poor' – the old, chronic sick and unmarried mothers and their illegitimate children – were housed.

The transformation of poor relief from a means of supporting the old and sick and single mothers and their children to a way of bringing up the incomes of the poor to something approaching subsistence levels increased the burden on rate-payers already faced with increasing taxation to help finance the war effort. Nor did farmers gain as much as one might expect from rising food prices, since they were faced with not only increased local and national taxation but also increased tithes payments. Whilst there was the option to bring marginal grassland under cultivation, this was a relatively expensive process if a reasonable yield was to be gained. Tenant farmers also faced steep rent increases, since landlords were quick to exploit apparently permanent increases in the price of farm produce.

O.R. Ashton has demonstrated a relationship between high wheat prices and an increasing mortality rate in Knighton Hundred during the 1790s,[6] though this is not entirely borne out by the Knighton parish data, possibly because the numbers involved are too small. The annual number of burials in Knighton in the period 1790-1811 tended to be in the 20s and low 30s. However, the number of burials in the parish in the years between 1812 and 1820 show a marked increase, with distinct peaks in 1814-15 and 1818-19, which suggests that the very high wheat prices of the closing years of the war and then the post-war slump had some impact on the mortality rate in Knighton.

In the struggle to survive in the era of high food prices, some people were reduced to desperate measures, stealing simply so that they and their families could survive. In the absence of an effective police force, the landowners and substantial farmers of Knighton, Whitton, Discoed, Llangunllo and Bleddfa formed the Knighton Association for the Prosecution of Felons in 1802 in an attempt to combat this. Members of the Association, which was by no means unique, paid a subscription and this was used to pay the costs of prosecuting an offender, in those days met by the victim of the crime rather than public funds, and to offer rewards for information. The largest reward – 5 guineas – was offered for information on burglaries and in cases involving the stealing or maiming of horses, cattle, sheep or pigs. Information on the theft of grain, threshed or unthreshed, carried a reward of 2 guineas, while information on stealing poultry, robbing any garden, orchard or fish pool, stealing turnips, cabbages or potatoes and breaking down a hedge or fence or stealing posts, rails or poles, brought a reward of half a guinea.[7]

Property owners clearly regarded the Association as successful since it continued to exist until at least 1830, though there does not appear, from press reports, to have been a marked increase in the number of cases of petty theft at Knighton Petty Sessions. Possibly the value of the Association to property owners was psychological, in that its existence gave reassurance and a sense of security; alternatively, punishment may have been inflicted on an unofficial basis. This was certainly the case in 1826 when an intruder broke into Ystrad House, the home of the Knighton lawyer Thomas Meredith. The intruder was seized by a servant and 'soundly thrashed' by the attorney.[8]

As in the rest of the county, serious crime was very rare in Knighton, and the murder of the Beguildy tailor Arthur Bedward by a Knighton labourer Samuel Harley, reported in the *Hereford Journal* of 10 October 1821, must have caused a sensation in the district. The unemployed Harley had been drinking with Bedward, who had come to Knighton to sell a small house, and noticed that Bedward was carrying £30 in cash. He thought wrongly that Bedward must have the purchase money on him, and when Bedward left in the late evening to walk back to Beguildy,

Harley followed him to Lloyney where he took a stake from the hedge, beat him to death and threw his body into a ditch.

At the inquest at Knucklas a verdict of wilful murder was found against Harley, who was imprisoned at the county gaol at Presteigne whilst awaiting trial. Two days after his arrest, Harley cut his throat, and for a while it seemed unlikely he would survive to stand trial, but he recovered and on 19 February 1822 was sentenced to death. He was hanged at Presteigne on Monday 22 April, the first execution in Radnorshire since that of Mary Morgan in 1805.[9]

The rarity of serious crime should not be taken to signify that everyone in the Knighton area subscribed to high standards of behaviour and morality. In his *History of the Baptists in Radnorshire*, John Jones wrote of the 1830s: 'Sabbath breaking, drinking, boxing, fighting and other brutal sports were prevalent in Knighton in those years.' The presence of a counter culture in the town is supported by the *Hereford Times* of 12 March 1853 which described how a few years earlier 'pugilistic engagements were prevalent in the place' while the Sabbath was 'desecrated by gymnastic exercises and the atmosphere of the tavern.' Press reports of a bare knuckle match in the Knighton area in the summer of 1829 suggest that such contests were organised by Ludlow supporters of the sport who recognised that the remoteness of the Knighton area ensured that the match would not be disrupted by the authorities.[10]

The Price and Rogers families

During the first half of the 19th century the dominant figure in Knighton was Richard Price II (1773-1861), MP for Radnor Boroughs from 1799 until 1847. His standing was such that in all that time he fought only two elections, in 1812 and 1820, on all other occasions being returned unopposed. He also served as lieutenant-colonel commanding the Radnorshire Volunteers between 1803 and 1808, and then as lieutenant-colonel of the Radnorshire Local Militia. He lived initially at Chandos House, before moving in 1838 to his newly built Norton Manor. He poured a great deal of energy into building up the family estate, and by the 1840s owned nearly 23% of the parish and more than 18% of the borough of Knighton by rateable value.[11] By 1871 the Price estate amounted to 8,775 acres with an annual rental value of £7,638.

Plate 11: Richard Price,
MP for Radnor Boroughs,
1799-1847

His younger brother, Charles Humphreys Price, was able to assist Richard's political career since he served Sir John Benn Walsh as steward of his estates in Radnorshire and thus exercised considerable influence in the contributory borough of Cefnllys, a Walsh possession.[12] His older sister, Margaret, followed family tradition and married well, her husband being George Green, the fourth son of the Revd Jonathan Green D.D. of Ashford Hall, Shropshire. Her second son, Richard, who inherited his uncle's estate in 1861, taking the additional surname of Price by royal licence, was to play a leading role in the later rapid development of the town and its economy.

At some time in the later 1790s a second major landowning family moved into the Knighton area when a wealthy East India merchant, Charles Rogers (1752-1820), purchased the Stanage Park estate from Thomas Johnes of Croft Castle. The house had been demolished by Johnes, and between 1803 and 1807 Humphrey Repton produced plans for a new house and remodelled grounds for Rogers, who laid the foundation stone of his new house in 1807. Charles Rogers was a younger son of the Revd Edward Rogers of The Home, Bishops Castle, an estate which the family had owned since the 14th century.[13]

Neither Charles Rogers nor his son, Edward (1781-1852), who moved into Stanage Park in 1822, involved themselves closely in the affairs of Knighton or Radnorshire. Edward Rogers served as one of Bishops Castle's MPs between 1820 and 1832, but thereafter steadfastly refused all the invitations of Richard Price to stand for either the Radnorshire or the Radnor Boroughs seat. It was not a question of finance, for in 1871 the Stanage Park estate amounted to more than 4,600 acres, producing an estimated rental of nearly £4,000.

Plate 12: Stanage Park by Jonathan Myler Lee

On Edward Rogers' death in 1852 the estate passed to his sister Harriet, and on her death in 1866 to a cousin, the Revd John Rogers, whose wife Charlotte played a prominent part in the social life of Knighton, taking a particular interest in the town's National Schools. Their son, Charles Coltman Rogers (1854-1928), besides playing a significant role in the musical and sporting life of Knighton, served in 1884-85 as the last MP for the Radnor Boroughs seat prior to its abolition in November 1885, and after the establishment of county councils he became the dominant figure in Radnorshire local government.

The presence of two gentry families in the Knighton area does not seem to have produced any clash of interests. Neither Richard Price nor Charles or Edward Rogers were active socially, and by the time Mrs Charlotte Rogers was active in Knighton's social life the Green Prices had moved to Norton Manor.

Post-war Knighton

The defeat of Napoleon at Waterloo in 1815 removed inflationary pressures from the British economy and produced a sharp fall in the price of agricultural products, which plunged the farming community into crisis since the level of rents, local taxation and tithes did not adjust to the new situation quickly. Farm costs however could be reduced speedily: marginal arable land was allowed to revert to low quality grazing, while in 1815 labourers' wages were cut to 8 shillings a week, a level at which they remained into the 1830s and beyond.

Yet it would be wrong to portray the farming sector of the Knighton area as lacking any sense of direction and simply retreating into low cost subsistence farming, for the number of fairs held annually increased in the post-war years. Prior to the 1790s Knighton had three main fairs: the 'mop' or hiring fair on 17 May (originally on 6 May), the fair on 2 October mainly for the sale of sheep; and the Llan Hollan or All Hallows Fair (famous as a butter fair) on the Thursday before 12 November. In the 1790s two new fairs were added: one was held on the first Saturday after 1 March in 1792, and an Easter fair was held for some years after 1795. In 1818 further fairs were introduced: one on 8 August and another, the Great Market, on the Thursday before Christmas Day; while in 1826 another fair was added, on 21 June, the day before Brampton Bryan Fair. Press reports of the Knighton fairs in the 1820s usually reported that markets were cleared relatively early in the day and that prices received were at least satisfactory, which suggests that the local farming sector was adjusting to the post-war economic situation.[14] However, other evidence suggests that Knighton's economic development was fairly stagnant until the 1830s.

The annual rents derived from the three Knighton gates of the Radnorshire Turnpike Trust – the North Gate on the road to Beguildy and Newtown at the bottom of Conjuror's Pitch, the South Gate on the Presteigne road, and the West

Year	£	Year	£	Year	£
1800	168	1811	266	1821	170
1801	131	1812	233	1822	140
1802	131	1813	216	1823	143
1803	161	1814	211	1824	144
1804	170	1815	223	1825	n.a.
1805	170	1816	216	1826	196
1806	184	1817	130	1827	176
1807	220	1818	145	1828	188
1809	184	1819	200	1829	166
1810	184	1820	n.a.	1830	166

*Figure 8: Annual rental received from the three Knighton gates
of the Radnorshire Turnpike Trust 1800-1820*
(Source: *The Hereford Journal*)

Gate on the Penybont road near the junction with Ffrydd Road – for the period 1800-1830 give an indication of the health of the town's economy in that period. Since the rents the tenants were prepared to pay depended upon the amount they expected to collect in tolls, the rents payable for the gates over the years provide some indication of the prosperity of the town. Apart from a boom in the later years of the war, the level of rents shows little fluctuation, which suggests that the town's economy was not growing. In 1800 the three gates produced a total rental of £168 in 1829, and 1830 rentals totalled no more than £166.

The census data of 1801-1841 shows that, after a sharp increase of 18.5% between 1801 and 1811, the population of Knighton parish grew more slowly than that of the remainder of Knighton Hundred until 1831-41. The lower growth rate probably stemmed from sustained out-migration, for while between 1811 and 1831 the population of the town grew by 145, baptisms exceeded burials by 316. There

	Knighton			The remainder of the Hundred	
	Population	%	Houses	Population	%
1801	938		225	2,721	
1811	1,114	+18.5	249	3,101	+13.8
1821	1,191	+6.9	253	3,547	+14.3
1831	1,259	+5.7	252	3,954	+11.4
1841	1,404	+11.5	285	4,326	+ 9.4

*Figure 9: The population of Knighton parish
and the remainder of the Hundred, 1801-41*
(Source: Printed census data)

is also some evidence that the mortality rate in the parish had not fallen as sharply as that of many parts of the kingdom. Between 1831 and 1841 the natural increase – the excess of baptisms over burials – was only 66, while in 1836 and 1839 the number of burials in the churchyard exceeded the number of baptisms recorded in the parish register. The marked increase in the town's population between 1831 and 1841 therefore must have come about by substantial in-migration, possibly from the neighbouring rural area. Certainly the population data of 1801-41 suggests that the town's economy for much of the first half of the 19th century was less than dynamic.

The increase in population growth level and the marked increase in the number of occupied houses between 1831 and 1841 indicates that the pace of economic growth may have been quickening by this time and this seems to be borne out by a comparison of the Knighton entry in the 1830 edition of Pigot's *National Commercial Directory* with that in the 1844 edition, which shows that the number of businesses in the town named in the earlier edition of the directory had almost doubled by 1844.

The two directories also show that Knighton's links with the country outside its immediate hinterland had strengthened in the period 1830-44. In 1830 the town was served by three carriers who made weekly journeys to London via Ludlow, Birmingham and Leominster respectively, carrying relatively small consignments of goods, packages and parcels. However, by 1844 four carriers were active in the town, two making weekly journeys to London via Ludlow and Bishops Castle respectively, another operating a weekly service to Presteigne and Kington and a twice weekly

	1830	1844		1830	1844
Academies	2	5	Maltsters	4	6
Attorneys	2	3	Millers	0	3
Auctioneers	2	2	Milliners	1	3
Bakers	2	7	Saddlers	2	4
Bankers	0	1	Surgeons	2	3
Butchers	3	3	Tailors	1	8
Carpenters	3	8	Tanners	2	2
Coopers	2	3	Tawers[x] and glovers	3	1
Drapers	8*	7	Saddlers	2	4
Grocers	8*	8	Shoemakers	3	8
Inns etc	13	18**	Wool staplers	0	2

Figure 10: Selected businesses in Knighton, 1830 and 1844
* described in the directory as 'grocers and drapers'
** including 3 'beer retailers'
[x] leather dressers

service to Ludlow and Worcester, and the fourth operating a weekly service to the two latter towns.

Though complaints over their poor condition continued, it seems clear that the local roads had improved. Certainly by the late 1840s the surrounding villages had their own means of transport to and from Knighton so that visitors now came in from Leintwardine, Bucknell, Bedstone, Clun and other places to Knighton market, and returned the same evening, for low fares.[15]

The building of the Penybont to Knighton road in 1836-37 also served to increase the custom of the Knighton shopkeepers, since it brought Bleddfa and Dolau within the town's orbit. However, despite the reform of the Welsh turnpike system, road users were still faced with tolls not only on the three roads formerly managed by the Radnorshire Trust, but also at the Shropshire tollgate on the Clun road near The Lee and the East Gate on the Ludlow road near the Milebrook. On all five of the main roads leading out from Knighton, farmers paying tolls to transport lime from the lime kilns at Leintwardine or Nash, or taking livestock to or from Knighton markets and fairs, felt particularly hard hit.[16]

The establishment of the Knighton and Kington and Radnorshire Bank in 1836 by Richard Green in conjunction with the Kington bankers James Davies and Richard Banks, enhanced the town's commercial standing. The steady improvement in quality of the stock offered for sale at Knighton from the 1830s increased the attractiveness of its livestock market to dealers, as did the absence, in practice, of market dues from the mid-1830s. The right to collect tolls on livestock – 9d per

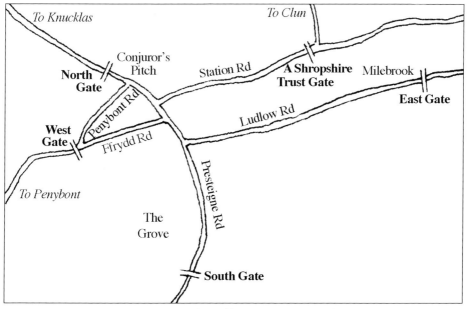

Figure 11: Turnpike tollgates in the Knighton area

horse, 3d per head of cattle, 2d per pig and 10d per 20 sheep – had been leased from the Crown by a Mrs Hester Cole, but from November 1836 an increasing number of dealers and farmers refused to pay. Initially Richard Banks, the Kington lawyer who was the Crown's steward, took a hard line and issued handbills threatening legal action, but over the next two or three years he failed to follow this up and evasion of the tolls became so common that from 1840 attempts to collect tolls were abandoned. By 1851, the authorities had come to the conclusion that any

Plate 14: The restored tollhouse on the Presteigne road

attempt to revive the tolls would provoke widespread opposition and probably very serious disturbances, though the tolls were not legally extinguished until 17 March 1883.[17]

The Knighton Poor Law Union

An early indication of Knighton's enhanced standing was the formation of the Knighton Poor Law Union in 1836 in the course of the reorganisation of poor relief on a national basis. Such a reorganisation was deemed necessary by most ratepayers since the old system was regarded as costly and ineffective, and there were fears that it would pauperise the rural labour force whose wages were usually supplemented by allowances from the poor rates. In addition to the parishes in Knighton Hundred, the Knighton Union also included townships and parishes in Herefordshire and Shropshire such as Brampton Bryan, part of Leintwardine, Bedstone, Bucknell, Stowe, Llanfairwaterdine, and Bettws. Within Radnorshire, the Union included not only the town's hinterland but also three parishes of the upper Ithon valley – Llanbadarn Fynydd, Llanddewi Ystradenni and Llananno – which were in Knighton Hundred, although many of their inhabitants regarded Rhayader rather than Knighton as their market centre. The total population of the Union was 8,719, of whom 6,266, about 72%, lived in Radnorshire.[18]

The three parishes of the Upper Ithon Valley were attached to Knighton Union rather than to Rhayader Union because the ratepayers of upper Radnorshire, mainly small tenant farmers, were hostile to the new regime which they feared would lead to increased wages, thanks to the elimination of wage subsidies, while keeping the poor rates high because of the administrative costs of the new system. By placing these parishes with those of the Welsh borderlands, where the influence of the gentry was stronger, it was hoped that the ratepayers' opposition to the new regime would be neutralised.[19] As a side effect, the extension of Knighton's influence into Rhayader's hinterland could not but raise the town's status and enhance its self-confidence.

The main objective of the new regime was to end the giving of outdoor relief – the making of payments to enable the poor to continue to live in their own homes – instead insisting that anyone wanting poor relief would have to enter a workhouse, conditions in which were harsh enough to deter all but the desperate from entering. Knighton Union Workhouse, designed to hold 120 paupers, was built on Ffrydd Lane at a cost of about £2,900, considerably more than the original estimate of between £1,600 and £1,800.[20] However, the system of outdoor relief did not wither away, for usually only about 10% of those in receipt of relief were to be found in the workhouse.

The new Poor Law regime certainly benefited the local economy since its officers – clerk, workhouse master and matron, nurse, chaplain, teacher, three medical officers and two relieving officers – were recruited locally wherever possible, on national pay scales considerably above the local going rate. Additionally, almost invariably, tenders for bread, meat and other foodstuffs, clothing, furniture, building repairs, painting, decorating and plumbing were awarded to local tradesmen.

The weakening of Knighton's links with the Crown

The de facto abandonment of the market tolls was symptomatic of the gradual erosion of Knighton's direct link with the Crown which began in earnest in the 1820s and continued into the 1880s. The link was already beginning to weaken under the stewardship of the fifth earl of Oxford. Between 1800 and 1824 no manorial courts were summoned in the Lordship of Farrington, while in 1823 there were only seven freemen in Knighton borough – not enough to empanel a jury for the manorial courts, a situation which put the existence of the borough under threat.[21]

The dismissal of the earl of Oxford from the stewardship of the lordship of Maelienydd in 1822 and the appointment of Richard Banks and James Davies, two Kington lawyers, did little to improve the situation beyond creating a few additional freemen in Knighton, for the Commissioners of Woods and Forests, who administered Crown lands, had decided to dispose of Crown assets in Radnorshire. The Crown properties in the Knighton area which were disposed of in the 1820s, along with the prices obtained and the names of the purchasers, are shown in Figure 12.

In addition to the properties listed in Figure 12, Richard Price also tried to buy 6 acres near Jenkin Allis Farm, but after waiting nearly 30 years to complete the transaction, gave up and demanded the return of the purchase money. The manor of South Rurallt included lands in the parishes of Llandegley, Llangunllo, Llanddewi Ystradenni, Llanfihangel Rhydithon, Pilleth and Whitton. The purchase of the manors by Price and Rogers involved only feudal dues, court fees and fines and the

Date	Property sold	Purchaser	Price
1823	Globe Close & the Old Pig Market Close	Henry Lloyd, Knighton, skinner	£250
1823	Swan Close	Richard Price MP	£450
1823	Castle Bank	Tomas Baxter, Knighton, surgeon	£50
1823	Site of Knucklas castle	Samuel Webb, Knucklas, carpenter	£40
1823	Land adjoining Knucklas castle	Richard Oakley, London, solicitor	££68
1824	Whitterleys	John Sayce of Kington	£1.599
1826	Manors of Farrington and Cwmgilla	Edward Rogers of Stanage	£397
1828	The manor of South Rurallt	Richard Price MP	£1.800
1832	The Slang, Temes Green	Richard Price MP	£135

Figure 12: Lands in the Knighton district sold by the Crown
(Source: TNA PRO CRES 49/4920-22 and LR1/242)

right of soil – the right to one-tenth of the commons, should they be enclosed; no land changed hands as a result of these transactions. However, Knighton remained a royal borough with the Crown retaining the right to collect tolls (until 1883), feudal dues and quit rents (a small residual rent payable on any former Crown possession).

Living conditions in Knighton in the 1840s

Some insight into living conditions in Knighton in the 1840s can be gained from the *Report ... on a Preliminary Inquiry into the Sanitary Condition of Knighton* by William Lee, published in 1849, which consists in the main of evidence provided by the leading townsmen. The general tenor of the report is provided by the concluding part of the evidence of Thomas Peters, one of the town's leading solicitors:

> We are much in need of a system of drainage; we have no sewerage. The paving of the town is very deficient; the water supply utterly inadequate, and the lighting discreditable. The general sanitary state of the town, from the existence of pigsties, privies and manure heaps, is very bad.

The evidence of Henry Warren, one of the district's Medical Officers of Health, as to housing conditions in the town, was particularly damning.

> The construction of the cottages is vicious with respect to morality, as well as injurious to health. Many of the houses are made of lath, plaster and thatch and have only one sleeping room for the whole of a large family. Others of them are built against the side of a hill without any attempt at drainage, and in consequence moisture exudes from the walls. The arrangements of the privies and conveniences are also very bad, producing offensive effluvia. Besides the injury to health, one serious evil resulting from the above facts is the gradual and certain loss of all the delicate feelings which ought to exist between the sexes.

At first sight the housing densities in the parish of Knighton in the censuses of the period 1801-1841, which show an average of between 4 and 5 persons per dwelling, suggest that overcrowding was not too serious. But a closer look at the census of 1841 shows that households of six, seven, eight and nine, though in the minority, were not uncommon in Cwm Bank and parts of the top of the town such as Castle Bank Alley, the Pig Market and the Butter Market, where the type of cottages described by Warren predominated.

The lack of street cleaning and of any drainage system meant that the road surfaces were normally covered with animal dung and refuse until the arrival of heavy rainfall. This would wash it down from the top of the town through the

Narrows and then through Church Street and Almshouse Street or through Broad Street and Bridge Street into the Teme or Wylcwm Brook, flooding cellars on the way with refuse and sewage. Overflowing cesspits were not unusual, and in 1849 Richard Green (Price) described how at Cwm Bank sewage was running over the road surface 'in a large semi-fluid stream'.

The town had had a commercial water supply water since at least 1807, and in 1818 the prospectus offering the 'valuable and desirable waterworks' for sale gave a description of it.[22] A spring on the Garth supplied a lead reservoir which in turn flowed into a supply tank in the Pig Market which supplied three main areas: Pig Market, Butter Cross and The Narrows; Broad Street; and from the bridge over the Wylcwm Brook to as far as Ffrydd House. The water company charged its customers 2s 6d or 5s, while those with taps paid between 4s and £1 per annum. In the lower parts of the town the better-off had sunk wells, while the poor without access to the town supply took water from the Teme and possibly the Wylcwm Brook, though the latter was clearly a health hazard.

❧ 6 ❧

THE GREAT REBUILDING

The third quarter of the 19th century saw Knighton emerge as Radnorshire's principal market town, leaving its main rivals, Presteigne and Rhayader, way behind in terms of size, amenities, population and prosperity.

The change in tempo

The innovations in Knighton of the first half of the 19th century had come about in a haphazard basis, but in the 1850s a concerted effort began to upgrade the town's commercial infrastructure, thus ensuring its future as a prosperous market town, and to enhance its civic amenities. This burst of energy and the civic pride which it engendered lasted into the late 1870s, waning with the advent of the agricultural depression of the closing decades of the century.

This co-ordinated drive to improve the town's amenities can be traced back to the dinner given on 6 October 1848 by John Edwards, the sheriff of Radnorshire, to celebrate the coming of age of his oldest son. Edwards, who hailed from Stowe, had made his fortune in business in London and had retired to Brampton Bryan. Following the dinner, held in a marquee at the Chandos Arms and attended by the local elite, the town's lack of a decent market hall, public room and other facilities was heavily criticised and a subscription opened to remedy matters.[1]

The Butter Cross

The first result of the initiative was a new Butter Cross on Market Street to replace the cramped Butter Cross of the 1750s, which was now considered not only dilapidated, but also 'unsightly and disagreeable'. A public meeting held at the beginning of August 1849, attended by the leading townsmen resolved:

> It was well known that Knighton was famous for a first rate market and people must no longer delay, but at once join hand in hand and build a handsome structure ... It is intended there should be an elegant and commodious building, fitted inside with tables and benches and sufficiently large to hold 200 to 300 people.

Plate 15: The Butter Cross c.1750

Plate 16: The Butter Cross c.1850,
later demolished to make way for the Market Hall

The new building was financed entirely by subscriptions raised after the dinner of October 1848. The single-storey building was designed by Thomas Nicholson of Hereford and was opened in mid-November 1849, though it was not quite finished, the *Hereford Times* expressing the opinion that, 'when quite complete it will be a comfort to the market people and a credit to the town'. The 'market people' consisted of two broad groups: the farmers' wives who brought in butter, sometimes cheese, eggs and dressed and live poultry for sale on market and fair days, and the 'higglers' who travelled the local countryside, buying similar goods from the farms they passed.

The decision to build the new Butter Cross on Market Street would appear to confirm the status of 'the top of the town' as the commercial centre of Knighton, containing at least 13 of the town's inns and beer houses on The Narrows, Market Street and Russell Street. However, its dominance was to continue for little more than a decade as, with the building of the railway, the centre of gravity was to shift downhill.[2]

The Farmers' Club

By the end of 1849 plans had been drawn up for the building of a market hall and an hotel, with iron gates between the two buildings opening out into a market place for the sale of sheep and pigs on the ground behind, which was the venue for the Knighton and Temeside Agricultural Show. The plan also specified two shops, one to be a coffee shop, and a large room on the first floor for public meetings. The scheme was to be in the hands of a public company which raised the necessary capital by the sale of £5 shares, the largest shareholder being Richard Green, with 120 shares.[3]

The original plans were subsequently scaled down and the new market hall was omitted. The construction of the two shops, the public room and the Farmers' Club began at the bottom of Broad Street on a site then occupied by the New Inn and a number of cottages. The accommodation at the Farmers' Club consisted of a dining room and kitchen, a library of 700 volumes together with a selection of newspapers and periodicals, and a reading room.[4] From its inception the Farmers' Club was managed by the Misses Tudge, who also undertook the catering for the public rooms, soon known as the Assembly Rooms.

In addition to its social function, the Farmers' Club which, at its formation in 1852, had more than 90 members, sought to publicise the latest agricultural innovations in the district. The club had four quarterly meetings, one being the annual general meeting, while the other three took the form of discussions on farming issues led by a member or guest speaker. In 1853, for example, the topics for discussion included the advantages of railways compared with other forms of transport; the production and general management of the turnip crop; and the management of farmyard manure.[5]

The club certainly fulfilled its social function initially, for its 'ordinary' or set dinner on market and fair days was well attended by the more well-to-do farmers of the district since its facilities were considerably better than those of the town's inns. The club also exercised great influence in the town. It succeeded in switching the fair held on the first Thursday after 4 February to the third Friday in January, while the wool fair held in June was abandoned in favour of one on 20 July.[6] This latter change was greeted with great satisfaction as a report from Knighton in the *Hereford Times* of 25 July 1857 makes clear:

> ... since the late alteration of the wool fair from June to July, it has advanced considerably, and now it can be ranked as decidedly popular and well attended. The change was made at the instance of the Knighton Farmers' Club. Now we are on a much better footing than formerly, when the farmers carried their wool to Newtown, then the principal market for the district. Thanks to some of our contemporary neighbours, we have now a market for any quantity of wool at our very door in the middle of a wool country ...

While the quarterly discussions served to spread knowledge of the latest farming innovations amongst the club membership, which was composed of the local gentry, substantial freeholders and well-to-do tenant farmers, they probably had little impact upon the deeply conservative small hill farmer, who tended to see the reduction of costs to the bare minimum as the way to prosperity. Such farmers often regarded a turnip course in their crop rotation, the use of artificial manures or the regular liming of land – all of which were consistently advocated by members of the Farmers' Club – as expensive and 'not for the likes o' we'.

By the mid 1860s attendance at the club's quarterly meetings had fallen off sharply and though the dining table was laid for 30 on such occasions, sometimes fewer than ten attended. Though the club's premises had been incorporated into the Norton Arms Hotel in 1867, it had effectively ceased to function by that date. However, in 1861 the club had set up a society to reward ploughmen, farm servants and other labourers for proficiency in such skills as hedging, ditching, thatching and ploughing and this, in turn, gave rise to the Knighton and District Agricultural Society in 1872, which was to survive, after several resurrections, into the 1920s.[7]

The Sheep Market

The Sheep Market was built on a field to the rear of the Farmers' Club which had been owned by Richard Price. When it opened in 1851 it could accommodate rather more than 6,000 sheep, normally sufficient for all but the September and October fairs in some years. Even after the market was extended to hold another 1,000 or 2,000 in the mid 1850s, on these fair days all the pens were often full by 6 or 7am. Thereafter the sheep were penned in the streets, to the great inconvenience of passing traffic and pedestrians. (Prior to the building of the Sheep Market the sheep pens were placed around the old Market Hall at the top of Broad Street and in front of the old Crown Inn. At this time cattle and horses were sold along Market Street and its environs at 'the top of the town'.)

The Sheep Market was seen as a great improvement, and in 1861 it was proposed to demolish the Chandos Arms and to use the site for a cattle market. Access was to be by a road running directly from north to south – the present Norton Street – while small cottages blocking the way between the proposed cattle market and the Butter Market were to be cleared away. However nothing came of the scheme, possibly as a result of financial difficulties, but partly because it sanctioned the continuation of the practice of selling sheep, cattle and horses in different parts of the town, which was inconvenient for the farmers. By 1863, on fair days, the cattle were to be found from the lower part of the Presteigne road to the crossroads with Ffrydd Road, the sheep and pigs in the sheep market with only horses sold at the top of the town.[8]

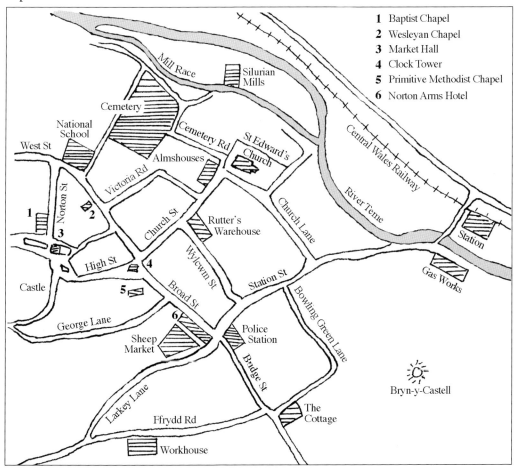

Figure 13: Knighton in the 1870s

The Demolition of the Market Hall

The Market Hall, which stood on the site now occupied by the clock tower, had had a very chequered history, having been rebuilt on several occasions, most recently in the 1790s and again in 1812. The hall served a number of purposes: market tolls on livestock and corn were collected there; it served as the town's law court, with a separate jury room; and it also housed the town lock-up. In the 18th century it had been the custom to lease it and the market standings around it on long leases, reserving only the court and jury rooms and the lock up for civic use.

At some point around 1790, when his lease of Knighton's tolls was on the point of expiring, Edward Lewis of Downton, MP for Radnor Boroughs between 1760 and 1790, or his sub-tenant, a Mr Williams, in accordance with a stipulation in the lease, produced ambitious plans to rebuild the hall. However the rebuilding was halted because the new, larger hall would have taken in too much of the street, and in revenge the new building that was constructed was deliberately much smaller and shoddily built. Thus by 1805, when the Welsh scholar Walter Davies visited Knighton, he described the hall as a ruinous building.[9]

In 1812, in the course of his unsuccessful attempt to defeat Richard Price for the Radnor Boroughs seat, Perceval Lewis, the son of Edward Lewis, built a new Market Hall on the same site. Once again the building was far from substantial and by 1837 it was sufficiently dilapidated to encourage a campaign to collect subscriptions to build a new hall. Success seemed likely in 1838 when a Mr Merrick, a London merchant who had been born in Knighton, gave a donation of £800 for the improvement of the town, but imposed a time limit within which it was to be used. Unfortunately, sustained bickering over a suitable site for the new hall meant that the time limit expired with nothing accomplished.[10]

During the late 1840s there were two schools of thought as to what should be done with the rapidly deteriorating Market Hall. Some thought that it should be patched up and made fit for use until funds were sufficient to build a new hall. In December 1848 a meeting decided that this should be done and that farmers should be encouraged to use the hall to revive the old corn market. Others, however, thought that the building was unsightly and beyond repair, and reflected badly upon the town, and eventually they took matters into their own hands. In September 1852 it was demolished, the *Hereford Times* of 11 November 1852 reporting:

> The Downfall of Mr (Town) Hall: the building had a few old friends (burgesses) who were determined to rally round him. But not withstanding all their care and watchfulness, authority and attention, Rebecca and daughters almost invisibly made their appearance.

Rebecca rioters had nothing to do with the demolition – their targets were tollhouses and tollgates – but blaming them served to shield the perpetrators. Surprisingly, no attempt was made to clear the rubble immediately. Not until early 1855 was the site cleared and levelled.[11]

The Local Board of Health [12]

The third quarter of the 19th century also saw a drive to raise public health standards in the town, and to improve its civic amenities. The task of raising public health standards was the responsibility of the Local Board of Health. This was formed in 1853, renamed the Local Government Board in 1872, and survived until 1894 when the Urban District Council was set up and took over its powers. The Board of Health consisted of eight members elected by the ratepayers, three members retiring annually. It financed its activities partly by levying a rate on householders, but with the town's rateable value assessed initially at rather more than £2,600, a shilling rate produced little more than £96. Capital projects were thus financed by loans, normally repayable over 30 years.

The board's initial priorities – the building of the town's sewers, the provision of a larger reservoir and a piped water supply – was financed by a loan of £2,100, with a further loan of £500 from which small sums could be advanced to less wealthy owners so that they could connect their houses to the mains water supply and to the sewers. However, connection was not mandatory, and standpipes were made available for those householders without a domestic water supply, while the owners of houses not connected to the sewers were persuaded to provide brick-lined cesspits or, later, earth closets.

The sewage system, which discharged the untreated sewage into the Teme some distance below the town, seems to have provoked few complaints, but the same could not be said of the town's water supply, for dissatisfaction with this was endemic. The town's existing water supply had been purchased for £600 in 1853, but an early attempt to increase the supply from the Garth spring by blasting deeper into the rock only succeeded in losing half the spring. To supplement the supply, three or four springs in the Woodhouse area and the Ffrydd were utilised and the Ffrydd reservoir was built, while later the Jackets Well spring was brought into use. Though both the Garth and Ffrydd reservoirs were enlarged on several occasions, the board was never able to guarantee a continuous supply as in periods of prolonged drought the supply from the springs could be sharply reduced, and the reservoirs did not hold sufficient water to maintain the supply to the town unless the water supply was shut off during the night.

As the Jackets Well spring was at a lower height than the other springs supplying the town's water, it could not be utilised as a source at the same time as the other springs. To make use of Jackets Well, the supply from the other springs had to be closed off, which meant that the upper part of the town was without a supply, since the pressure of the Jackets Well source was insufficient to supply that part of the town. Any sustained period of dry weather meant that all or part of the town found its water supply cut off at some point in the day. The continuing growth of the town and its population, together with increased water consumption on the part of households and businesses, meant that this situation persisted into the 1920s.

	Population	Occupied houses
1841	1,404	285
1851	1,566	319
1861	1,853	326
1871	1,946	387
1881	1,905	393
1891	1,853	390
1901	2,139	448

Figure 14: Knighton's population and housing 1841-1901
N.b. The data refers to the parish, *not* the town. The increase in population 1861 and 1871 and 1901 resulted partly from labourers working on railway and water pipeline construction respectively. (Source: Printed census data)

The major preoccupation of urban authorities in the mid-19th century was the prevention of epidemics of diseases such as cholera, and this led the board to intervene closely in the life of the town, issuing bye-laws and checking that all new dwellings met its minimum standards. The board's officers, the Inspector of Nuisances and, after 1872, the Medical Officer of Health, regularly inspected the town's housing stock and sought to remedy deficiencies such as dampness, lack of ventilation, and poor sanitation, as well as curbing overcrowding. Their task was by no means an easy one, for in August 1872 it was reported that only 91 of the 269 houses in the borough were in a good or satisfactory condition. Lodging houses, slaughterhouses and dairies were also regularly inspected. The Inspector of Nuisances, in his other capacity as Surveyor of Highways, was also responsible for keeping the streets and pavements in good repair, a task in which, judging from the frequent complaints in the Hereford newspapers, he had no more than mixed success.

The board achieved only limited success, as the report of the Local Government Board Inspector, a Dr Airy, made clear in his report of 1878. He criticised the limitations of the water supply, while noting that the sewage system made no provision for the flushing or ventilating of the sewers. Moreover, most of the poorer houses in the town relied on common privies emptying into unlined cesspits. Airy reserved his most severe criticisms for the housing standards to be found at the top of the town:

A semi-circle of most miserable houses, closely investing the old castle mound, half-buried in the castle ditch and backed into the castle bank, damp, ill-ventilated, unwholesome, a disgrace to the town.

The situation in the Cwm was just as bad:

Several rows of low class dwellings, terraced into the steep hillside and presenting all the bad features of dampness, insufficient ventilation and close contact with filth which usually belongs to dwellings so situated.[13]

However, one should not be too critical of the board: its financial resources were limited, as were its powers to borrow, while board members were dependent upon the goodwill of the ratepayers, few of whom were ready to see a steep rise in the rates they paid. The board members and their officers were well aware of the circumstances of the ratepayers, most of whom they knew well, and were naturally reluctant to impose anything beyond the mildest sanctions upon offenders, preferring to wear them down over the years by a policy of attrition.

Since it was the only body with any claim to authority in the town after the court leet met for the last time in 1862, the board found itself charged with an increasingly wide range of responsibilities: in 1866, the management of the church clock; in 1872, the management of the town clock; in 1877, the establishment of a fire brigade; and in 1879, the location of notice boards in the town and the provision of name plates for the main streets in the town.

The Gas Works [14]

The speed with which the town's establishment could act, once a course of action had been decided upon, is well illustrated by the way in which a gas supply was obtained for the town. The possibility of lighting the streets by gas first came up at a public meeting at the Chandos Arms in September 1851. It was stated that setting up a gas works would cost £500 and it was unanimously agreed to raise this by the sale of £5 shares; by the close of the meeting more than a quarter of the total sum required had been raised. The Knighton Gas, Coal and Coke Company was duly formed with the main objective being to light the town and its streets by gas, and in June 1852 a board of directors had been elected and officials appointed. Richard Price of Norton Manor presented the company with a site for the gas works near Teme bridge, free of charge. By September the mains had been laid through the town, the lamp posts and fittings were being erected and connected, and the gasometer and the other buildings at the gas works were reported to be 'in a forward state'. By late November the work had been complete and the town lit by gas.

By this time responsibility for street lighting had passed to the board. Although anxious to dispense with the old and inefficient oil lamps, the board drove a hard bargain and initially the agreement was for 28 street lights to be lit from an hour after dusk until 10pm from mid-September to mid-April at a charge of £2 2s per lamp. The number of street lamps increased steadily, to 36 in 1864 and 70 in 1921. The new form of lighting seems to have been taken up with enthusiasm by the town's retailers and businessmen, and the company met with a measure of financial success, William Archibald, the chairman of the board of directors, being able to declare in August 1863 a modest half-yearly dividend of 5%.

The Central Wales Railway [15]

Interest in railways began to develop in Knighton late in 1849 with the promotion of the Shrewsbury to Hereford line which, at Craven Arms, would pass within 12 miles or so of Knighton. In 1852-53, when the construction of the line was underway between Ludlow and Leominster, the possibility of a branch line to Knighton from either Craven Arms or Leominster was greeted with enthusiasm in the town for it brought the prospect of cheaper coal, lime, guano and artificial manures, coupled with wider markets for Knighton's products and livestock.[16] However, such a line was not an attractive investment prospect, for the town's hinterland was sparsely populated.

The emergence in the early 1850s of schemes to develop Milford Haven as a deepwater port with rail links to the manufacturing areas of Lancashire and the west Midlands, made the construction of a railway line through Radnorshire a real possibility. Two rival schemes soon emerged: a Mid Wales line which envisaged the extension of the existing Shrewsbury to Newtown line through Rhayader and western Radnorshire to Builth and Llandovery, to link up with the line from Milford Haven; and a Central Wales line running from Craven Arms on the Shrewsbury to Hereford line through Knighton, Llandrindod Wells and Builth to Llandovery. Advocates of the latter scheme, including Richard Green and many of the Knighton establishment, together with many of the leading landowners in the Llandrindod area, met in 1854 at Penybont to raise funds to cover preliminary expenses, but the outbreak of the Crimean War and the resulting sharp rise in interest rates led to the scheme being postponed.

It would have been difficult to raise sufficient funds to finance the building of the whole line in one share issue, so instead it was decided to build it in three phases, thus spreading the demands upon investors' funds over a number of years, as well as enabling the promoters to tap into more local sources of capital as the line progressed. The first phase was the construction of the line between Craven Arms and Knighton, and so The Knighton Railway Company was established by an Act passed in mid-May 1858, news of which was celebrated in Knighton by the ringing of the church bells.

The company was to have a capital of £66,000 in £10 shares and was empowered to borrow a further £22,000. Little immediate difficulty was experienced in selling the shares, the two largest local purchasers being Richard Green and Mrs Harriet Rogers of Stanage Park, each of whom held shares to the value of more than £2,000. Other local shareholders included the doctor Henry Warren, William Banks who had recently set up the Silurian Cloth Mills, Charles Edwards of Skyborry and three High Street shopkeepers: Edward Weyman, ironmonger; William Bowen, grocer; and Benjamin Taylor, draper.

The contract to build the line was awarded to Thomas Brassey, the well known railway contractor, and his partner, William Field. Their tender of £50,000 did not include the cost of the stations, while the average cost of £4,000 per mile, excluding the cost of land, reflected the very few difficulties which the contractors expected to meet. A single track was to be laid, but the construction of the permanent way, bridges and earthworks was such as to permit a second line being added if required. The ceremony of cutting the first sod on the line took place on 19 August 1858 and was performed by Lady Jane Walsh, the wife of the MP for Radnorshire. The town's buildings and streets were bedecked with flags and banners, and the celebratory lunch in a marquee near the Chandos Arms was followed by a series of speeches and toasts and then dancing. More unofficial celebrations went on in the town's inns, to such effect that two local police constables were subsequently fined for being drunk and absent from duty.[17]

Though it had been intended to open the line to Knighton by 1 May 1860, bad weather in the winter of 1859-60 and a wet summer in 1860 combined with a shortage of labour, meant that the line did not open to Bucknell until 1 October 1860. A few days later the first passenger train arrived at Knighton from Craven Arms, the journey, according to the *Hereford Times* reporter, being 'marked by the wonderment of the rustic population and the enthusiasm of the inhabitants'. Goods trains were using the line early in 1861 but it was not formally opened to passenger traffic until 6 March 1861, and even then the station was far from complete.[18]

Originally it had been intended to commemorate the coming of the railway by erecting a monument on the top of Garth Hill, but nothing came of the plan.[19] No formal celebrations had been planned to mark the official opening of the line, but even so, on the arrival of the first train at 9.15am, the *Hereford Times* of a week later reported that when the first train arrived:

> ... the platform in front of the station and the bridge was crowded with hundreds anxious for the first glimpse of the train. The town band was in attendance and the church bells were rung throughout the day.

The line had cost some £72,000, £48,000 raised by the sale of shares and £24,000 raised in loans, much of this from Richard Green, the first company secretary, on the security of his estate. The company made no attempt to pay off its borrowings; instead, the debt was extinguished when the creditors accepted shares in the company in lieu of repayment.

Richard Green had been the driving force behind the Knighton Railway Company and he was largely responsible for the extension of the line from Knighton to Llandrindod Wells, a distance of nearly 20 miles. The Act incorporating the Central Wales Railway Company and authorising the building of the line had been obtained in 1859, in spite of stiff opposition from the promoters of the Mid Wales line, and the unexpected withdrawal from the scheme of the original contractors, Brassey and Field. From the start the company faced financial problems, for although the Act had authorised a share capital of £160,000 and the power to borrow a further £53,000, only £18,000 was raised initially by the sale of shares, and Richard Green had initially to borrow £30,000 from Coutts of London and later to raise substantial sums on the security of his family estates.

The financial difficulties were made worse by the high cost of the Knucklas viaduct which, at 70 feet high and with 13 arches, each 36 feet wide, cost £10,000, while the Llancoch tunnel, 637 feet long and at its highest point 980 feet above sea level, posed considerable technical difficulties. The situation was saved by the contractors, Hammersley and Morton, agreeing to take half their fee in the form of shares, combined with heavy investment in the line by the London and North Western Railway and the Shrewsbury and Hereford Railway. There was some revival of local interest in the shares after the Llancoch tunnel had been completed, when Sir John Walsh invested £5,000 in the company.

The line reached Penybont in 1864 and the formal opening of the line to Llandrindod Wells took place on 10 October 1865, when the banner 'Whither bound? To Milford Haven', first seen at Knighton in August 1858, was again very much in evidence. By this time the construction of the Llandrindod Wells to Llandovery line, some 27 miles long, was underway, the Act authorising the Central Wales Extension line having been obtained in 1860. The line was completed to Builth in 1866 and reached Llandovery in 1868. The Knighton Railway was amalgamated with the Central Wales Railway in 1863, the line being worked by the LNWR who acquired all three elements of the railway in 1865.

The impact of the railway upon Knighton was considerable, for the social and commercial horizons of this 'small town shut up in a narrow valley' were transformed. For the first time the town was in direct contact with all parts of the kingdom, not least with those parts of Wales beyond upper Radnorshire, while the ease of rail travel encouraged more frequent visits to the town by those who lived in the surrounding countryside, much to the advantage of its shopkeepers.

Plate 17: Knighton Station on a Fair day;
the sheep are waiting to be let into the loading yard

The potential benefits of the railway for the town's livestock trade were illustrated by the March Fair of 1861, which took place two days after the official opening of the railway to Knighton. The *Hereford Journal* of 13 March reported that the fair was well supplied with stock and attended by many dealers, and that much business was done. The report continued:

> Through the facilities afforded by the railway company the town was attended by many dealers whose visit to Knighton was their first. ... A special train was provided, drawn by two engines which conveyed 20 trucks of cattle to Birmingham, Wolverhampton and distant parts.

The *Hereford Journal* of 29 May 1861 hinted at another potential advantage for the town, pointing out that as a result of the Shrewsbury to Hereford line, Craven Arms had developed as a depot supplying the surrounding villages with coal, timber, lime and artificial manures, earthenware goods and building materials – a pattern that Knighton was soon to follow. The coming of the railway was not without its disadvantages for some, but the less beneficial results are best left to a future chapter.

The National School[20]

The trade directories of the 1830s and 1840s show a number of small private day schools in Knighton. Most of them charged a few pennies a week and taught little more than the three Rs, but sometimes a school with greater social pretensions took in boarders and day girls. In 1846 a National School set up by the Church opened in rooms in the Great House. It was funded by 'School Pence' paid by the pupils each month, subscriptions and Church collections. The accommodation was considered 'indifferent' and both the master's classroom and the infants' classroom were very overcrowded.

Matters seemed likely to improve when in the spring of 1855 W.S. Woodburn, a visitor with no family connections or property in the locality, endowed the school with £1,000 vested in trustees. He also signified a wish to purchase a site on which a new school could be built, but apparently no suitable site could be found. There matters rested until the summer of 1861 when Richard Green Price – the latter surname added when he inherited Richard Price's estate – gave the upper part of Crabtree Meadow as a site for the new National School. A committee of prominent townsmen, chaired by the vicar, the Revd J.R. Brown, was established to collect subscriptions and oversee the project.

The committee eventually secured promises of subscriptions totalling £1,200 and Thomas Nicholson, the Hereford diocesan architect, was commissioned to prepare plans. In early April 1864 Mrs Green Price laid the foundation stone for a

Plate 18: The National School

74

building that would provide for up to 300 pupils and comprise an infants' hall in the centre with boys' and girls' wings on each side, and houses for the master and the mistress. The school was built of Kinsley stone by George Watkins, a Knighton contractor, and the building was completed on the day of its opening, 21 April 1865. The day began with a service at St Edwards, after which the pupils, prominent townsmen and guests processed to the school on Conjuror's Lane, now West Street, for the formal opening, followed by tea for the 217 pupils.

The building of the school had cost £1,900, more than had been raised, and so right from the start it faced considerable financial difficulties. Richard Green Price had not only given the site but had also subscribed £200 and could hardly be expected to come to the rescue. In early July a two-day Grand Fancy Bazaar was held in aid of the Building Fund with the stalls manned by the local elite – Lady Brydges of Boultibrooke, Mrs Green Price, Mrs John Rogers and Mrs Covernton, the wife of Dr Covernton, a leading Churchman. Even so, the financial difficulties continued despite annual fund-raising events, many organised by Mrs Rogers, while on two occasions a shortfall of £100 was made good by the Revd M.H. Ricketts. On his death in 1901, amongst his bequests Ricketts left £1,800 to the National Society, the income from which was to go to the National School in Knighton. It was this endowment which in 1914 funded the building of two new classrooms and the conversion of the caretaker's house into a kitchen to enable the teaching of home economics.

The Norton Arms Hotel [21]

In the spring of 1864, a consortium of Knighton businessmen that included Richard Green Price announced plans to build a new hotel in the town. A limited company, the Knighton Hotel Company, was formed, which purchased the Farmers' Club, the Sheep Market, the Globe Hotel and some houses to the south of the club, and commissioned Thomas Nicholson to design the new building, which was to incorporate the Farmers' Club premises and the Assembly Rooms.

In July 1864 the contract to build the hotel was awarded to 'a London building company of great experience', Messrs Drake and Co.. But problems soon arose, and by September 1865 Nicholson was advertising for tenders to complete the hotel and outbuildings. The hotel was an ambitious project for a town of Knighton's size: it consisted of a coffee room, commercial room, Assembly Room, billiard room, smoke room, bar, bar parlour, bar sitting room, 30 bedrooms, kitchens, larder and cellarage. It opened in the autumn of 1867, under the management of Jonathan Green, the company secretary.

The motives for building a hotel of this size in the mid-1860s are not entirely clear, though it is likely that Richard Green Price was the driving force in this as in many of the other projects of this period. It may have been an attempt to breathe new life into the Farmers' Club, while another factor may have been a blistering attack on the town's lack of accommodation made in the course of the report on Knighton races in the *Hereford Journal* of 11 April 1863:

> No provision whatsoever has been made in the town for the accommodation of visitors, indeed the present accommodation for man and beast is disgraceful … In fact beds could not be got for love nor money and people had to take coach for Presteigne or take rail and proceed 'down the country'.

This was not the image which the town's champions wished to see portrayed.

The building of the hotel was a manifestation of the town's optimism and confidence in its future, and was by no means the only new building of the 1860s to grace the junction of Bridge Street and Station Road. New shops had been built on the north side of Station Road, while opposite the hotel, where the war memorial now stands, a new court and magistrates' room was built together with a police station and lock up. Invariably others in the town found it necessary to modernise; many of the shopkeepers of Broad Street and High Street fitted new shop fronts, while Mrs Chandler of the Swan Inn, Broad Street, converted her 'old fashioned and dilapidated house' into 'a handsome hotel'. Both the Primitive Methodists and the

Plate 19: The Norton Arms Hotel and Assembly Rooms in the early 20th century

Wesleyans built new larger chapels in Broad Street (1860) and West Street (1870) respectively, while in 1865 the Baptists built their chapel in Norton Street.

To assist the new hotel, Richard Green had closed the Chandos Arms, but even so press reports suggest that the Norton Arms was not living up to expectations, and early in 1873 the Norton Arms and Knighton Hotel Company was wound up, paying its creditors a dividend of 12s 7d in the pound. The *Hereford Journal* of 29 March reported that the hotel was now in the management of 'a gentleman who already owns the larger amount of the property of the town' – Richard Green Price.

The Market Hall [22]

By the 1860s the single-storey Butter Cross of 1849 was considered by some to be inadequate and not in keeping with the town's growing status. In 1868 a Market Hall Company was formed, £1,200 was subscribed and the Butter Cross was demolished; a new two-storey Market Hall was built on the site of the old (Seven) Stars Inn on Market Street. The first trustees of the company were the vicar, the Revd J.R. Brown, Robert Phillips, and Richard Hatfield. According to a letter to the Commissioners of Woods and Forests of January 1883 the hall was built

> for the sole purpose of securing the market being held on the site occupied [since] time immemorial, and more fully to do so [the Company] granted a considerable space to the use of farmers' wives etc. selling butter, poultry etc. free from toll.

Plate 20: The Market Hall, also called the Town Hall, built in 1869, on the eve of demolition in 1987

To this end an area equal to that of the old Butter Cross on the ground floor was given to the town, while the top floor contained a hall which was used for social events.

The siting of the Market Hall is interesting, for in the previous 15 years or so the town's centre of gravity had shifted downhill from the top of the town as a result of the coming of the railway, and the building of the Market Hall may well have been an attempt to reverse this shift. If so it had little success, for by 1880 came the first of many attempts to persuade first the Local Board and then the Urban District Council (UDC) to buy the hall.

Many dealers, finding the hall too far removed from the centre of the town and difficult to access, started to sell their goods elsewhere in the town. The inhabitants of the top of the town, including those who were building houses on the recently built Norton Street, objected strongly to the potential removal of the market since it was felt that its loss would reduce property values in the upper part of the town. However, there was little which could be done: the Local Board could not take control of the market since market rights were vested in the Crown; and later the UDC found that the Company's valuation of the hall was in excess of what it was prepared to pay.

All that could be done by the advocates of the hall was to bring pressure to bear on the more influential townsmen such as Richard Green Price, and later on the more influential councillors. This kept the hall in an uneasy existence until 1987, but such pressure could not reverse the continuing shift in gravity.

The Clock Tower

The first mention of the possibility of a town clock came in 1857, when civic pride in Knighton was in its first flush. It was proposed that the clock – which was to have a diameter of 5 feet and be illuminated by gas – should be erected on the site of the dilapidated market hall which had been demolished in 1852. The donor of the clock was Henry Miles of Downfield, a native of Knighton and a former sheriff of Radnorshire. Not everyone supported its erection on the proposed site: some living nearby thought that the clock chimes would be too noisy, while others thought it unwise to infill an open space large enough to house the stalls of the market and the town's many fairs. Instead Henry Miles' 'unsolicited gift' was placed in the church tower.[23]

The present clock tower was presented to the town by Thomas Moore

Plate 21: The clock tower, built on the site of the old Town Hall, seen from West Street

of Old Hall, Llanfihangel Rhydithon, who, with his brother Richard, had been the main promoter of the Penybont to Knighton road and backer of the Knighton and Central Wales lines. The town was given no say in the matter beyond accepting or rejecting the proposal, for at the beginning of 1872 the leading townsmen were invited, by circular, to a meeting at the Swan Hotel where Moore, supported by his solicitor William Stephens, a friend, William Price, and the Hereford clockmaker A.W. Bezant, presented his proposal. The resulting 'useful and ornamental remembrance' was built to the plans of the Hereford architect, George Haddon, by the contractors Walsh and Co. It had been intended to complete the project by August 1872, but the installation of the clock mechanism by Bezant was not completed until January 1873, the total cost amounting to £800.[24] There remained the task of ensuring that the two public clocks gave the same time and that this corresponded with 'railway time', otherwise potential customers of the railway could have been seriously inconvenienced.

The improvements in Knighton's commercial infrastructure and its civic amenities in the third quarter of the century were certainly impressive. To obtain an approximate current equivalent of the sums invested in the projects undertaken in the Knighton area between 1849 and 1870, it would be necessary to multiply them by at least 50.[25] For example, the building of the railway between Craven Arms and Knighton cost, in terms of current values, at least £3.3 million. Investment on this scale could only have occurred if both the agricultural and commercial sectors of the local economy had been buoyant.

The Agricultural Sector
Since farming in Radnorshire was essentially pastoral it had not had to adjust as radically as the arable sector to the repeal of the Corn Laws in 1847 and the fall in cereal prices caused by imports of foreign grain which had resulted. At the same time its landowners gained from the increased availability of loans at favourable interest rates to improve farm buildings, roads and drainage, which had been introduced to assist the arable sector.

Thus the third quarter of the 19th century saw no large changes in farming patterns in the Knighton area. The tithe commutation survey of 1839 suggests that the arable acreage of the parish amounted to about 21% of the total acreage, while the crop returns of 1877 for Knighton show that the arable acreage accounted for 26% of the total acreage – the increase being probably accounted for by the Farrington and Cwmgilla enclosure of 1844 and the Knighton enclosure of 1853, which saw nearly 1,000 acres of commons brought into private ownership. The predominance of the livestock sector in the Knighton area can be seen from the large proportion of the arable acreage – one-third – devoted to oats in 1877.[26] The local farming community certainly benefited from the increased demand for meat from the industrial areas, where the boom of the third quarter of the century had greatly increased both employment and wages.

The pattern of livestock farming in the Knighton area had not changed, the main business being in store cattle and wethers for fattening on English grasslands, along with ewes bought for breeding purposes. There are hints, however, that farmers on the better grasslands were taking advantage of railway links with the west Midlands to produce fatstock and sheep for immediate slaughter by the butchers of Wolverhampton, Birmingham and other industrial towns of the region. The general quality of sheep produced in the area was also improving as a result of crossing the native Radnor Forest sheep with at first the Ryeland breed, and later the Shropshire Down or Southdown breeds.[27]

The press reports of Knighton fairs suggest that increased demand was responsible for encouraging local farmers to increase both the quantity and quality of livestock they produced, particularly in the later 1850s and the 1860s. The efforts of the Farmers' Club to encourage improvements in farming methods has already been noted, and these were augmented by the annual shows organised by the Knighton and Temeside Agricultural Association founded in 1848, which offered prizes for sheep, cattle and crops of swedes and turnips.[28]

Show Day at the end of September or the beginning of October was a day out for many of the 'grey coated' farmers of the Knighton district, so called because they wore coats made of the traditional grey cloth produced in the county. There they were brought face to face with high quality livestock produced by careful breeding, the latest farm implements and machinery, and salesmen offering a wide range of seeds, artificial manures and lime. The show was followed by a dinner for the members of the Association, the theme of the after-dinner speeches usually being aspects of agricultural improvement which might be usefully applied in the Knighton area. Thus at the dinner in October 1857, attention was drawn to the need for farmers to breed from a bull of quality rather than from the farm bull or that of a neighbour, and the desirability of growing more turnips for winter, utilising hill land and artificial manures to do so.

Though the Association enjoyed the backing of Richard Green and the leading gentry and farmers of the area, it had a surprisingly short life, for it came to an end after the show of 1858 which was adjudged 'a complete and decided failure', since there were few entries in any of the classes and only three new implements on display, all by Messrs Cooper and Black of Ludlow. The local press attributed the failure of the Association to two main factors. The first was that it did not break up the classes into several sub-groups to reflect farm sizes – which led to most of the cash prizes in the show being carried off by two or three local 'celebrities', wealthy improvers with whom the 'grey coats' couldn't hope to compete. Secondly, when such sub-groups were created, a decision was made to award medals rather than cash prizes, which led to an almost complete lack of entries, since, as the *Hereford Times* explained, 'farmers would not compete without some solid advantage'.[29]

Contemporary authorities consistently bewailed the failure of the small hill farmer to embark upon agricultural improvements, usually blaming their innate conservatism and their attachment to a low cost approach. However, many farmers did not have the necessary financial resources, while others were tenants at will and insecurity of tenure made them reluctant to upgrade grassland and make other improvements, the benefits of which might be largely reaped by a succeeding tenant. Market forces may have had more success than exhortation. Since inferior livestock either made low prices or were driven home unsold, small hill farmers found it made sense to improve the quality of their livestock over time by investing in a few rather better quality ewe lambs or a better ram lamb every few years. Similarly, the quality of bulls used for breeding by small hill farmers also improved, though they could not afford to purchase heifers or utilise bulls produced by prominent local breeders such as John Rogers of Pilleth, James Rea of Monaughty or William Tudge of the Great House, Llangunllo. Thus the quality of the livestock offered for sale at Knighton improved steadily.

Plate 22: Broad Street c.1865. The building on the left is the George and Dragon, those in the middle of the picture were demolished in the 1880s

The Commercial Sector

If the local farming industry was doing well, the town's service and retail sectors serving the farming community would clearly share in its prosperity, as did the small scale local industries – the tanners, skinners, maltsters, timber merchants and straw hat manufacturers who processed the produce of the surrounding countryside. However, Knighton's prosperity in the third quarter of the century stemmed not only from organic growth, but also from a surge in economic activity stimulated by the presence in the area in the later 1850s and 1860s of 600 or so labourers involved in building the Knighton and the Central Wales line, and by the formation of three new enterprises: Isaac Rutter's wool business; William Banks's Silurian (flannel and clothing) Mills; and the Radnorshire, Coal, Lime and General Supply Company, better known as the Radnorshire Company.

Isaac Devereux Rutter (1824-97) was born in Forden, Montgomeryshire, and moved to Knighton in 1848. During the early 1850s he had set up a wool stapling business, possibly initially in partnership with an older brother, buying the wool from local farmers, sorting and grading it and then selling it on to the textile industry. His was not the only wool stapling business in the town, but his concern was on a completely different scale to the others. William Banks was primarily concerned

with securing wool for his own business, while the two other Knighton wool staplers seem to have been little more than intermediaries for larger concerns in Ludlow and Shrewsbury. Local farmers were happy to deal with Rutter for it saved them transporting their wool to Newtown, previously their only major wool market, and even in 1855 he was able to purchase wool to the value of £1,200 in a few hours at the Knighton July wool fair. He was also active at other wool fairs in Radnorshire, Herefordshire and Shropshire, competing against major wool merchants such as Pease of Darlington and Parkingstone of Bradford.[30] His main warehouse in Knighton was at the junction of Church Street and Almshouse (now Wylcwm) Street, and he had a smaller warehouse on Conjuror's Lane, now

Plate 23: Rutter's wool warehouse on the corner of Church Street and Wylcwm Street

West Street. In the wool season – late summer and early autumn – he was said to employ 'a large number of hands', but the number of permanent workers was small. Unfortunately his business did not survive the difficulties created by the large imports of wool from Australia in the 1880s.

Rutter played an important role in the affairs of the town, in 1862 being appointed the last bailiff of the borough, and he continued to exercise some authority in succeeding years since he had no successor. A leading member of Knighton Primitive Methodist Church, he also served on the Local Board of Health, in some years as chairman. Politically he was a prominent Liberal and at one time served as chairman of the Radnorshire Liberal Association. He withdrew from public life after his business failed in 1888, and the closing years of his life were marred by ill health.

William Banks was born in Shrewsbury in 1801 and little is known of his early life. By the early 1840s he was involved in several business ventures in Knighton for in *Pigot's Commercial Directory of South Wales* of 1844 he is listed as a miller, a draper, and, in partnership with John Russell, a wool stapler, while by 1849 he was also the manager of the Knighton Water Company. How active a role Banks took in these ventures is difficult to judge, for in a speech made on 15 September 1854 on the opening of his Silurian Mills in Knighton, he claimed that he had had five years' experience as a partner of Thomas Duppa at a woollen mill at Church Stretton.[31]

The laying of the first stone of the Silurian Mills or 'The Knighton Flannel and Clothing Manufactory', took place in early April 1853, and the report of the ceremony in the *Hereford Times* of 16 March 1853, which may well have been written by Banks as he was an accomplished self-publicist, made great play of the advantages which the enterprise would give the town in terms of increased employment and business:

> Knighton has hitherto been, like our neighbouring towns entirely dependent upon agriculture, and when the farmers were suffering dull markets or bad crops, of course they had less money to expend with tradesmen in their market town. To a stranger entering this town, nothing is more remarkable than the number of strong, able-bodied boys idling about the street.

The new enterprise was formally opened on 15 September 1854, amidst great celebrations. A lunch was held in a marquee near the Chandos Arms for nearly 300 guests and Banks was presented with a silver breakfast service, while tea and cakes were provided outside for 'the poorer classes'. Later in the day a ball was held in the Assembly Rooms attached to the Farmers' Club – and all was reported at length in the *Hereford Times* of 23 September.

The machinery in the mill was worked initially by waterpower, but a boiler had also been installed to allow the use of steam power at some time in the future. The mill was to manufacture conventional Welsh flannel and tweed as well as a new type of cloth –'Silurian cloth' – which it was claimed was a material of great durability, elasticity and warmth. With his shrewd eye for publicity, in 1855 during the Crimean War, Banks dispatched a quantity of this cloth to British officers serving in the trenches outside Sebastopol. This was duly reported in the *Hereford Times* of 15 September 1855, the opportunity being taken to inform the public that the mill was now using both water and steam power.

At the opening of the mill it had been anticipated that it would employ more than 50 operatives, and to ensure that relatively unskilled local workers could be employed, 'self-acting' machinery had been installed which, it was asserted, 'a common labourer may learn to work ... in a few days'. However the 1861 and 1871 censuses suggest that neither of these aims was fully met. The former shows that the mill provided employment for 21 operatives, while the census of 1871 gave the number of employees as 45. Nor were the majority of the employees local people. The 1861 census showed 17 to have been born in Montgomeryshire and no more than 7 as of Radnorshire origin, while the 1871 census suggests that Radnorshire-born operatives were very much in the minority.

While most press reports were highly favourable to Banks and the Silurian Mill, the second of a series of articles on Knighton by a correspondent using a pseudonym, published in the *Hereford Times* of 6 June 1861, was more negative. It was suggested that although the mill had been 'fitted up with the most modern and costly machinery', much of this had been dispensed with because of difficulties experienced in getting skilled mechanics, capable of maintaining and repairing it, to settle in Knighton. The report also stated that Silurian tweed had declined in popularity and that production now centred on the traditional Radnorshire grey cloth.[32]

Even so Banks' approach continued to be bullish and the *Hereford Times* of 6 March 1875 announced the formation of The Knighton Silurian Cloth and Welsh Flannel Company (Limited) with a capital of £30,000 in £10 shares and William Banks as managing director, while the prospectus painted a glowing picture of the mill's future. The existing factory with its plant was valued at rather more than £15,000, which would have made Banks the major shareholder.[33] However, it seems likely that the flotation failed, for there are no references to the company in local newspapers after March 1875. By the time of the 1881 census Banks and his son William O. Banks were no longer active in the textile business, nor were they wealthy men, Banks senior being described as an agent for Norwich Union and his son as unemployed. Nor are any spinners or factory operatives to be found in the Knighton census returns for 1881 or 1891, and only one weaver, who may have been working independently. The Silurian Mills did not appear in trade directories of 1880 and 1895, while an advertisement in the *Brecon and Radnor Express* of 21 February 1896 which stated that the new proprietor, Thomas F. Wills, was prepared to manufacture wool supplied by customers into stocking yarn, blankets and other woollen goods, or to card and spin the wool into yarn for the customer's own use, suggests that the business he had acquired was at best small in scale.

If the stimulus to the town's economy provided by Isaac Rutter and William Banks was only short term, that given by the Radnorshire Company was to last well into the 21st century.[34] The Radnorshire Coal, Lime and General Supply Company – which was to take the name The Radnorshire Company in 1946 – was incorporated at the end of November 1865 with capital of £10,000 in £5 shares. Initially there were six directors: Isaac Rutter, Thomas Peters, John Evans (farmer of Llangunllo), John Wilson (tanner of Knighton), George Morton (railway contractor of Penybont), and Henry Ayre (of Laurel Villa, Knighton), who was to be the chairman of the board, managing director and company secretary. The company remained an essentially local business until the second half of the 20th century, with the bulk of the shareholders residents of Radnorshire, Herefordshire and Shropshire.

In addition to supplying coal and lime, the company dealt with other heavy goods such as bricks and slates, guano and later, basic slag and artificial manures. By January 1866 depots to stock such goods had been established at Broome, Hopton Heath, Bucknell, Knighton, Knucklas, Penybont and Llandrindod, each with a salesman. Contracts to supply coal and artificial manures had been signed with the Cannock Chase Company and the Nottingham Mills Company respectively, while 25 wagons had been hired from the Midland Wagon Company, a further 25 being hired a few months later.

The first year's trading produced profits of £555 and half yearly dividends of 10%, and plans were soon laid to set up depots at Llangunllo, Dolau, Presteigne and Newbridge-on-Wye, and at the stations on the Mid Wales line as far as Llanwrtyd Wells. The modest prosperity of the company did not produce a marked increase in employment in the town until it developed a large scale sawmill in the late 19th and early 20th centuries. By this time the firm's activities were almost exclusively in the agricultural sector and its continued success stemmed from an ability to diversify, first into seeds and then into milling and processing of animal foodstuffs.[35]

Richard Green Price 1803-87

The transformation of Knighton's economy and townscape in the third quarter of the century was very much a co-ordinated effort on the part of the town's establishment and was carried through with remarkably little bickering and dissension.

However, the initiative and drive needed to push through projects to a successful conclusion seems to have come largely from Richard Green Price who, after serving his articles in Worcester, had set up a flourishing legal partnership in Knighton with Thomas Peters in the 1820s, moving into banking in 1836 when he became a partner in the Knighton and Kington and Radnorshire Bank. He also managed the affairs of his uncle, Richard Price of Norton Manor, and during the 1850s served as county treasurer, and he was an experienced local politician having acted as political agent for Thomas Frankland Lewis, Sir John Walsh and George Cornewall Lewis.

He thus brought considerable legal, business, administrative and political expertise, together with his family's wealth and influence, to the task of transforming Knighton. As his uncle's man of business he played an influential role in the enclosure in 1844-45 of 592 acres on Llanwen Hill in Farrington, and 333 acres in Cwmgilla involving commons and waste on Bailey Hill, Garth Hill and Little Cwmgilla. Both Farrington and Cwmgilla lay in the parish of Knighton, though outside the borough, and the two main landowners, Edward Rogers and Richard Price, received 33% and 30% respectively of the land enclosed. As the enclosure solicitor Richard Green Price succeeded in negotiating favourable terms with the Crown for the enclosure of common land in the borough of Knighton in 1852-53. This involved 71 acres and was essentially a tidying up process, which was of benefit to eight landowners who shared the waste land between them, with Richard Price and his cousin Robert Henry Price between them receiving nearly 35% of the land enclosed. In 1859 Richard Green Price purchased the quit rents – small residual rents on former Crown properties – in order to allow them to lapse, and in doing so eliminated a potential cause of friction between the town's property owners and the Crown.[36]

Though he moved from The Cottage to Norton Manor in 1861, Green Price continued to show considerable interest in Knighton's affairs, his motive being probably enlightened self-interest, for as his family was the largest property owner by far in the town, he stood to gain materially from the town's growing prosperity. Again, as the major landowner in the district, he also stood to gain from the rising land values created by the coming of the railway. Unfortunately Sir Richard's – he was created baronet in 1874 – interest in railways was little short of an obsession, and his reckless investment in them was to do considerable harm to his family's fortunes.

≫ 7 ≪

LATE VICTORIAN AND EDWARDIAN KNIGHTON

In the 1870s the economic situation in Britain began to deteriorate, with the agricultural sector the hardest hit initially. The optimism and energy which had characterised Knighton's 'great rebuilding' began to wane, but investment in the town continued, though it was more defensive in character, designed to maintain the town's status rather than to encourage further development.

The Impact of the Agricultural Depression

In the last quarter of the 19th century British farming found itself facing severe competition in its home market as cheaper farm produce from North and South America and Australasia was imported into Britain after technical improvements in steam shipping had led to greatly reduced freight charges. The arable sector was first to feel the competition as cheap cereals began to flood in from the North American prairies in the 1870s, but in the 1880s the development of refrigeration enabled the beef producers of the Argentine pampas and the Australian grasslands, along with the sheep and dairy farmers of New Zealand, to target the British market. Between 1871-74 and 1894-98 wheat prices fell by 51%, while the livestock sector saw price falls of 25% in the same period, with wool prices falling by 50%.

Initially, however, the farmers of the Knighton area were more concerned with short-term crises – the outbreaks of foot and mouth of 1872-76 and 1881-3. In the week ending 10 August 1872 there were 3,515 cattle affected in Radnorshire, 925 of them in the Knighton district. The disease died out locally by the end of the year, only to break out again in the early autumn of 1875 with 57 farms in the area affected in the week ending 25 September, though the number of stock affected this time was much smaller. Again the disease had died out by the end of the year. The Knighton area was not affected directly by the outbreak of 1881-83, though neighbouring areas in Shropshire were, with adverse effects upon the town's trade.[1]

The epidemics hit local farmers hard, for the movement of stock was seriously affected, though the transport of unaffected stock to slaughterhouses via the railway was permitted, as only diseased animals were slaughtered rather than whole herds that contained infected stock (as was the case in the outbreak of 2011). The impact on farm incomes of the epidemics was thus not as severe as one might have expected, although the impact upon Knighton market is difficult to assess. Surprisingly, the livestock market does not seem to have been closed during the epidemics, though movement restrictions meant that stock from affected areas were barred until such areas were free from infection. Thus livestock from the Shropshire parishes of Bettws, Llanfairwaterdine, Clun, Clunbury, Hopton, Bedstone, Bucknell and Stowe was barred from the September Fair of 1883.[2] The volume of trade at Knighton livestock market was thus reduced from time to time, though the impact of this upon the town's economy may well have been no more than marginal since such disruptions were few and of short duration.

Of much greater impact was the importation of farm produce from the Americas and Australasia, as shown by the Knighton crop and livestock returns. A comparison of the returns of 1875 and 1905 shows a fall in the arable acreage (excluding rotational grass) from 720 acres to 490 acres. The decline in the wheat acreage was particularly marked, for in 1875 wheat accounted for 22% of the arable acreage, but in 1905 it accounted for rather less than 10%. The dominant cereal crop in Knighton parish throughout the period was oats, reflecting its continuing importance as a feedstuff for livestock: whereas it accounted for 31% of the arable acreage (excluding rotational grass) in 1875, it accounted for nearly 45% in 1905.

The increase in the grassland acreage between 1875 and 1885 suggests an initial tendency to convert arable to grassland, the figures for 1895, 1905 and 1914 suggesting that in turn some grassland was allowed to revert to rough grazing. The proportion of cattle under two years of age rose from 30% or so in the 1870s to 42%+ in the 1880s and 1890s, and reached 48% in 1914. This suggests that there was a growing tendency towards marketing stock at a younger age – under two years – rather than two to three years which had previously been the norm, thus increasing the farmers' cash flow. It would also be in line with the growing demand for smaller and leaner joints on the part of the consumer.

The figures for sheep suggest that as yet the demand for lamb had not yet overtaken the demand for mutton, since the returns of the 1870s, 1880s and 1890s show the number of sheep over the age of a year to be about twice the number under that age. This would suggest that the number of wethers remained broadly equal to the number of breeding ewes and to the number of lambs being produced – mutton had not yet lost out to lamb on the country's dining tables. However the data for the 1900s suggest that this was beginning to change, since the proportion of lambs in the flocks in the parish was increasing from the 34-35% of the late 19th century to 37-38%.[3] The shift in consumers' taste from mutton to lamb had begun. The Shropshire Down had been the dominant breed in the Knighton area for much of the second half of the 19th century, but in the 1900s was giving way to the Kerry Hill breed, itself facing competition from the smoky-faced Radnor Forest, which was thought to produce a better cross from mountain ewes.

The fall in farm incomes in the last quarter of the 19th century and, to a lesser extent, the slight shift to the less labour-intensive pastoral farming gave large farmers an incentive to reduce labour costs by dispensing with one or two farm labourers, replacing them as and when necessary by general labourers employed by the day or on piece work on such tasks as hedging, ditching or laying field drains. An analysis of Knighton census returns for 1851, 1871 and 1891 seems to support this hypothesis. As Figure 15 shows, the number of farm workers, which includes those described as farm labourers, fell sharply after 1851, while the number of labourers in Knighton, excluding labourers attached to specific trades such as builder's labourers or mason's labourers, and thus approximating to general labourers, increased sharply after that same year.

	1851	1871	1881	1891
Farmer	18	21	19	21
Farmer's son	11	11	9	12
Bailiff	1	2	-	2
Shepherd	1	1	-	2
Farm worker	105	38	36	39
Labourer	27	102	73	57

Figure 15: Some occupational categories in Knighton
(Source: Knighton census returns)

The formation of a branch of the West of England Agricultural Labourers' Association at Knighton in 1872 was possibly a response to the shedding of labour by the farmers, but should not be regarded as a militant move.[4] The objective of the Association was not to encourage strikes but to promote emigration to those parts of the country where farm labourers' wages were higher than those paid on the Welsh border.

There seems to have been no further union activity in the Knighton area until the years of industrial unrest preceding the outbreak of war in 1914. Rumours were circulating in the town in 1913 that a branch of the Workers' Union was to be formed, and after a well attended meeting near the clock tower in July 1914, held under the auspices of the Hereford district of the union with Mr William Parker of Plough Road in the chair, it was indeed decided to form a branch of the union in the town. The news was greeted with alarm by the Knighton branch of the Brecon and Radnor Farmers' Union which had been formed in 1909, and which acted as a pressure group seeking lower auctioneers' fees, lower charges from blacksmiths and better rail facilities for livestock at Knighton. However, the outbreak of war in August 1914 averted the possibility of a confrontation between the farmers and the Labourers' Union for the duration, as the country buried many issues under a surge of patriotism.[5]

The fall in farm incomes in the closing decades of the 19th century was no doubt reflected by a fall in the receipts of Knighton shopkeepers and other businesses, but other factors were also at work. The Malt Tun Act of 1880 introduced changes in taxation which favoured large-scale malt producers, with the result that of the four malting businesses in Knighton in 1880, only one remained in 1891. Other businesses which had disappeared by the 1890s were the tannery and the other leather dressing concerns – the fellmongers, skinners and curriers.

Moreover, the railway had opened the way for an influx of cheap, mass-produced goods which soon led to the decline in the business of the town's shoemakers, tailors and dressmakers, some of whom, in order to survive, became retailers of ready-made boots and shoes or men's and women's outfitters. Another trade to disappear in the town was that of the cooper – by 1891 the three coopers in business in 1880 had lost out to the mass produced zinc bowls and washing tubs on sale in the town's ironmongers. The railway also made it possible for the 'big houses' of the locality to order most of the goods they required from the fashionable London stores, rather than from Knighton tradesmen.[6]

Plate 24: Mr Davies, a maltster, at the entrance to the Maltings in Broad Street which were demolished in the 1890s

Employment opportunities in Knighton had begun to shrink as early as 1881. The census of that year suggests that a small proportion of the town's labour force had lost hope of finding work in their trade, for 24 workers – 13 men and 11 women – listed their status as 'Unemployed'. Of the unemployed women, 8 were domestic or general servants, all of them aged 25 or younger, while of the unemployed men, 8 were labourers, their ages ranging from 17 to 57. The apparent suspension of operations at the Silurian Mills – neither the 1881 nor the 1891 census shows any spinners or factory workers and only one weaver living in the town – and the closing of Rutter's wool stapling business reduced employment opportunities further.

	Population	Occupied houses	Unoccupied houses
1871	1,946	387	6
1881	1,905	393	28
1891	1,813	390	32
1901	2,139	448	9
1911	1,886	420	46

Figure 16: Population and Housing in Knighton 1871-1911
(Source: Printed census material)

The census data gives a clear impression of the town's decline at the turn of the century, though the fall in population is masked by the influx of construction workers involved in building the water pipe from the Elan Valley dams to Birmingham. The construction of the pipeline in the Knighton area was completed by the beginning of 1902, from which date the decline

Plate 25: Sawing wood in Owen's Yard

in the town's population was renewed. A more graphic impression of decline is provided by the data on unoccupied houses, which show 11% of Knighton's housing stock unoccupied in 1911. Knighton's rural hinterland was also losing population – about 10% between 1871 and 1881. The trend continued into the 20th century with the population of the Knighton Rural District falling 8½% between 1901 and 1911, by which time 115 houses – 10% of its housing stock – were unoccupied. This sharp decline in customer base did not augur well for Knighton's retailers and businessmen.

Some left Knighton for work in the industrial areas of south Wales and the west Midlands 'where work is fairly plentiful, wages higher and life more attractive', while others emigrated in search of greater opportunities, mainly to the USA and Canada.[7] Reports in the local press suggest that the rate of emigration from the Knighton area quickened after 1900, with the Nanton district of Alberta and the Yorktown district of Saskatchewan favourite destinations. In the *Radnorshire Standard* of 1 March 1913 'Corner Boy' commented:

> Knighton, like so many agricultural towns has become infected with emigration fever. I hear that from 20 to 30 townspeople will be leaving for Canada this spring. There must be quite a colony of Radnorshire folk who have settled during the last few years in Alberta and Saskatchewan, and by all accounts they're doing very well.

Certainly by 1914 the former Knighton confectioner Charles William Still had found it worthwhile to become a full-time shipping agent. Nor was it only farmers and artisans who were emigrating, for amongst the emigrants were members of some of Knighton's leading business and professional families such as the Hamars and the Medlicotts.[8]

Meeting the challenge

The response of the town's authorities was to take steps to secure Knighton's future as a livestock market. To this end, in 1897 the Urban District Council purchased the Sheep Market from the Birmingham and District Counties Bank, securing a loan of £1,800 to do so after a public meeting had approved the purchase. (The Bank had bought the Sheep Market along with the Norton Arms Hotel from the Green Price family in 1891.[7]) The UDC purchase ensured that it would be run in the long-term interests of the town as long as it met its costs, rather than on purely narrow commercial motives.

Many felt that further development of Knighton's livestock market was held up by the inadequate facilities for stock at the railway station, which had been the subject of complaint for decades. In 1899 the *Radnor Express* entered the fray, in the

Plate 26: Knighton Station before the First World War

issue of 14 September urging the UDC to bring pressure to bear on the LNWR to improve the facilities at the station. The railway company however was not prepared to do more than offer minor improvements, presumably arguing that apart from the great spring and autumn fairs, the existing facilities were sufficient. The issue was raised again in 1911, but again to no effect.

An attempt was made to increase the market's throughput in 1904-5 by introducing new fairs in February, June, August and towards the end of October. To what extent this ploy was successful is debatable, since other livestock markets in the area such as Kington and Penybont were using the same tactics. The introduction of fortnightly auction sales in 1904 may well have fared better. The establishment in 1902, by the auctioneers Morris, Marshall and Poole, of an annual September auction sale of wethers, ewes and lambs was undoubtedly the most successful innovation as it began a new line of trade that increased hugely in size over following years. The first sale was of 3,000 sheep with the numbers offered for sale rising substantially within a few years. More importantly, it proved to be the start of the large sheep sales which were to make the town well known in agricultural circles in the inter-war years and the decades following 1945, and confirmed Knighton's status as a major livestock centre.[10]

An attempt was also made to improve the town's commercial infrastructure. From the 1860s onwards an attempt had been made to modernise the town's shops, in particular the shop fronts, improved display facilities and, in the case of food shops, a more hygienic environment, the butchers' shops being the last to be brought into line. By 1883 the *Hereford Times* could report:

> The constant state of progression has deprived the town of much of its original quaintness and eradicated much of its primitive Welsh appearance.[11]

During the early 1890s, in addition to spending £1,500 improving the water supply, the Local Board borrowed £610 to finance the paving, kerbing and channelling of rainwater in the main streets. Even so the criticisms of the town's streets continued. Thus in 1905, 'Rambler' writing from 'Llanbistershire' complained of the town's lack of a water cart to lay the dust in dry weather:

> People went to Knighton Fair,
> Looking for enjoyment,
> But the dust was awful there,
> 'Twas a real torment.
> We'd expect a town so smart
> To possess a water cart.

In the following week's *Radnor Express* 'Rambler' renewed his criticism:

> Knighton is a pretty town,
> With lovely scenery all around,
> But if the wind should blow at all,
> There'll sure to be a dusty squall.
> Amongst your goods the dust will go,
> In your face, your eyes, your nose
> In your food I also fear,
> Also in the poor man's beer.

The UDC decision in 1912 to tar spray the principal streets eased the problem, if it did not eliminate it.[12]

While many saw the town's future prosperity as resting on the consolidation of its role as a market town, others favoured a policy of diversification, and in the autumn of 1899 the Knighton Development Association was set up. Possibly influenced by the discovery of sulphur springs near the Gwernaffel tunnel, built to house the Birmingham water pipe, and impressed by the rapid rise to prosperity of Llandrindod Wells, the Association thought that the town could also become a holiday resort and spa. The Association was unabashed by the decision of the UDC that any development of the mineral spring was a matter for private enterprise, and in 1900 undertook a survey which discovered that more than 40 visitors had made an extended stay in the town. It then commissioned a guidebook for the town

Plate 27: A collection of whinberry baskets in The Narrows packed ready for collection or transportation from Knighton Station. Picking whinberries from the surrounding hills was usually a family affair that involved a picnic at the same time as raising some extra money

stressing the area's picturesque scenery and its many historical remains of general interest.[13] However Knighton had to wait more than 60 years before its potential as a holiday and touring centre received any significant recognition.

Given the difficult economic climate, the town authorities were reluctant to increase the burden on ratepayers by financing any developments which did not directly impact on Knighton's commercial prospects. One exception was the establishment of a town fire brigade in 1878. The town had possessed a fire engine since at least the 1830s, affectionately known as 'the Old Squirter', a timber box containing a cylinder filled with water pumped from a river or a pool, or filled by buckets. It had low-slung wooden wheels with metal rims, was unsprung and was staffed by eight men, six to keep the container filled with water, one to operate the pump, and one to direct the water. If it was needed any distance from the town, the fire engine had to be hoisted on to a wagon and drawn to the scene of the fire.

Mary Cadwallader's *Knighton* suggests that 'the old squirter' was replaced shortly after 1850, but the minutes of the Local Board makes no mention of a new fire engine at this time. According to these minutes the new fire engine and modern equipment was ordered in December 1876, and the first steps to organise a new fire brigade were taken a few months later. In October 1877, F.C. Cobden, the town's leading cricketer (see chapter 8), stepped in and undertook to form and train an eight-man brigade at his own expense, provided that it was placed under his personal control. His motivation for taking this step is far from clear; possibly he was influenced by the recent public adulation afforded Captain Shaw of the newly formed London Fire Brigade by fashionable London society ladies. His enthusiasm was short-lived, for by July 1878 he had withdrawn his offer and the Local Board set up a five-man brigade, each man under-taking to attend a three-hour

Plate 28: The 'Old Squirter' with members of Knighton Fire Service in the 1970s on its way to be displayed at Knighton Library

drill each month in return for pay of £1 1s per annum. No fee was to be charged for the attendance of the Brigade within the borough, but attendance beyond was at the rate of £1 10s plus 3 pence per mile together with the associated cost of the horses and driver to pull the engine to the scene of the fire.[14]

Another exception to only funding activities which enhanced the town's commercial prospects was the provision of a cemetery in 1879. This was an obligation which could not be evaded, since the churchyard had room for only a few more graves, while the nonconformists disliked the fact that their own clergy could not officiate at funerals held there. The Baptists were particularly aggrieved in that, by canon law, an Anglican clergyman could not bury an unbaptised child in the churchyard. The former incumbent, the Revd J.R. Brown, had ignored this, but the new vicar, the Revd M.H. Ricketts, a High Churchman, was less flexible.

The decision to provide a public cemetery was made in mid-1878 and a Burial Board was set up with the tasks of finding and buying a site. The first site it selected – at the junction between the Ludlow and Presteigne roads – was objected to strongly by Sir Richard Green Price who felt that it was too expensive, that its location might inhibit the expansion of the town along these roads, and also that it was too close to his own property, Frydd House. In the end the Burial Board purchased Crabtree Meadow (to the west of the churchyard) from Green Price for £600, together with a right of way past the National School.

The cemetery was designed by Thomas Gough and was equally divided between the church, which had the east side, and the nonconformists, who had the west side. Building the walls, making the walks and providing two entry gates, for the church section from Church Street, and for the nonconformists from West Street, cost a further £675, the work being carried out by Messrs Williams and Jones of Knighton. The Anglican section was consecrated by the bishop of Hereford in July 1879, after the churchyard had been formally closed on 30 June.[15]

By the opening decade of the 20th century the economic situation had eased, and the UDC felt able to enhance the town's amenities. Thus in 1907 the land next to the National Schools was leased from Sir Richard Dansey Green Price for use as a Recreation Ground, while in 1911 land was purchased from the estate of the late Col. R.H. Green for use as allotments, the necessary funds – £1,200 – being borrowed, to be repaid over 50 years. The land was adjacent to 3 acres on the Garth that had been allocated as 'field gardens' by the Knighton Enclosure Act of 1853 and organised in 1885 as allotments, each of about quarter of an acre, to be let at the rate of 10 shillings per acre. The UDC had taken over the administration of these allotments in 1905.[16]

Perhaps the most serious blow to the town's esteem came in the early 1890s when it failed to be chosen as the location for one of the new Intermediate Schools – which were to provide a secondary education – to be set up under the Welsh Intermediate Education Act of 1889. The Radnorshire Joint Education Committee found itself under pressure from all Radnorshire's towns, as each wanted an Intermediate school. Knighton found itself squeezed by Presteigne and Llandrindod since the former had the Beddoes endowment, the income from which Radnorshire would not wish to lose, while the rail link with Llandrindod made access to that town's schools for Knighton pupils very convenient. Initially it seemed likely that a girls' Intermediate school would be located in Knighton, but in the end it was decided to establish a dual school at Llandrindod catering for boys and girls of the Llandrindod and Rhayader areas which girls from the Knighton area might attend, while Knighton boys had the choice of Llandrindod or Presteigne Intermediate schools.[17]

Civic Dissension
One of the most striking features of mid-19th-century Knighton is the manner in which the town's elite consciously sought to act together, thus avoiding any personal rivalries or factional disputes. This was noted by Sir Thomas Frankland Lewis in 1846, when in a letter to his son Cornewall Lewis, he wrote

> Richard Price, Mr [Edward] Rogers and Mr Green [Price] ... act cordially together and when united, nothing can make any headway against them.[18]

Certainly a characteristic of the 'great rebuilding' of the third quarter of the century had been the virtually unanimous backing given by the town's middle class to each commercial and civic innovation. This stemmed partly from the unchallenged dominance of the Price family in Knighton, and partly from the lack of any great difference between the views of mainstream Liberals and Conservatives. The latter led to some politicians, including Richard Green Price initially, describing themselves as Liberal Conservatives.

In the 1880s, however, the situation began to change as Gladstone, the Liberal leader, who was strongly supported by Sir Richard Green Price, adopted radical policies such as backing Irish Home Rule, eroding Anglican dominance in the interests of Welsh nonconformists and eventually advocating the disestablishment of the Welsh Church, by which it would secure its special status and also its endowments. For their part the Conservatives also developed distinctive policies such as protecting British industry and agriculture from cheap imported manufactures and foodstuffs (in complete contradiction of long-standing Liberal advocacy of Free Trade), building up an extensive empire, and defending the interests of the Church.

Thus on a wide range of subjects Liberals and Conservatives were diametrically opposed and exchanges could become heated. In the Radnor Boroughs election of 1880, supporters of the Conservative candidate, Captain Otway, attempted to break up a Liberal election meeting at Presteigne, and Liberals attempted to return the compliment at a Conservative meeting at Knighton. Green Price won the county election by 337 votes, which led to a Knighton Conservative writing to the *Hereford Times* claiming that Green Price had been returned 'by a majority of 337 liars' – presumably their canvass returns had indicated a Conservative majority.[19] The political temperature in Knighton remained high, and in the 1880s and 1890s elections to first the Local Board and then the UDC were conducted on party lines, as were most debates on local issues.

Sir Richard's dominance in the Knighton area was by no means as secure as it had once been. It was well known that he was in financial difficulties as a result of the agricultural depression, his heavy investments in local railways and the need to provide for his large family, and this led some to suspect the motives behind his enthusiastic support for the enclosure of commons in the Radnorshire uplands. Others suspected that there may have been some truth in the allegation made by his opponents, that the baronetcy granted him in the Dissolution Honours of 1874 was the result of his giving up the Radnor Boroughs seat in favour of the Marquis of Hartington, a potential member of Gladstone's Cabinet who had been defeated in the general election of 1868.

In the late summer of 1881, after Green Price had demolished six almshouses in Wylcwm Street, his right to do so was questioned by some who thought they were the property of a charitable trust. In a letter to the *Hereford Times* of 3 September,

Sir Richard pointed out that they had been bought by Richard Price in 1810 for the occupation of poor persons, nominated first by Richard Price and then by himself. In the autumn of 1880, when they were no longer fit for habitation, he had had them demolished only after the Charity Commissioners had confirmed that they were not connected with any charitable trust. He went on to point out that he had then provided, without charge, a large site near the parish church on which his sister had erected six much more substantial almshouses, which had then been conveyed to the Charity Commissioners. Dr Welsh, who had raised the issue, had the good grace to apologise, though he insisted he had not intended any personal attack on Sir Richard.

Sir Richard Green Price's second spell in the Commons was not a particularly happy one. His health was deteriorating, partly as a result of old age – he was 77 in 1880 – and he had suffered from asthma since the late 1860s. Health problems led to long absences from the Commons and visits abroad in winter to benefit from a drier climate. In the early spring of 1884 he fell seriously ill and spent most of the year convalescing and away from the Commons. It was suggested, rather unkindly, that some in the county were wondering whether Sir Richard was 'the representative of Radnorshire in the House of Commons, or the representative of the House of Commons in Radnorshire'.[20] Sir Richard did not contest the election of December 1885 but, ever loyal to Gladstone, contested the election of 1886, but without success since the seat was won by Arthur H.J. Walsh, the eldest son of Lord Ormathwaite.

While the town remained, in the main, loyal to Sir Richard and the Liberal cause, there is no doubt that the Liberal advocacy of disestablishment of the

Plate 29: The Almshouses, Church Street, built by Miss Margaret Green, the sister of Sir Richard Green Price, in 1881

Welsh Church and Irish Home Rule cost the party some support in the Knighton area at large. Some, including most members of the Green Price family (after the death of Sir Richard in 1887), switched their support to the Conservatives, while others, such as Charles Coltman Rogers, became Liberal Unionists. Although Francis Edwards, who had settled at The Cottage, the old Knighton home of Sir Richard Green Price, won the Radnorshire seat for the Liberals in 1892, he lost it in 1895, and although he won it back in 1900, his tenure was not particularly secure.

Plate 30: Sir Richard Green Price, MP for Radnor Boroughs 1863-69 and for Radnorshire 1880-85

'Passive Resistance'

A topic which provoked considerable ill-feeling in the town at the turn of the century was the management of the National Schools. These were essentially Church schools, managed and staffed by Anglicans, largely funded from Anglican sources, and teaching a religious education syllabus which reflected Anglican doctrine. Knighton's National Schools were always in financial difficulties and dependent upon local fundraising events, particularly the annual bazaar. The Revd. J.R. Brown had recognised that many of the pupils came from nonconformist families and that much of the money raised to support the schools came from nonconformist pockets, and had cultivated an inclusive approach. Nonconformists had been appointed as school managers and close inquiries into the religious beliefs of pupil teachers had been avoided.

The situation changed when the Revd M.H. Ricketts became the incumbent. A High Churchman, he avoided close co-operation with nonconformists, and in 1887 he resigned the chaplaincy of the workhouse rather than work alongside a nonconformist clergyman ministering to nonconformist inmates. He also insisted that the rules of the National Society be followed to the letter in the administration of the National School. When he was asked in 1898 to appoint one representative from each nonconformist church as a trustee and to waive the requirement that pupil teachers should attend the parish church, he refused and pointed out that trustees and pupil teachers had to sign declarations acknowledging that they were bona fide members of the Church of England.[21]

The Revd Ricketts died in 1901, but such suspicion had been created amongst the town's nonconformists that when the Education Act of 1902 was passed providing for Church schools to be financed in part from the rates, it provoked as much resentment in Knighton as it did in the Radnorshire heartland where nonconformity was much stronger. Thus when in 1903 Radnorshire County Council fixed the county rate at 6½d in the pound, of which 2½d was to be spent on elementary education, some withheld payment of that portion. (The county rate was collected separately from the road rate and poor rate.) The refusal to pay would lead to a summons to appear at Petty Sessions which would give the 'passive resister', as such a withholder of payment became known, the opportunity to state his views publicly (ratepayers were overwhelmingly male).

The first passive resister to appear before the Knighton magistrates was William Weale, a builder and contractor from Stowe. In February 1904 summons were served on a further 21 passive resisters at Knighton, including the Baptist minister, the Revd W. Williams, and Mr A.C. Wainwright, a leading Primitive Methodist. They duly appeared in court, but refused to pay. Bailiffs were therefore ordered to distrain upon their goods which were then to be sold to meet the costs of the action and the withheld rates. The goods were to be auctioned near the clock tower at 4pm on Friday 10 March, when the livestock fair had finished. The auction was conducted by the Presteigne auctioneer, Philip Davies, from a cart and was said to have been witnessed by 'some thousands'. Davies was a prominent Liberal and made a stirring speech in support of the passive resisters before the sale, which was then conducted

Plate 31: The sale of the goods of 21 'passive resisters' at Knighton in March 1904

with good humour and ended with all the distrained goods back with their original owners. Even the Conservative *Radnorshire Standard* considered the proceedings to be farcical. A further four passive resisters, including Thomas Hughes, the county councillor for Llanbister, and the Revd D. Mills, the Baptist minister at Gravel, were summonsed before the end of March, while at the beginning of July 1904 a passive resister's watch was sold by Dutch auction outside the Market Hall.[22]

Beyond getting publicity for the cause, passive resistance achieved little, however. The decision of the Knighton and Builth Poor Law Unions, responsible for collecting the county rate from their component parishes, to withhold their share of the rate was potentially more serious, for it made the Unions liable to a 10% surcharge and raised the local political temperature significantly.[23] However in the county council elections of 1904 the Liberals gained a majority and promptly waived the surcharge.

The Disestablishment Controversy

The Education Act of 1902 did not have the disastrous consequences that the nonconformists had feared, and over the following years the political temperature in Radnorshire fell. The Liberal MP for Radnorshire, Francis or Frank Edwards, nursed the constituency assiduously from his home at The Cottage, Knighton, giving generously to local good causes, 'reading a chapter' in many Radnorshire chapels and attending markets and fairs 'with the regularity of a drover'.[24] The Knighton Conservatives turned to ridicule as a weapon. In the columns of the *Radnorshire*

Plate 32: Sir Francis Edwards, MP for Radnorshire 1892-95, 1900-10, 1910-18

Standard Edwards became 'the Caliph' and J.R. Bache, the leading Knighton Liberal, 'the Vizier'. Edwards was made a baronet in 1907.[25]

In 1909-10 bitterness returned to Radnorshire politics with 'the People's Budget', whose central issues were a proposal to increase taxation on the wealthy to finance social reforms and build up the navy, and a plan to curb the power of the House of Lords. In Knighton, however, the proposal to disestablish and disendow the Welsh Church also became a contentious issue, thanks to the energy and determination of the Revd D.G. Macpherson who had become the incumbent in 1908. The first public meeting held in the town to rally opposition to the proposal came at the beginning of June 1909.

In Knighton, as in some other towns along the English border, the Church was numerically much stronger than nonconformity. The Religious Census of 1851 gives the average attendance at the two services at the parish church as nearly 57% of the town's population.[26] In east Radnorshire the issue was complicated by the fact that many of the parishes, including Knighton, Presteigne and New Radnor, lay within the English diocese of Hereford. Macpherson, the secretary of the Church Defence Association in Radnorshire, was also its most effective speaker and quite prepared to challenge Sir Francis Edwards to a debate on the issue, a challenge which Edwards declined.

The *Radnorshire Standard* dubbed the Disestablishment Bill the 'Church Robbery Bill', potentially a shrewd move since a major argument in favour of taking over the endowments of the Church on behalf of the community was that in most Welsh parishes church-goers were greatly outnumbered by chapel-goers, whereas in Radnorshire parishes such as Knighton, Presteigne and New Radnor, this was not the case. However, outside the Church the issue of disestablishment never really engaged public opinion – it had little to do with the life of the average man or woman and meetings were rarely well attended. The local press only reported two cases of public disorder at a Church Defence Association meeting, both at the Pound, Llanbister. In the first instance the speaker was howled down by four 'outsiders', while on another visit the same speaker was disturbed by 15 'hobblede-hoys' deliberately making a great deal of noise at a nearby blacksmith's shop.[27]

Even so, Macpherson and his neighbouring clerics succeeded in rallying Anglicans to oppose the measure, and a petition of communicants to the bishop of Hereford against disestablishment was signed by 318 of a total of 340 communicants in Knighton.[28] The Act, which passed the Commons in 1912 (although opposed by the Lords), was due to come into effect in 1914, but this was deferred by the outbreak of the First World War. Macpherson and his allies secured one concession, that Welsh parishes in the diocese of Hereford were to vote whether to remain in the diocese or join the disestablished Church of Wales. Disestablishment was implemented in 1920 and in 1923 Knighton, along with the other Radnorshire parishes in the diocese of St David's, was included in the newly created diocese of Swansea and Brecon of the Church in Wales.

Knighton personalities

In addition to Sir Richard Green Price, Isaac Rutter and William Banks, three others who played an important role in life of the area were Dr Charles James Covernton, Charles Coltman Rogers and J.R. Bache.

Dr Covernton, FRCS (1833-1890), a Canadian by birth, received his medical training at Edinburgh University and for a number of years worked as a ship's doctor with the P & O and the Royal Mail lines.[29] He settled in Knighton in

1860 and in addition to his private practice, served at various times as Medical Officer for Llanbister, Beguildy, Brampton Bryan, Knighton (parish and borough) and Knighton workhouse. He also served as surgeon to the Offa's Dyke Lodge of Oddfellows.

As Medical Officer for Knighton borough, Covernton had the backing of the Local Board which had in the 1850s already begun to improve public health in the town. His task was to prod the board into continuing its good work, to nag private house owners into improving the quality of the town's housing, and to encourage everyone to recognise the importance of a good water supply and efficient sanitary arrangements.

In those areas covered by the Knighton Poor Law Union outside Knighton borough, the Rural Sanitary Authority was established in 1872 in response to the poor quality of housing of both labourers and farmers. Sanitary arrangements were primitive, and most villages had no healthy public water supply. In 1874 Covernton reported that typhus had been present in the Beguildy district for three years due to poor sanitation and the lack of a pure water supply, and that in 1873-74 there had been more than 70 cases in the district. In 1876 he reported that of the 1,032 houses in the upper Teme valley, only 502 had privies, the worst case being Llanbadarn Fynydd, where only 46 out of 117 houses had privies.[30]

The two major landowners by far in the higher reaches of the Knighton Union were Lord Dunsany in the Beguildy area and Lord Ormathwaite in Llanbister and Llanddewi Ystradenni, so Covernton concentrated on persuading the agents of the two peers to embark on a programme of upgrading the housing on their estates. By doing so he hoped to establish a standard that would serve as a model for other property owners. In the last resort the Rural Sanitary Authority could declare houses as unfit for habitation, but he hoped to avoid using this measure, particularly as many of the cottagers' houses were frequently owned by the occupiers. His aim here was to use inspection as a means of ensuring that the cottages were kept clean and not overcrowded.

His words were sometimes more frank than the authorities would have wished. In April 1882 a boy of nine in Knighton workhouse was severely beaten on his bare back for saying that the chaplain's Religious Education classes 'did not do him any good'. Covernton wrote an indignant letter to the *Hereford Times*, denouncing such treatment, for which he was admonished by the Knighton Guardians. The newspaper took Covernton's side, pointing out that while the 'cat' had been abolished in the army, the chaplain still considered it useful in correcting small workhouse boys.[31]

Dr Covernton was an Anglican and served for a time as a churchwarden, but was more ecumenical in his outlook than the Revd Ricketts. He sometimes spoke at nonconformist services and meetings and also served as president of the Knighton branch of the non-sectarian YMCA. He was closely involved in the restoration of

St Edward's church in 1876-77 to which, in 1878, he gave two small memorial windows, one in memory of his wife Jane who had died in 1871, and the other in memory of an Elizabeth Covernton, possibly his mother, who had died in 1849.[32]

A Liberal, Dr Covernton represented the town on Radnorshire County Council. At the time of his death in 1890 he was acting as chairman of the council's finance committee and was campaigning to secure an Intermediate school for girls for Knighton. A vestry in St Edward's in memory of Dr and Mrs Covernton designed by J.L. Pearson and built by Cadwallader and Evans of Knighton, was dedicated in 1892.[33]

Charles Coltman Rogers (1856-1929) of Stanage Park was educated at Eton and Oxford, served as High Sheriff of Radnorshire in 1882 and initially seemed set for a career in politics. In 1884 he was returned unopposed as the last MP to represent the Radnor Boroughs constituency which was merged with the county constituency in November 1885, when he was the unsuccessful Liberal candidate for the new combined seat against Arthur H.J. Walsh, the son of the second Lord Ormathwaite.[34]

He was elected as a Radnorshire county councillor in 1888 and became an alderman in 1889. In 1890 he became chairman of the finance committee and was vice-chairman of the county council between 1892 and 1895. In 1896 he became chairman of the council, chairman of the Local Education Authority and then of its successor the Radnorshire Education Committee and chairman of the Joint Standing Committee (the Welsh equivalent of the Watch Committee), positions he held until his death in 1929. He enjoyed the trust and respect of people holding a broad spectrum of political opinion, partly because, as a Liberal Unionist, he held some views in common with both Liberals and Conservatives. During the First World War he was the chairman of the Radnorshire War Agricultural Committee, and of the County Appeals Tribunal which made the final decision on appeals for deferment from military service. In 1922 he succeeded the third Lord Ormathwaite as Lord Lieutenant of Radnorshire.

He was deeply interested in agriculture in general and in arboriculture in particular, becoming a member of the Council of the Royal Agricultural Society in 1896 and Vice President in 1918. He was chairman of the Society's botanical and forestry committees. He was on the Council of the Welsh National Pony and Cob Society and editor of its Stud Book. The

Plate 33: Charles Coltman Rogers, MP for Radnor Boroughs 1884-85

author of *Characteristics of Conifers* and a fellow of the Linnaean Society, he planted many trees at Stanage Park, collected by Wilson and Forest on their expeditions to China.[35]

Given his wider commitments, his attention was drawn more sparingly to matters in the immediate Knighton locality. Although not a gifted cricketer, he did turn out for the Knighton club on occasions. In the 1870s and early 1880s he played in matches between teams organised by various country houses, sometimes playing for Downton Castle, and he also organised matches at Stanage Park. On such occasions he was often responsible for providing the musical entertainment during the evenings, and it was in the musical sphere that he made his major local contribution. With the help of his mother and his sisters he set up the Knighton Choral Society in early 1882. Though it ceased to function for a few years after 1884, it was reformed again in 1887 and continued to function until the outbreak of war in 1914. He was also a gifted violinist and in the 1880s led a small orchestra composed largely of his family and his friends, such as J.H. Arkwright of Hampton Court near Leominster, which gave concerts in aid of various charities and local clubs and societies. Thus in June 1886 the orchestra gave a concert to raise funds for Knighton Cricket Club.[36]

The third major Knighton figure was John R. Bache (1849-1932), who was born at Rushock, near Kington. He was educated at Broughton House School and then at Hereford Proprietory School, after which he began training as a chemist, but returned home to help on the family farm.[37] In 1874 he married and moved to a farm at Staunton-on-Arrow, moving to the Grove Farm to the south of Knighton in 1879, before taking The Farm, now the Stud Farm, in Stowe, in 1886. He was a committed Liberal, serving as president of the Radnorshire Liberal Association in 1902.

He had a distinguished record in local government. He became a member of the Local Board in 1882 and subsequently its chairman. In 1894 he was elected to Knighton UDC and served as chairman from 1900 until 1912. He was elected as a guardian of Knighton Poor Law Union in 1887 and served as its chairman from 1905 until it was abolished in 1930. He succeeded Dr Covernton as county councillor for Knighton and subsequently chaired several county council committees, including the Education Committee and the Joint Standing Committee, and served for a time as vice-chairman of the council. He was also a JP, at first in his capacity as chairman of Knighton UDC, but when he resigned from that position he was appointed a JP in his personal capacity.

He was also prominent in agricultural circles. He bred Kerry Hill sheep and Shire horses which he showed, winning 46 'Firsts', and he also became a well known judge, serving in that capacity at the Royal Show and at the National Show of the Welsh Mountain Pony Show in London in 1915. In 1924 he claimed to have

198 judging rosettes, 'nearly enough to paper a room'. He served as secretary of the Knighton and Temeside Shire Horse Society from its inception in 1888 until his death, and played an important part in reviving the Knighton Agricultural Improvement Society in 1909 and in setting up the Knighton branch of the Brecon and Radnor Farmers' Union in the same year, serving as its first secretary. He also served as one of the joint secretaries of Knighton Show for a time.

During the First World War he played an important role in driving up farming productivity in Radnorshire, serving as District Sub-Commissioner for Brecon and Radnor under the Food Production Department of the Board of Agriculture and Fisheries, and also as a member of the Radnorshire Agricultural Committee. He was also a member of the Knighton Rural and Urban Tribunals which decided on applications for deferment of conscription into the Services, and of the Radnorshire Appeals Committee, the final adjudicating authority on deferment.

At first sight his career would appear to be that of a born administrator, worthy but dull, but it is clear that through his various public appointments he would have touched the life of virtually every inhabitant of Knighton. It would seem that he enjoyed the respect of a broad cross-section of the community. Thus, following a very bad tempered soccer match between Knighton and Presteigne in February 1888, after which stones were thrown at the omnibus carrying the Knighton players home, injuring one of them, there was a discussion as to how to referee the return match in March. In the end, the option of each side nominating a referee to adjudicate in their half of the pitch was rejected in favour of Bache acting as referee for both sides. The *Hereford Times* of 24 March reported that the Knighton spectators had treated the visitors courteously and that the game had been 'very pleasant throughout'. Again, when Major Careless, who had bought the Norton Manor Estate, decided in 1923 to dispose of some of the estate farms, the sale was handled by Bache, who valued them and fixed the prices. Clearly Bache's judgment was valued by the vendor and by prospective purchasers.[38]

A few Knightonians of the period succeeded in making a name for themselves, if only briefly, in the wider world. One such was John Griffith Goulstone MD, born in Knighton in 1833. He was the oldest of ten surviving children of John Griffith Goulstone, 1809-1868, a Llandovery man who had been a druggist and chemist in Knighton since the 1830s, dealing not only in medicines but also in seeds as well as manures such as guano. By 1855 his son had qualified as a medical man for in that year he served as the ship's doctor on the *Cynosure*, travelling from Liverpool to New York with 162 Mormon passengers. By 1859 he had become a surgeon and an MD and during the early 1860s came to public notice as surgeon in chief on the *SS Great Eastern*, the largest ship built in Britain during the 19th century, during its brief and hardly glorious spell as a passenger ship travelling between Milford Haven or Liverpool and New York. The *New York Times* of 12 May 1861, in its account of the *Great Eastern* and its facilities, described Goulstone as 'one of the most skilful of English surgeons'.

The later highlights of his career are supplied by brief notices in the *Hereford Times*, no doubt submitted by his proud father. The newspaper of 2 October 1861 describes a presentation to him of a 'handsome gold chronometer', while that of 28 June 1862 announced his election as a Fellow of the Royal Medical and Chirurgical Society. In the issue of 4 March 1865 it was announced that he had been created a chevalier of the Legion of Honour by Napoleon III of France, 'for services rendered on different occasions to several of his officers and subjects'. The *Great Eastern* had ceased service as a passenger ship by this time, but Goulstone seems to have continued as a ship's doctor for the *Hereford Times* of 3 June 1865 reported another presentation to Goulstone,

> by his shipmates and friends in remembrance of this kindly officer, his strict attention to detail and a courteous bearing which marked his service with them in the employ of the Liverpool, New York and Philadelphia Steamship Company.

Doctor Goulstone died at his Liverpool home in 1878.

The success of another Knightonian, William Garnet Evans, was much briefer. He was born in 1887, one of seven children of Charles Evans, a tailor of Station Road. If not prosperous, Charles Evans could afford to employ a servant, but even so Garnet chose to become a jockey, hardly a safe career choice, though the censuses for Knighton reveal that it was by no means unique in the area. In April 1905 he seemed to be on the brink of a successful career when, aged only 18, he won the Jubilee Stakes, worth £3,000, at Kempton Park. However at the Epsom meeting of June 1805 he was thrown by his mount and died of a fractured skull. He was buried in the cemetery at Knighton, his gravestone funded by his fellow jockeys.[39]

Plate 34: The gravestone of Garnet Evans in Knighton Old Cemetery

8

SOCIAL LIFE IN VICTORIAN AND EDWARDIAN KNIGHTON

Knighton at work

As a market town Knighton was geared to serving the needs of its rural hinterland and commercially the town was at its busiest on market days – Thursdays – and on fair days. Shops were also busy a day or so before, preparing their stock in readiness, with grocers' shops particularly busy as the assistants weighed out and packaged tea, sugar, butter, cheese and other goods to suit the customers' anticipated requirements. Farmers' wives and higglers added to the bustle of the town as they sold eggs, dressed poultry, butter, rabbits and other produce at the clock tower, the Butter Cross and later at the Market Hall. Itinerant traders were also busy at their standings around the Butter Cross or Market Hall, and outside inns and other commercial buildings on the main streets of the town. Nor were retailers the only beneficiaries of market days for the town's professional men, craftsmen and tradesmen did much of their business on such days, while the town's inns and eating houses also did well.

Fair days were very much market days writ large, for if not all the local farmers attended every market day, they usually made a point of attending the fairs, if only to get an idea of the state of trade. The busiest fair days were usually those in March – mainly cattle and horses, September – mainly sheep, and October – sheep and cattle. Business was particularly brisk in the autumn fairs, and it was not unusual for the penning of sheep to begin at 3am and for the Sheep Market to be filled to capacity by 6 or 7am. Thereafter sheep or cattle were penned or tethered in the adjoining streets, to the great inconvenience of passing traffic.[1]

Though some livestock changed hands at the May Fair, this fair was primarily a mop or hiring fair where farm servants, male and female, including boys and girls as young as 10 or 12, were hired for the year. In 1883 the *Hereford Times* reported that there were so many farm servants seeking work that it was difficult for pedestrians to negotiate the High Street. On coming to terms, the farmer would give his new employee 'earnest money' which was sometimes spent in a nearby inn, earning

January	Third Friday in the month. Started in 1854
February	First Thursday after 4 February. Replaced in 1854 by the January fair
March	First Friday in the month. Changed in 1850 to the first Friday after 6 March
May	May 17-18. A livestock, hiring and pleasure fair
June	21 June. A lamb and wool fair
July	First Thursday after 10 July. Began in 1856. Replaced the June fair
August	18 August. Mainly sheep and horses
September	13 September. Started in 1850. Extended to two days in late 1870s
October	1 and 2 October. First day sheep and pigs, second day cattle and horses
November	The Thursday before 12 November
December	The Thursday before Christmas Day. Sometimes coincided with the Christmas Poultry Market when thousands of turkeys, geese and poultry were bought by dealers from the west Midlands

Figure 17: Knighton's Fairs
(Sources: W.H. Howse, 'Old Fairs of Radnorshire', *TRS* xvii, 1947, p.57
and the *Hereford Times* and *Hereford Journal*)

mop fairs a bad name amongst those who deemed themselves to be the respectable members of society, so much so that in its issue of 28 April 1860 the *Hereford Times* urged their abolition. The Knighton hiring fair continued into the 20th century, however, though on a much reduced scale, finally coming to an end in 1947.[2]

Plate 35: All the fun of the fair in the early 1900s

The May Fair and, to a much lesser extent, the October Fair, were pleasure fairs, but whereas the livestock trade at the May Fair slowly declined in significance, at the October Fair the livestock trade always greatly overshadowed the pleasure fair. At the May Fair the streets were lined with stalls selling gingerbread, oranges and nuts. The roundabouts and swings were normally to be found in Market Hall Square, as Nelson Square was sometimes called or Castle Bank, while the waxwork shows, Aunt Sallies, Punch and Judy, shooting galleries, photographic studios, 'cheap Johns [Jacks]' stalls, peepshows, theatres, dancing booths, refreshment booths and games of chance were located at first on Stedman's Field on Frydd Road, near the workhouse, and from 1907 on the Recreation Ground on West Street.

Plate 36: The stalls along the streets at the May Fair in the early 1900s

Each fair was always well attended, particularly after the coming of the railways, when special trains brought in as many as 2,000 country folk, and large crowds invariably attracted pickpockets, cardsharps and ladies of pleasure. The fair also offered locals who had taken too much drink and nursed a grievance a chance to settle a score. The police always attended the fair in numbers and often dealt with troublemakers forcefully. Almost invariably the police cells were full by the end of the night with drunks, 'amateur pugilists' and rogues – both male and female, while the police court next morning was kept very busy.

Trade directories of the period suggest that the town was at its busiest in the later 1860s and early 1870s – a trade directory of 1868 shows more than 145 commercial businesses in the town at that date, compared with 120 in 1858-59 and 110 or so in 1844. After 1868 the number of businesses in the town tailed off and trade directories of 1880, 1891 and 1914 show the number of commercial concerns falling to about the 1858-59 levels.

During the last three or four decades of the century, two issues preoccupied the town's shopkeepers: the shift in the town's commercial centre of gravity away from the top of the town and High Street to the junction of Broad Street, Bridge Street and Station Road; and the issue of half-day closing. The shift had begun before the building of the Market Hall in 1868-69 and its erection did not halt the drift away from the top of the town. In 1882 the Local Board received a request from ratepayers and property owners in the locality asking that it buy or rent the Market Hall, equip it, improve access to it and take control of the stallages, rents and tolls, in order to maintain the market 'in the place in which it had always been held'. Rutter, the last bailiff, had already vested the fees and rents for stallages in the board, while the tolls had been abolished in practice in the late 1830s. Nevertheless, the board approached the Crown with a view to purchasing the right to collect tolls to be told that the right was owned not by the Crown, but by the burgesses – a body no longer in existence.[3] However, the Market Hall Company had gifted the centre of the ground floor to the town, and the board was prepared to finance the decoration of the hall and the provision of toilets. Even so the commercial drift continued, while an approach made in 1904 to the UDC to purchase the hall came to nothing, as did further tentative approaches in 1909 and again in the 1920s. The UDC finally bought the Market Hall from the company in March 1939.

Though a 12-hour day was the norm for working men except in the depths of winter, shop assistants worked considerably longer. In the mid-19th century Knighton shops opened at 8am and closed at 9pm on weekdays and 10pm on Saturdays. Since shop assistants were expected to be at work an hour before opening time in order to clean the premises and prepare for the day's business, they could expect to work an 85-hour week. An attempt in 1854 to persuade shopkeepers to close at 8pm instead of at 9pm during the winter seems to have had some success, while in 1861 shops agreed to close at 5pm on Fridays in order to allow their assistants who were members of the Knighton Volunteers to attend

Plate 37: P.B. Abery's photograph of stalls around the clock tower in the 1920s or early '30s

112

Plate 38: P.B. Abery's photograph of Broad Street in the 1920s or early '30s

drill, but it was not until the closing decades of the century that a weekly half-day holiday became general in the town for most shop assistants.[4]

By the 1880s most shops closed at 2pm on Fridays in the summer and by 1895 also during the winter months, and normal closing time during the week had become 8pm. However grocers refused to grant their assistants a half day, probably because Friday half-day closing was highly inconvenient for them. Most of the tea, butter, cheese and other goods that had been weighed and packaged earlier in the week would have been sold on market day, and a Friday half-day would leave little time to prepare packages for sale on Saturdays, another busy day for grocers. Thus when in 1907 shopkeepers agreed to close at 7pm from Monday to Thursday, 3pm on Friday and 10pm on Saturday, the town's three major grocers, Allcock, Tudge and Clee, refused to agree to the arrangement.[5]

The Relief of Poverty

Most working people, particularly labourers, lived at or just above the subsistence level, had little or no savings, and unemployment or inability to work as a result of illness, accident or old age therefore left them with no option but to apply for poor relief. After the reorganisation of the Poor Law in 1834, those wishing for poor relief were, in theory at least, compelled to enter workhouses where living conditions were inferior to those endured by the poorest souls living outside such an institution.

Dickens' *Oliver Twist* paints a very bleak picture of the reorganised Poor Law and the new workhouses, but the evidence from the Knighton Poor Law Union papers along with those of the Rhayader and Builth Unions at the National Archives suggest that he exaggerated, at least in terms of the local Unions. As Figure 18 demonstrates, less than 10% of those in receipt of poor relief in the Knighton Poor Law Union were in the workhouse in the 1840s. The remainder were in receipt of 'out relief' – they continued to live in their homes and received a few shillings a week to maintain themselves. Those responsible for the local administration of the Poor Law were anxious to keep the number of workhouse inmates as low as possible, not on compassionate grounds, but because it was cheaper to give out relief and so the poor rates could be kept low. In 1841, one of those in Knighton responsible for administering the Poor Law wrote to the Poor Law Commission in London complaining that it was costing 55 shillings a week to keep two widows and their large families in the workhouse, whereas to give them out relief would have cost the Union just 10 shillings per week.

But if those involved in managing and running the local Unions were less harsh than many, nevertheless those in receipt of out relief received barely sufficient to keep them alive, and those without relatives in the locality were particularly at risk, especially if the local Poor Law officer was careless or incompetent. In January 1864 a Llangunllo woman admitted to Knighton workhouse 'in a state of exhaustion and destitution' died five hours later. The verdict at the inquest was that she died of natural causes, 'accelerated by exposure to cold and want of proper nourishment'. Clearly the relieving officer had delayed too long before taking action. Again, in January 1875, at the inquest on a widow living at Cwm Bank, Knighton it was

Plate 39: The workhouse in the early 1900s

	In the workhouse	Total number of paupers relieved
1846	74	791
1847	77	905
1848	83	870
1849	97	1038
1850	83	879

Figure 18: Numbers in receipt of poor relief in Knighton Union 1846-50 (Source: TNA PRO MAF/16691 dated 22.2.1850)

found that the local relieving officer had failed to read part of the Medical Officer's note and so had not realised that the widow had neither, fuel, food or sufficient clothing in the house and had taken no action. The relieving officer was charged with manslaughter, but was found 'not guilty' at the Easter assizes.[6]

An analysis of the number of inmates of different ages and sexes in the workhouse listed in the censuses of 1851 and 1871 shows that local administration of the Poor Law was not as intended originally by the central authorities, for most of the aged poor and unemployed adults of working age continued to receive out relief. Of the 20 females in the age group 16-59 in 1851, five were widows with children and 11 were women with illegitimate children. If these are discounted, of the 86 inmates only nine were of working age. On the basis of surnames, of the 54 children 23 were apparently orphans since they were not accompanied by an adult. However writing to the authorities in London in August 1847, Edward Mason, the clerk to Knighton Poor Law Union, admitted that many of the orphaned children in the workhouse were illegitimate children whose mothers had been advised by parish officers to abandon their children as it was cheaper than keeping both mother and child in the workhouse.[7]

It would seem that the situation had not changed by 1851. In how many cases the arrangement was purely temporary it is impossible to tell. At the time of the census of 1871, the number of inmates had fallen to 59 and the number in the age group 16-59 was small – 2 men and 9 unmarried women, at least 5 of them in the workhouse with their children. 41

Age group	Males	Females
60+ yrs	5	2
16-59 yrs	4	21
Under 16 yrs	35	19

Figure 19: Inmates in Knighton workhouse in 1851

of the inmates were children, at least 23 of whom appear to have been abandoned.

By the closing decades of the century the number of inmates was about

Age group	1881	1891
60+ yrs	17 males, 1 female	8 males, 3 females
16-59 yrs	16 males, 8 females	9 males, 15 females
Under 16 yr	4 males, 15 females	14 males, 11 females

Figure 20: Inmates in Knighton workhouse in 1881 and 1891

the same, but although the proportion of the inmates in the 16-59 age group had risen significantly since 1871, the central Poor Law authority still believed that the Knighton Guardians were spending too much on out relief.[8] The sharp fall in the number of children in the workhouse since 1871 was the result of the authorities deciding to board some of them out with householders in the Union and send others to orphanages, while some of the boys were sent to industrial schools.

The regime in the Knighton house was not as harsh as critics of the workhouse system have suggested. The inmates' accommodation was drier, warmer and better ventilated than the houses in which the poor generally lived, they were adequately clothed and had three square meals a day, even if the meals were stodgy and consisted in the main of bread and potatoes. The inmates also received free medical attention, whilst the children received a free education in the 3Rs. In addition, boys were taught gardening and to knit stockings, and the girls knitting, sewing and house-work. Nor was the work provided arduous or degrading. The women were occupied in cleaning and washing clothes and bed linen, while the men were put to work in the garden. A later suggestion to employ some of the male inmates to pick oakum – untwisting and unpicking old rope into fibre – seems to have been rejected by the central authorities. Vagrants, however, were expected to break stone – men for three hours and women for two – in return for their meals and a bed for the night. The administration of the workhouse was sometimes more lax than one might expect. The steady stream of workhouse inmates sentenced to short spells of imprisonment in the county gaol by the magistrates in the 1850s and 1860s for insubordination or fighting suggests that the workhouse authorities – in particular the workhouse master – sometimes found it difficult to maintain order.[9]

The quality of life of the inmates depended upon the provision of reasonable standards of food, heating, accommodation and other amenities. Unfortunately, the elected guardians charged with administering the system locally saw their first responsibility as being to the ratepayers and thus to keep the poor rate as low as possible. The food was therefore of the lowest quality, as were the clothes, footwear, sheets and blankets provided, and the minimum was spent on repairs and main-tenance, with the result that by the mid-1870s the accommodation was markedly sub-standard, the workhouse being described in 1875 as 'comfortless and dilapi-dated'. Even so, it took the guardians more than a decade to build a new workhouse. Roast beef and plum pudding on Christmas Day, and the gifts provided by the Green Prices and other benefactors, did not make up for mean-spirited treatment the inmates experienced during the rest of the year.

Though Knighton workhouse was better than the workhouse as portrayed in literature, working people dreaded the prospect of spending the closing years of their lives there, bringing as it did a loss of personal identity and of control over one's life. Dressed in a cheap uniform, living in strict accordance with myriad rules and regulations, with husbands, wives and children in separate wards and for the most part strictly isolated from other family members, inmates could soon become institutionalised. However, only one case of cruel and inhumane treatment in Knighton workhouse is known of from local press reports and the records of the national Poor Law authorities, the case described in the previous chapter of the boy of nine severely beaten on his bare back in April 1882.

Severe winter weather caused hardship not only for the old, the sick and the poor, who lacked the means to buy warm clothing or additional fuel, but also for many in regular employment who were laid off temporarily. At such times it was customary for the local gentry to provide funds to buy coal to sell to the poor at a much reduced price, and to provide meat, bread and warm clothing for them. A series of severe winters in the later 1870s led to the formation of a town relief committee, while St Edward's and the chapels set up clothing funds. The most sustained effort came in February and March 1886, when more than £530 was subscribed to the fund, as a result of which 240 of the town's poor were each provided with two hundredweight of coal (approximately 10kg), and 400 4lb (2kg) loaves were distributed. During the winter of 1886-87 a soup kitchen was set up by the women of St Edward's and the town's chapels, while the Knighton Relief Fund gave out coal tickets to the 'deserving' poor. Soup kitchens and other relief schemes were also organised in 1900, 1905, and 1908.[11] In the winter of 1907-08 the soup kitchen distributed 60 quarts of soup and 20 quarts of milk twice weekly to 70 poor families and widows.

Perhaps the most important innovation in Knighton in the decade or so before the outbreak of the First World War, was the formation of a district nursing system covering the town and surrounding countryside. Since at least 1902, Nurse Ffoulkes of the Church Army had served in the town, two-thirds of her salary being paid by the Church, the other third by the members of the Nursing Club in subscriptions. The nonconformists, led by the Primitive Methodists, set up a similar Nursing Club. In September 1908 the clubs were replaced by a Nursing Association under a management committee of four church women, four nonconformist women and four men, two elected by the church and two by the nonconformists. During the first year of operation, 1908-09, the district nurse, Nurse Ellis, attended 185 cases and made 4,689 visits. When she resigned in May 1912 her place was taken by Nurse Tate. Fees charged to members of the scheme depended upon the rateable value of their house: under £8 per annum, the fee was 2 shillings; under £25 per annum, 5 shillings; over £25 per annum, 10 shillings. Honorary members of the association made an annual donation. Later the football club gave the proceeds of their Nurse's Cup competition to the association, while the proprietors of the May Fair gave one night's proceeds from their major entertainments. Since a doctor's fees could place a heavy burden on the ordinary family budget, the presence of a district nurse in the town was invaluable since she was able to deal with routine illnesses and give advice as to care and treatment.[11]

Church and Chapel

By the early 1840s, the church of St Lawrence, built in the 1750s, was distinctly old-fashioned, while the presence of so many privately owned pews left little seating available for the general public. In 1844 the first steps to improve the situation were taken: the 'squeaky old instrument' was replaced by a 'neat and pretty organ', a barrel organ 'of the finest quality' built by Child of Hereford, and the entrance to the church was shifted from the side to the rear, allowing 50 new free sittings. In 1857 the old church clock was replaced by one given by Henry Miles of Downfield. In 1861-62 an extensive programme of renovating the churchyard and the exterior and interior of the church meant that it was closed for public worship, and services were held in the Assembly Rooms for several months. In 1869, thanks to the drive and enthusiasm of William Banks, a new organ built by Clay and Davidson of London costing some £250, was installed.[13]

However, the mood in the country as a whole was for the wholesale rebuilding and restoration of parish churches and Knighton was no exception. In 1869 a public meeting was held to consider building a new church. Plans prepared by S. Pountney Smith of Shrewsbury, which would provide a further 350 free sittings, were approved and a committee was appointed to collect subscriptions. However nothing further was done. The *Hereford Times* of 1 November 1873 published a letter from 'Parishioner' denouncing the situation:

> The pews are monopolised by a few and one half of the parishioners cannot have a seat, and many who have are actually paying for them. The money, however, does not go into the exchequer of the church, but into the pockets of individuals who claim their ownership.

The Religious Census of 1851 suggests that this assertion was correct since it revealed that the church contained 50 free sittings – those provided in 1844 – and 700 'others'.[14]

In 1875 it was decided to implement Pountney Smith's plans of 1869, a subscription list was opened and a building committee set up, with Sir Richard Green Price as chairman and J.P. Medlicott of the North and South Wales Bank as treasurer. The most generous subscribers were Lord Hartington who gave £200, Richard Green Price and the Revd John Rogers who each gave £150, and the Revd J.R. Brown who subscribed £100. The restoration involved the rebuilding of the nave and the north and south aisles at a cost of £3,500. Originally both the chancel and tower were to be left as they were, though in the end a further £250 was spent restoring the tower. The cornerstone of the new nave was laid on 5 June 1876 by Mrs Green Price, and the re-opening of the church took place in November 1877. The restored church was dedicated to St Edward, King and Martyr.[15]

Letters published in the *Hereford Times* suggest that the atmosphere in Knighton was not one of sweetness and light during the course of the restoration. The issue of 21 July 1875 contained a letter complaining that the subscription lists published in the newspaper only included those whose subscriptions amounted to £5 or more. Once the restoration was complete the complaints mounted. A letter to the issue of 24 November complained of the use of the 'Romanising hymnal' *Hymns Ancient and Modern*; while the issue of 1 December included a letter complaining of 'the mummeries of Rome' used at the re-opening service – the choir wore gowns and the prayers were 'intoned' – in spite of the fact that many nonconformists had contributed to the building fund. A fortnight later a Knighton parishioner complained that the restoration had been unnecessary since the old building had been sound and seating sufficient for those who attended; moreover the position of the curfew bell had been altered and it could not now be heard 500 yards away, while the gas lighting, which had cost more than £100, lit up the roof rather than the hymn books of the congregation.

The restoration was completed in 1896-97 by the rebuilding of the chancel to a design by J.L. Pearson, the pause probably stemming from financial constraints. The replacement of the chancel – a 'small and inadequate building' – was to be part funded by the incumbent, the Revd M.H. Ricketts, who subscribed £700 and hoped that parishioners and friends would subscribe the balance. The scheme was not without its problems. It was envisaged that the new chancel would have a new east window to celebrate Victoria's Golden Jubilee, but this would necessitate the removal of the existing window installed in 1860 by Mrs Breeze in memory of her husband, Edward Breeze, a former high sheriff of Radnorshire. A faculty to remove the window and to

Plate 40: The tower of St Edward's is the oldest part of the church. The clock, given in 1857, was originally intended for the clock tower in the centre of the town

place it at the east end of the north aisle was applied for on the grounds that the window would be too small for the enlarged chancel, and was 'not in character with the taste of the present day'. The Breeze family objected, but Ricketts was supported by Pearson and in the end carried the day.[16]

The demolition of the old chancel began in mid-February 1897 and in April Mrs Ricketts laid the cornerstone of the new building which was to be constructed by the Knighton firm of Cadwallader and Weale. The work was now estimated to cost about £3,000 of which Ricketts was to subscribe £1,000 and Francis Edwards £500. The final cost of the new chancel was £2,900 and with subscriptions and other sources totalling £2,700, the shortfall was made up by the proceeds of a fête held on Bryn-y-Castell. In addition, the Jubilee window cost some £250, of which £200 was subscribed by the Revd and Mrs Ricketts.[17]

The rebuilding of the nave and chancel of the parish church was akin to the surge of energy and confidence which produced the secular 'great rebuilding' in the town during the third quarter of the century. But those involved with the church were by no means solely concerned with renewing the building. The churchwardens were often instrumental in distributing coal and bread during spells of severe winter weather whilst the ladies, together with those of the chapels, staffed the soup kitchens in such times. The donations of the wealthier churchgoers helped to subsidise the church's clothing club, while special collections helped to finance the town's

Plate 41: St Edward's church: the nave was built in 1876 and the chancel in 1896-97

National Schools, the sole providers of elementary education in the town. They were also firm supporters of the anti-slavery North in the American Civil War, and when the North blockaded the Southern States, preventing them from supplying Britain with cotton and thus causing textile workers in Lancashire to be laid off in the autumn of 1862, St Edward's raised more than £25 and also provided several loads of clothes to assist them.[18]

The incumbencies of the Revd J.R. Brown and the Revd M.H. Ricketts almost covered the entire reign of Victoria. Both were wealthy, able and well educated clerics, graduates of Emmanuel College, Cambridge and Exeter College, Oxford respectively, but their theological stances differed markedly. Brown was a Broad Churchman, sometimes described as a 'squarson', none too concerned with the finer detail of doctrine and able, as we have seen, to establish a working relationship with local nonconformists. Ricketts possessed considerable academic ability, a Fellow of Exeter College, who preached the sermon at Evensong at St Paul's Cathedral on a Sunday in mid-November 1879. He was a High Churchman, very conscious of his priestly status, and found it difficult to work with nonconformists.[19]

The first of the nonconformist churches in Knighton was the Wesleyan church built on Castle Bank, near Plough Lane, in 1802 and said to be the oldest Methodist chapel in Radnorshire. By 1844 it was considered too small to seat more than half the congregation, but this would seem to be an exaggeration for the Religious Census of 1851 lists the seating as 20 free sittings and 40 other sittings, along with standing room for 40. On the day of the census 80 attended the afternoon service and 30 attended that in the evening. The most conservative branch of Methodism, the Wesleyans nevertheless had a strong social conscience and early in 1863 were raising funds to assist the Lancashire textile workers laid off as a result of the Northern States' blockade of the Southern States. The Wesleyan cause in Knighton continued to grow in the middle decades of the century and in 1870 a new chapel was built in West Street on a site given by Richard Green Price.[20]

Another branch of Methodism, the Primitive Methodists, was established in Knighton in 1826 by the 'Preacher Poet', the Revd Richard Jukes. At first the 'Prims' met in a house belonging to Thomas Owen near the present entrance to the railway yard. The Primitive Methodists were far more evangelical than their Wesleyan cousins and held open air 'camp meetings' in order to reach the general public, a tactic which sometimes aroused great resentment. By 1844 their numbers were such that a chapel was considered necessary. 400 tickets were sold for the first fundraising event, a tea meeting, which was held in the Duke's Arms and at which 300 sat down for tea. These numbers should not be taken as an indication of the numerical strength of the Primitive Methodists in the town, however, for the event was attended by other nonconformists from both the town and the surrounding area.[21]

By 1851 funds were sufficient to start building a chapel on part of the site now occupied by part of the railway station, the foundation stone being laid by John Wilson, the tanner, who had given the site. The church, which cost £1,400 to build, was opened in 1852, but within a few years proved to be too small and in 1860 the foundation stones for a new chapel were laid on a site on Broad Street by, amongst others, Isaac Rutter and John Wilson. The new church, which was designed by Henry Lote, a local architect, could hold a congregation of 500 and cost £1,100. It was formally opened in January 1862, the *Hereford Journal* claiming: 'It exhibits considerable taste and architectural neatness and will be an ornament to Broad Street.'[21]

The origin of the Baptist church in Knighton can be traced back to 1833 when a few Baptists began to meet regularly in a cottage to the rear of the present Norton Arms Hotel. For a couple of decades small Baptist meetings continued to be held in various cottages in the town, but membership began to grow rapidly in the 1850s, thanks to the leadership of a Mr D.C. Chapman, the cashier of the railway contractors Morton and Hattersley, who were building the Central Wales line, and whose presence in the town coincided with an influx of textile workers from Montgomeryshire brought in to man the Silurian Mills, many of whom were Baptists. By 1860 funds were being gathered to build a church at tea meetings

Plate 42: An early photograph showing the Wesleyan Chapel in the foreground and what was to become known as Norton Street Baptist Chapel above and to the right. The photograph was taken before Norton Street had been completed and Victoria Road built

attended by over 200 supporters. The Presteigne Baptist minister, the Revd T.L. Davies, gave the Knighton Baptists a more formal church organisation and by 1862 they could claim a membership of 41. A building committee was set up and a site for a chapel was purchased from Richard Green Price on the newly built Norton Street, the foundation stone being laid on 8 June 1864. The church was built of Kinsley stone, given by Richard Green Price, and so cost just £650. It was opened on 25 June 1865, and by the 1870s the Knighton Baptists claimed a membership of between 200 and 300, with 220 scholars and 20 teachers in its Sunday School.[23]

Baptist churches enjoyed a considerable degree of local autonomy, meaning that strong views uncompromisingly held could lead to deep divisions, and as early as 1859 the young Knighton Baptist church was in danger of splitting into factions. In 1901 strong divisions of opinion led to 14 Baptist members being suspended, and they and their supporters, popularly known as 'the Splits', set up another Baptist church which met at a number of locations including the Market Hall and the Working Men's Club, before deciding to build their own church. Towards the end of June 1904 the foundation stone of the new church was laid in Victoria Road. The church, designed by E.J. Morris of Llandrindod and built by Messrs Weale and Lloyd cost £750 and seated 200.[24]

The nonconformist churches, particularly the Primitive Methodists and Baptists, demanded a high level of commitment from their members, who were expected to attend services and other meetings on a regular basis, to ensure their children attended Sunday School and to adhere to the high standards of conduct expected from them. 'Backsliders' could expect to be admonished privately or publicly, with expulsion the final sanction. Members found much of their social life revolved around their church: the choir (both women's and men's), youth and children's clubs and associated organisations. The nonconformists exercised considerable influence, for each of their churches included amongst its members individuals and families of considerable standing in the town – the Wesleyans, the Oldbury and Allcock families; the Primitive Methodists, Isaac Rutter and John Wilson; and the Baptists, Edward Davies, the manager of the Radnorshire Company.

However, we should bear in mind that a substantial proportion of the town's population were not churchgoers. If we take the optimistic average attendances reported at the parish church and Wesleyan church in the Religious Census of 1851 – 890 and 122 respectively – at face value and add a generous 60 as the attendance at each of the Primitive Methodist and Baptist house churches, 1,132 of Knighton's population of 1,566, 72% of the population, were church or chapel-goers. But at least 28% were not, and many of these had little time for the temperance campaigns conducted by the Baptists and the Primitive Methodists in the town in the second half of the century.

Of the social life of this non-churchgoing minority we know little, since local press reports tend to deal with the doings of the local establishment and the more respectable elements of the town. The town's inns and public houses – 22 in 1879 – offered warmth, light, congenial company and small-scale gambling on card games and dominoes. Serious gambling was reserved for less public venues such as Pinner's Hole (see below). In the mid-19th century, prize fights, dog fighting and cock fights were also popular with the less reputable elements in the town. In 1851 and 1854, respectable public opinion in the locality was shocked by the sale of wives in the town. The *Hereford Times* of 1 March 1851 reported that the Knighton town crier announced 'the sale of a woman by public auction at the Town Hall in this town, being the property of a Jockey', while the edition of 6 May 1854 reported that on the previous Saturday the sale of the wife of a William Jones was to have taken place in the market place, but did not occur as the wife was sold privately. The paper denounced this 'outrage on public decency'.

The Maintenance of Public Order
Serious crime was rare in Knighton and most cases involved petty thieving, drunkenness, brawls, poaching for the pot or 'coursing' – a farmer or his shepherd using dogs to chase off the flock of another from a choice piece of grazing on the common – and were heard at Petty Sessions. This was perhaps just as well, for the only police force available consisted of the untrained and usually elderly parish constables. When the county authorities were offered an opportunity to set up a rural police force in 1840 they declined, preferring to appoint a paid superintendent constable in each of Radnorshire's market towns – jointly with Breconshire in the cases of Hay and Builth – to supervise the parish constables and the lock-up.

Magistrates always feared an outbreak of public disorder since it not only threatened property, but also reflected badly upon their competence. In the autumn of 1843, when tollgates in the Rhayader area were being destroyed by Rebecca rioters – groups of armed men with blackened faces, often wearing women's clothes as a disguise – rumours reached the town of an impending attack on Knighton workhouse. As a result Richard Green (Price) immediately arranged for a detachment of troops from the 6th Regiment of Foot at Newtown to be sent to Knighton to maintain order.

Green Price must have panicked for he had not contacted the Knighton magistrates or his uncle Richard Price. The evidence upon which he had acted was certainly weak: a rumour from a highly unreliable source had been relayed to Mr Thomas of Treburvaugh; and there had been a report that a woman – thought to be a Rebeccaite in disguise – had been seen sketching the workhouse. Green's panic was clearly infectious for the Knighton magistrates ordered special constables (unpaid men of standing) to be sworn in, and six other constables were hired at 18 shillings a week to patrol the town at night.[25]

By the end of 1843 the trouble in the Rhayader area had died down and the detachment of the 6th Regiment of Foot at Knighton returned to Newtown, though the expensive constables continued to patrol the town at night – much to the annoyance of the people of Knighton who bore the cost. The *Hereford Times* of 10 December probably reflected the townspeople's feelings accurately:

> These uncalled for and (to the inhabitants) annoying so-called protective measures will not soon be effaced from their memories.

The constables were finally stood down in January 1844.

Serious crime was not entirely absent from the wider Knighton area. The sparsely populated uplands of the upper Teme valley were an ideal base for sheep-stealers since the sheep could be slaughtered, skinned and cut into joints safe from prying eyes and quickly transported to the industrial areas of Staffordshire and the west Midlands before they had been missed by their owners. The authorities tended to punish any offenders severely. The *Hereford Times* of 28 August 1844 reported that two Beguildy men convicted of sheep stealing had been sentenced to transportation for ten years, while the issue of 4 September reported that a gang of 11 sheep-stealers active in Beguildy and Bettws had been rounded up. Some were committed to prison by the Knighton magistrates and the remainder remanded for trial at the Assizes.

Any other serious crime in the locality created a major sensation. Two highway robberies perpetrated by two Knighton men and an accomplice in November 1847, one on Stonewall Hill and the other towards Ludlow, led the new Knighton super-intendent, John Constance, to set off in hot pursuit. Aided by the Leintwardine police officer, he caught up with and arrested the Knighton men a few miles from Ludlow, where their accomplice was taken a few days later. The incident provoked much excitement in the town, for the brothers' parents were of 'a highly respectable character'. All three men were initially sentenced to transportation for life, but this was subsequently changed to imprisonment for life.[26]

Since the authorities sometimes over-reacted to the threat of public disorder, the superintendent constables and their successors, the Radnorshire Constabulary which was formed in 1857, were initially highly unpopular, especially among the less respectable elements, who saw the constables as protecting the interests of the landowners, for example by arresting poachers, at the expense of the ratepayers. In May 1840 a pistol was fired at Henry Verdon, Knighton's first superintendent constable, wounding him in the arm. A suspect was subsequently arrested and charged, but was found 'not guilty'.[27]

For their part the superintendent constables and the county police could, on occasions, be overzealous. Verdon's successor, John Constance, believed in anticipating trouble, as this report in the *Hereford Times* of 18 March 1848 illustrates:

> We never noticed so many of the light fingered gentry at this season as there were at this fair. On night approaching, Constance and a body of constables went through the streets, public houses and beer shops, giving them an entire sweep out, driving before them the whole of the bridle and whip vendors, orange sellers etc, to their several houses and lodging houses.

As a result the pickpockets, cardsharps and ladies of the night were unable to ply their trades.

The initial unpopularity of the Radnorshire Constabulary is best illustrated by incidents which occurred on the evening of the March Fair in 1858, when there was a confrontation in the town between five policemen and several groups of men who had been fighting. Some were persuaded to go home, but others stood their ground and as their numbers swelled they attempted to rush the police, crying 'What do the police want here?', while 'many an ill taught urchin' shouted 'Down with the police'. The heavily outnumbered police stood firm and refused to be provoked.[28] In the early 1860s, when the railway line to Llandrindod was being built, the task of the Knighton police was not made easier by the arrival in the town each Saturday of 150 or so navvies to collect their pay and celebrate pay day. The situation was just as bad in the late 1890s when the water pipe to Birmingham was being laid in the vicinity of Knighton.

Even so, serious disorder was a rare occurrence and for the most part the police were concerned with trivial issues, one of which, illegal gambling, was a perennial problem in Knighton throughout the century. On summer evenings and on Sundays, groups of 20 or 30 men and youths often gathered in Garth Lane or Pinner's Hole to gamble, a favourite game being 'Banker', but the police found it difficult to prosecute successfully. It was easy to prove that card games were being played, but very difficult to provide corroborating evidence that money had changed hands.[29]

The police were also getting many complaints about unruly boys and young men: the glass in gas street lamps and on the town clock had been broken by catapults; gangs of 10 to 15 year-olds were gathering in the streets in clusters, yelling, swearing and using obscenities; and, later, groups of rather older youths were in the habit of passing offensive comments on passers-by, both male and female. Sometimes however, the police seem to have over-reacted. Under the headline 'A Police Ridden Town: Ridiculous Cases at Knighton', the *Radnor Express* of 4 May

1899 described how seven young Knighton men had been charged with disorderly conduct, attempting to interfere with a street light, using bad language and singing 'The Holy City' – all of which had occurred on Christmas Eve! In the face of contradictory evidence the offenders were let off with a caution and a reprimand. The newspaper summarised the Chairman of the Bench's closing speech as 'Not guilty, but don't do it again'.

In part the trouble was the lack of leisure facilities in the town for the local young men not connected with church or chapel, and not attracted by the non-sectarian YMCA, which had been set up in Knighton in 1871. The problem was eased a little with the formation of the Gymnastic Club in 1891, the formation of several youth football clubs, and the opening of the Working Men's Club in 1900 with its full-size billiards table and facilities for bagatelle, table tennis and card playing – but not for money.

The local establishment was particularly exercised by the over-enthusiastic celebration of Bonfire Night. The *Hereford Times* of 22 November 1851, describing the celebrations in Knighton on 5 November, reported:

> The town was in the greatest tumult ever known. About 11 o'clock at night a mob, the very dregs of the town, congregated and bid defiance to all law. We think it is high time these lawless proceedings were putdown.

Celebrations the following year were even livelier: the Guy was burned on a bonfire on the site of the old town hall, guns and pistols were discharged, fireworks were thrown around and a window was broken.

Later the town authorities sought to reduce the risk of disorder and damage on 5 November by banning fireworks in the streets, but ensuring a site was made available outside the town where Guy Fawkes Night could be properly celebrated. In 1872, after such a site had been provided, the police employed the town crier to announce that anyone letting off fireworks in the streets would be prosecuted. The magistrates however subsequently ruled that the few who had offended should be cautioned rather than prosecuted. In 1888, the *Radnorshire Echo* of 9 November reported that 'Young Knighton went in torch light procession to the old quarry near the railway station' for their noisy Bonfire Night celebrations. Thereafter the celebrations of 5 November died out, possibly because official sanction had spoiled the fun, and the *Radnorshire Standard* of 7 November 1908 reported:

> It is some years since the streets of Knighton were lighted up with torches on 5 November ... This time not even a cracker was heard.

Knighton at leisure

Given their long working hours and subsistence level wages, most working people had neither the time nor the resources for much in the way of leisure activities. On the other hand their homes were far from comfortable since they were sparsely furnished, gloomy and cold, as when the fire was not needed for cooking it was 'banked up' with peat or turf. Some attended church or chapel meetings, while for others the public house provided an escape from the drab daily grind – though sometimes at the expense of a sore head and short rations until next pay day, costs which Baptist and Primitive Methodist teetotallers never failed to stress.

The May and October pleasure fairs provided welcome breaks in routine, as did the public celebrations of royal occasions such as the marriage of the Prince of Wales in 1863 or Queen Victoria's Golden Jubilee in 1887, or more local events such as the marriage of Richard Green in 1837 or the coming of age of his son, Dansey Green Price, in 1859. The celebrations on such occasions had a common pattern; the funds were raised by subscriptions on the part of local shopkeepers and businessmen (even to celebrate marriages of the local elite); a bullock and a number of sheep were bought, killed and roasted; the friendly societies and schoolchildren walked in procession bearing the wagon carrying the joints of meat through the town led by the town band; meat and bread were distributed amongst the poor of the town, and the children and old people treated to tea and plum cake. Celebrations were rounded off in the evening by rural sports such as climbing the greasy pole, and a bonfire.

Many shopkeepers and skilled craftsmen were members of the Savings Bank which had opened in 1855, and many also belonged to friendly societies which, in return for a monthly or weekly subscription of a few pence, provided small payments if a sickness or accident prevented a member from working. They also covered burial expenses. The oldest of these societies was the Crown Friendly Society, founded in 1771. Other Knighton inns such as the Fleece, the Globe, the Duke's Arms and the George also had friendly societies, and yet others included the Victoria Society and the Knighton branch of the Radnorshire Friendly Society founded in 1858. During the second half of the century most of these societies ceased to function and their place was taken by the Oddfellows, the Foresters and the 'Buffs' – the Royal and Ancient Order of Buffaloes.[30] The most important event for the members was the annual club 'walk' when the members gathered at their headquarters, usually an inn, then in full regalia and with their elaborate banners aloft marched in procession, led by a brass band, to the church for the anniversary service. Then the procession made a circuit of the main streets before adjourning for lunch and a series of formal speeches, followed in the late afternoon and evening by sports and dancing.

Until the late 1850s the major social events for the town's establishment were the Christmas Ball, sometimes referred to as the Card and Dancing Assembly, the

May Fair Ball and the ball held on the second evening of the Knighton races. By the late 1860s the Christmas Ball/Card and Dancing Assembly had been replaced by the Invitation Ball. The latter event was not initially as exclusive as one might expect for its full title was the Agricultural and Tradesmen's Ball, and though it was attended by the town's professional and commercial elite and the more prosperous farming families, only the younger members of the local gentry attended. By the end of the 1860s the Ball had risen in status, for Lady Brydges and Richard Green Price presided as patroness and patron, while in 1878 the stewards included Herbert Lewis of Harpton Court, Richard Dansey Green Price and Captain Otway. By the later 1880s, however, and the advent of the County Ball at Presteigne, the Invitation Ball had become 'the Agricultural and Commercial Ball' once more.

From time to time the everyday rhythm of life in the town was broken by the visit of professional entertainers, such as Sanger's or Howes' or Cushings' circus, while in 1840 and 1865 touring acting companies were performing in Knighton's theatre at the top of the town, though its precise location is not known. Amateur entertainment became a regular feature of the social life of the town in the 1860s, most notably in the form of 'Penny Readings'. These were normally held on a weekly basis between November and March in aid of the National Schools and were organised by the young wife of the lawyer Jonathan Green and a committee of ladies. One half of the proceedings consisted of recitations, readings of comic or dramatic extracts from such authors as Dickens and occasionally short plays, the latter always read by men, and the other half of instrumental and vocal items performed in the main by the wives and daughters of the local elite. The proceedings were chaired by an eminent townsman such as Thomas Peters – the partner in Richard Green Price's original Knighton legal practice, William Banks or the Revd J.R. Brown.

The readings were well supported in the town and sometimes had an audience of more than 250, in the main members of the town's elite families and the very respectable – a favourite Victorian adjective that encompassed shopkeepers and white collar workers. Only on one occasion did some of the audience misbehave, at the reading of March 1867 when the failure of the lighting in the hall seemed to have unsettled some of the boys who had been attending the fair, who began to make a great deal of noise. The chairman, Dr Scott, lacking the moral authority of the more established figures in the town, was unable to restore order and 'the most unpleasant evening of the series' came to an unhappy end.[31]

Convention dictated that women of the gentry and the middle class should lead their lives away from the public gaze, except in connection with their good works or in connection with society events. The charitable purpose of the Penny Readings meant that their appearance at such events was permissible, but convention decreed that they should not take part in amateur dramatics. Thus, when the recently formed Amateur Dramatic Club gave two performances of a play in aid of the Church Organ Fund in 1873, the female roles were taken by two professional actresses hired from Manchester. The public invisibility of gentlewomen in the mid-19th century is best illustrated by an incident at the last Penny Reading of the 1863-64 series, for when Isaac Rutter thanked Mrs Green for organising the series, convention dictated that Jonathan Green should reply on behalf of his wife.[32]

The second half of the 19th century saw a new musical tradition being established in the town with the development of choral singing. This grew out of the church and chapel choirs and was socially much more broadly based. The first choral society was formed in 1855, its conductor being Mr Starkie, a weaver at the Silurian Mills who was also the organist of the parish church. The choir had a short life for nothing is heard of it after 1859 when, after a concert in October 1859, a patronising report in the *Hereford Times* of 2 November commented:

> The Society has not attained the proficiency after another twelve months' practice as might have been expected.[33]

Another choral society was formed in 1882 by Charles Coltman Rogers of Stanage Park assisted by his mother and his sisters. It was discontinued for a few years while Rogers was MP for Radnor Boroughs and then contested the county seat, before he started it again in 1887, initially with 16 members, some being members of the Stanage Park domestic staff. It continued, with a few breaks, until 1914 and the outbreak of war.[34]

The decision to form a Volunteer Rifle Corps in Knighton was made at the end of January 1860 when, in face of a perceived threat from France, it was decided to form a company of between 60 and 100 men who were to drill on eight days over four months, each drill being of two or three hours' duration, and also to practice on a rifle range at Panpunton. By the end of February, 43 effective members had signed up under the command of Captain Richard Green, with his son Dansey as ensign.[35]

One of the attractions of joining was probably the uniform, with trousers of light grey with red cord down the outside of the trouser legs, a jacket with a scarlet collar and a cap with red braid and a badge showing the Prince of Wales' feathers. The uniform was expensive – in the region of £3 5s – more than a month's pay for most young men, but for those unable to afford it, the cost was borne by honorary members of the Corps who paid an annual subscription of at least three guineas. A surgeon and chaplain were appointed, and a drummer, bugler and fife player were recruited, an ensemble that later grew into a full band.[36]

While the members of the 2nd Radnor Rifle Volunteers cut a dash in their uniform, much to the delight of the more impressionable young ladies in Knighton, they were by no means popular in all quarters. Thus on their first Church Parade, when they assembled at the Farmers' Club and marched to church,

> The services of the band was, doubtless judiciously, dispensed with, as it would have excited the idle curiosity of some hundreds of navvies and others, at present located here, without producing any good results.

The ploy may not have been completely successful for the next week's *Hereford Times* reported that a Knighton man had been bound over to keep the peace after abusing the Volunteers.[37]

In 1875, when Richard Green Price and his son resigned and no persons of sufficient standing to take their place had been found, the Knighton Volunteers were disbanded, to be revived in 1882 under the command of Captain Otway as a contingent of the Herefordshire Volunteers. Later, like the other Radnor Rifle Volunteer companies, the Knighton Rifle Volunteers, under the command of Lt E.T.P. Rogers, became part of the First Battalion of the Herefordshire Regiment.[38]

One of the most important events in the Knighton calendar during the 20th century, Knighton Show, began in 1891 on the last Friday in August as 'The Horticultural and Bee Exhibition and Athletic Sports' and was held on the ground of Knighton Cricket Club at Bryn-y-Castell by the new Floral and Horticultural Society. A horticultural society had existed in the town since 1869, when it held

Plate 43: Crowds on their way to Knighton Show in the 1900s

Plate 44: The Fancy Dress Parade and Procession in 1922

its first show in a field adjoining the National Schools. The new show was on a much larger scale and covered a wider range of interests, and as early as 1897 it was attracting an attendance of 7,000.[39] The organisers continued to introduce new attractions: in 1900 the Knighton Horse Show joined with it and the fancy dress procession was introduced; in 1908 a brass band competition was added, whilst a quickstep competition in the streets attracted thousands of spectators; in 1913 a torchlight procession was added, along with a flying exhibition by Gustav Hamel, who also took passengers on short trips. By this time Knighton Show was generally considered the largest show in central Wales. Whereas Knighton Races had the reputation of bringing bad weather, Knighton Show, certainly down to the 1930s, was known for fine weather, which tended to encourage a good attendance.

Knighton at play

Of all the sports enjoyed in the town, horse racing was of the longest standing, having been started in the reign of Queen Anne by two officers of Marlborough's army who had rented Hill House and Dolyfellin. The original course had been near White Anthony on Beacon Hill, but in 1784 it had been moved nearer Craig-y-don, which was more accessible from the town. With the coming of the railway, however, the course was clearly too far from the station and in 1862 a new course was established at the end of Gas House Lane on land owned by Richard Green

Plate 45: Spectators at Knighton Show in 1922

Price.[40] The races were an important event in the local social calendar and well supported by the local gentry, led by the Green Prices, for both Richard Green Price and his son Dansey maintained racing stables.

Until 1847 the meeting was a two-day event, usually held in June, but on occasions later in the summer, with special breakfasts held on the Bowling Green and a dinner and ball at the Chandos Arms at the conclusion of the second day. From 1833 it was recognised as an important meeting in the Welsh racing calendar and listed by Weatherby's. It had always been a flat race meeting, but in the 1860s first a hurdles race and then a number of steeplechases were introduced.

In 1862, on the opening of the new course largely on Green Price land, a determined attempt was made to build up the status of the meeting. However, as Richard Green Price had not been able to use a piece of land owned by a Knighton farmer, the course was in the form of a figure of eight and was later described as 'exceedingly tortuous'. In 1863 a two-day meeting was organised and a special train was laid on from Craven Arms to bring visitors from Shrewsbury and Hereford. But the meeting attracted considerable criticism: it was felt that insufficient accommodation was available in Knighton for visitors, and that the race organisers had failed to make satisfactory arrangements for the racing correspondents.[41]

In 1864, although a grandstand had now been provided, the event reverted to a one-day meeting, but between 1868 and 1870 and between 1875 and 1879 the meeting became a two-day event once more. The meeting continued into the 1880s, but support was declining and considerable difficulties were experienced in adapting the course to the Grand National Hunt rules, meaning that the last Knighton race meeting was held in 1883 independently of National Hunt regulations. Not until 1945 was there another well supported race meeting in Knighton.[42]

Fox hunting was late to establish itself in eastern Radnorshire, where shooting was the field sport of choice for the local gentry. Local interest in the sport seems to have developed in the early 1860s after Captain Beavan founded the Radnor and West Hereford Hunt in Presteigne in 1864, and in April 1864 a meeting was held at the Farmers' Club to consider the formation of a pack to hunt the country south of the Teme. No other reference to this precursor of the Teme Valley Hunt has been traced, and only one reference to the Knighton Harriers which existed in 1878 with Thomas Bowles of Stanage as master.[43]

The Teme Valley Hunt was founded in 1892 by T.A. Lote of Brookside House, but initially met with little support since the pack was sold at the Swan Hotel by Lote in 1902. By 1909 it was functioning once more with Lote again the master, and apparently receiving more support since it began to hold its own Hunt Ball. The early struggle of the hunt to establish itself stemmed from the fact that it was squeezed to the east by the Ludlow and United Hunts and to the west by the Radnor

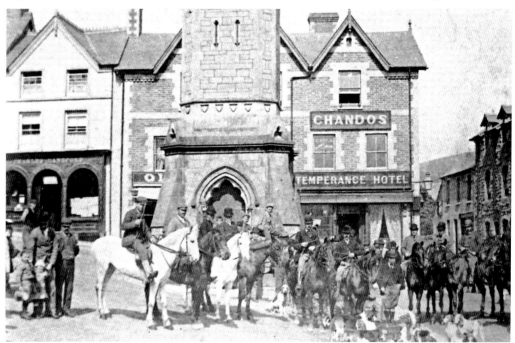

Plate 46: The Teme Valley Hunt at its traditional Boxing Day meet at the clock tower. The photograph probably dates from the 1920s and shows the section of the Chandos that was demolished in order to widen West Street

and West Hereford, while the Green Price family and their connections gave their support initially not to the Teme Valley but to the Radnor and West Hereford, whose master, Colonel Price, was a kinsman.[44]

The first reference to a Knighton cricket club in the local press comes in the *Hereford Times* of 25 August 1858 and it seems likely that the club had been founded in the mid 1850s at the earliest, since in 1860 it was described as a young club. At first the club played at Panpunton, but later moved to Bryn-y-Castell. This late date for the formation of the club is surprising given that Kington and Presteigne had cricket clubs in the 1840s. Despite the important role played later by the local gentry, they seem to have played little part in the club initially, though Richard Dansey Green (Price) took the chair at a dinner at the Farmers' Club after a match against Presteigne in 1859.

Membership of the early teams suggest that it was dominated by the Knighton professional and commercial families – in 1863 the team was captained by C.W. Ayre, the son of the future managing director of the Radnorshire Company. The club members clearly enjoyed their food, for after a match against Clun when rain had stopped play, both teams adjourned to the Chandos Arms to enjoy a meal which consisted of salmon and vegetable soup for the first course; a second course of lamb, roast chicken and roast duck; followed by a third course of lobster, leveret, plum pudding, tarts, cheese and salad; finished by dessert of apples, pears, nuts, raisins and gooseberries.[45]

By the early 1870s gentry influence on local cricket began to grow as a result of the development of country house cricket, with both Downton Castle and Stanage Park fielding teams, the formation of the Radnorshire Ramblers which in the main were drawn from the gentry families in the county, and the formation of county cricket teams in Herefordshire and Shropshire.

The early 1870s also saw the arrival in Knighton of F.C. Cobden, a fast (round arm) bowler and a dashing batsman, who made his name in the Oxford University v Cambridge University match at Lords in 1870, taking a hat-trick in Oxford's second innings to secure a win for Cambridge by 2 runs. The grandson of a baronet who had left him £20,000, Cobden rented The Cottage and in 1874 became the captain of the Knighton team. Prospects for the team improved still further in 1876 with the arrival in the area of A.M. Bannerman, a Scots rugby and cricket international, another fast (round arm) bowler and rapid scoring batsman. However, both Cobden and Bannerman were much in demand and received many invitations from senior teams, including Maesllwch Park, Shropshire, Free Foresters, the MCC and I Zingari, and never played regularly for the town team. The club therefore often had to rely on its own resources and, realising that the club subscription of 10 shillings for a playing member was beyond the resources of young working men, reserved the right to reduce or waive it.[46]

The main developments in Knighton cricket in the 1880s were: the arrival of yet another outstanding fast bowler in the person of W.P. Campbell, the landlord of the Norton Arms Hotel; the establishment of a Radnorshire cricket club; and the introduction of the Knighton Cricket Week over the August Bank Holiday week. Cobden suggested the formation of the county club in 1882, but it was not until 1884 that it began to fulfil fixtures, since first a pavilion had to be built on the town club's ground at Bryn-y-Castell and other improvements carried out. The first Knighton Cricket Week featured two day matches between Radnorshire and I Zingari and Herefordshire and two one-day matches, Knighton v Builth and the Radnor Hunt v the Ludlow Hunt. Other prominent clubs to feature in Knighton Cricket Week in the 1880s included the Free Foresters and the strangely named MCC Club and Ground. The Cricket Week owed much to the links of Cobden, the Green Prices and the Evelyns of Corton and Kinsham with their old public schools, and also benefited from timing: the Hereford and Ludlow Cricket Weeks, featuring senior cricket touring teams, took place each side of August Week, leaving that week free of competing fixtures.[47]

Cobden's services to Knighton cricket were recognised in 1887 by the presentation of a silver claret jug and a silver salver, but after he left Knighton, probably in 1889, the town club's playing record fell away. The side still possessed able players such as the batsman W. Harris and the fast bowler C.H.M. Nixson, but lacked ability in depth. In the later 1890s and in the 1900s the club usually engaged a professional, who also acted as groundsman, at a salary of £18 a week for the season of 18 weeks. Amongst the professionals were the gifted Knighton cricketer and footballer James (Jimmy) Cooper, and Ralph Whitehead, who went on to score a century for Lancashire in his first match for the county in 1908.[48]

The first reference to a Knighton football team comes in September 1884 when the Football Club met at the Chandos Temperance Hotel. This was not the inaugural meeting of the club since its secretary resigned and was replaced, and an alternative captain was nominated should F.C. Cobden decline to act. It is possible that the club had existed for some years, since as early as 1880 a football match had been played at Knighton between Beguildy and Bettws, while a football club was functioning in Llangunllo in September 1883. The report also suggests that Cobden who, like the Green Prices and the Evelyns at Presteigne, attended a soccer-playing public school, played a significant role in the formation of the Knighton club.[49]

Soccer in the 1880s differed greatly from the game today – each team had its own version of the rules, and the custom was for games to be played in accordance with the rules of the home team. The Rhayader rules for example provided for the ball to be kicked into play rather than thrown in, and did not recognise any offside rule. As goals had no nets and often a rope rather than a crossbar, there were many disputes as to whether or not a goal had been scored. Thus the *Radnorshire*

Echo of 15 April 1887 gave two reports of a game between Knighton and Ludlow. The report by the Ludlow correspondent gave the result as Ludlow 2 Knighton 1, whereas the Knighton correspondent gave the result as Ludlow 2 disputed goals, Knighton 1 goal – a victory for Knighton.

In the 1880s the Knighton spectators gained a bad reputation for seeking to influence the game in their team's favour. The *Kington Gazette* of 9 December 1884 reported on a bad-tempered game between Knighton and Kington which was abandoned with the score at 3 goals each. At one stage six Knighton supporters joined in the game to prevent Kington scoring, and after Knighton disputed a Kington goal, the Kington captain led his team off the ground. The *Hereford Times* of 16 January 1886 contained a letter from a member of the Stokesay team which had played Knighton at Knighton:

> We consider we were not treated very generously by Knighton in not seeing that the spectators treated us fairly. The hooting did not hurt us – but when several of the spectators started throwing, it was a disgrace and a discredit to them. The writer was struck on the forehead by a dry pellet of mud, as were the goalkeeper and several others.

The Knighton players also suffered at the hands of hostile spectators. As noted in the previous chapter (see page 107), after an ill-tempered match at Presteigne in February 1888, prior to which both clubs had accused the other of playing guest players, the Knighton players returning home in an omnibus were pelted with stones by the Presteigne spectators, causing injury to one player.[50]

Press reports in the 1880s and 1890s suggest that the Knighton team were reasonably successful, winning about two-thirds of the matches they played and reaching the semi-final of the Welsh Cup in 1897, losing by the only goal of the match to Newtown at Shrewsbury. In the early 1900s they did even better, winning the Mid Wales League in three successive seasons between 1901 and 1904 and again reaching the semi-final of the Welsh Cup in 1904. The club produced a number of outstanding players: in the 1890s Frank and Andrew Mills, the latter later playing for Blackburn Rovers, Swindon Town, Brighton and Leicester Fosse; and in the 1900s Jimmy Jones who played for Hereford Thistle and had a Welsh trial in 1904, and W.C. 'Billy' Davies, who won six amateur international Welsh caps and played for Shrewsbury, Stoke and Crystal Palace.[51] As away fixtures in the Mid Wales League involved some lengthy and expensive journeys, Knighton opted instead to play in the South Shropshire League in the mid-1900s and again in the 1913-14 season.

Golf was another sport which gained in popularity in the town in the years prior to the outbreak of war in August 1914. Press reports suggest that the first course on Upper Woodhouse land had opened in 1890 or 1891. By 1910 the existing course was considered as not up to standard and the directors of the Norton Arms Hotel, Tom Norton, J.B. Boote, Sir Robert Green Price and Roland Tench, anxious to improve the town's facilities in order to attract visitors, commissioned Harry Verdon, the famous golfer, to design the new course on Grove Farm land. Work began in October 1912 and in May 1913 the nine-hole course was opened with Verdon playing a medal round with the newly appointed club professional, Harry Owen. Within a few months of the outbreak of war, however, the golf club closed its doors for the duration.[52]

Cricket, football and golf were by no means the only sports enjoyed in Knighton, for the town had had a bowling club since the mid-19th century at least, while in the opening decade of the 20th century a hockey club enjoyed much support and fielded both men's and women's teams.

‍ 9 ‍

KNIGHTON 1914-19: WORLD WAR
AND THE WORLD SLUMP

*The loss and destruction of the Great War was followed by two decades when the threat
of unemployment was ever present, for as a market town Knighton was largely dependent
upon the prosperity of its rural hinterland and agriculture was far from prosperous in the
inter-war years. Yet despite the shadow cast by the war and the uncertainties surrounding
employment, the town did not stand still.*

Knighton at War, 1914-18

On mobilisation on 5 August 1914 the Knighton members of the local Territorial
Army unit, G Company of the Herefordshire Regiment, led by Lieutenant E.T.P.
Rogers and Sergeant J. Evans, left the town to join their regiment.[1] Elsewhere in
the Knighton area, members of the Montgomeryshire Imperial Yeomanry and of
the Territorial units of the King's Shropshire Light Infantry were also reporting for
duty. The three local regiments served on the Western Front and in the Middle East,
at Gallipoli (but not the Montgomeryshire Yeomanry), Egypt and Palestine.

Until conscription was introduced in 1916, the British armed forces depended
entirely upon volunteers, and the Knighton pleasure fairs of May and October
presented ideal opportunities for recruiting young men. On fair days bugle bands
played military music and local dignitaries such as the lord lieutenant Sir Powlett
Milbank and Radnorshire's MP Sir Francis Edwards made stirring speeches at the
clock tower, whilst soldiers home on leave and wounded soldiers from the town's
military hospital and their Red Cross nurses, led by Mrs Rogers, were also used
to induce men to sign up.[2] The local press also brought pressure to bear, thus the
Radnor Express of 20 May 1915 commented:

> A casual walk around [Knighton Fair] showed that the district still contained
> a wealth of strong, healthy men of military age.

Nor was the recruiting drive solely on behalf of the three local regiments.

With the introduction of conscription in 1916, all men between the ages of 18 and 51 were eligible for compulsory military service and some local administrative machinery was needed to identify those who, for medical, social or economic reasons, were to be exempted, or perhaps deferred for the moment, from military service. To this end tribunals for each rural and urban district were set up to hear applications, along with a Radnorshire Appeals Committee to hear appeals. The members of such panels tended to be made up of 'the good and the great' of the locality, but it was recognised that in an agricultural area such panels needed to have men of a farming background, Thus J.R. Bache represented the Board of Agriculture on both the Knighton rural and urban tribunals and the county appeals committee.

A few adventurous local young men opted to wage war in the air. The first Knighton man – and possibly the first in Radnorshire – to fly was W.L.T. Allcock, the son of a leading Knighton grocer. He had emigrated to Canada but returned on the outbreak of war and joined the Royal Flying Corps as a lieutenant in 1915. He was promoted to the rank of wing commander, mentioned in dispatches twice and spent some time as an instructor, but was reported missing in June 1917; when last seen his plane had been surrounded by hostile aircraft. Two young members of the Hamar family who had joined the RFC also met their deaths: in April 1917 Lt A.J. Hamar died making a crash landing on his return from a bombing raid in which his plane was shot up by enemy aircraft; his younger brother, C.R. Hamar, who had emigrated to Canada, died in July 1917 at the Canadian Aviation Training Camp in Ontario, when his plane crashed after gunnery practice.[3]

The exact number of Knighton men who were under arms in the war is not known, but contemporary estimates suggest that about 240 Knighton men served in the armed forces during the war and of these, 32 did not return home.[4] Nor were all those who returned fit and healthy, some had lost a limb, some had been gassed and others never recovered fully from their wounds, physically or psychologically.

The Home Front

The outbreak of war was accompanied by a sharp rise in food prices, caused in part by panic buying, but public opinion suspected that part at least of the price rise stemmed from profiteering on the part of shopkeepers, and protest meetings were held at the clock tower. In the *Radnor Express* of 13 August 1914 'Rambler' showed clearly where his sympathies lay:

> Why, tuppence on the sugar,
> Three ha'pence on the luf,
> And double price upon the rice,
> This sounded rather ruf,

A penny on the taters,
And tuppence on the cheese,
This selfish job our poor will rob,
Now, stop it if you please.

The war produced an unprecedented degree of government control over every aspect of everyday life, with food, fuel and petrol supplies strictly regulated. For much of the war food prices rose faster than wages, thus food tended at first to be rationed by price, but by the end of 1917 shortages led to the introduction of strict rationing of some foodstuffs – notably sugar, meat, butter and jam. The rise in prices produced great hardship for those families where the breadwinner was on active service, and the UDC appealed to able-bodied men to assist such women in cultivating their gardens.

Even so, food shortages and rationing bit less deeply than in urban conurbations since the area's orchards, gardens, hedgerows and moorland meant that fresh fruit and vegetables were relatively plentiful. In addition, the sugar ration could be supplemented by honey and the meat ration by the occasional rabbit or trout obtained by a little poaching, or more often through the network of family relationships and mutual obligations built up over the generations. This same source might also produce a piece of bacon, a few eggs, or some farmhouse butter and an occasional load of firewood.

The farming sector also found its activities closely supervised as the government sought to maximise food production by switching production where possible from livestock to cereals – particularly wheat – and potatoes, under the supervision of the county War Agricultural Executive Committee. In Radnorshire one of the major figures in this push to increase production was J.R. Bache, the sub-commissioner for Brecon and Radnor under the Food Production Department of the Board of Agriculture and a member of the Radnorshire Agricultural Committee. As this drive to increase food supply took place against a background of a shortage of horses and labour, particularly after the introduction of conscription, farmworkers' wages rose sharply, from 18 shillings a week in 1914 to 30 shillings a week in 1918. The labour shortage was partly made good by the Women's Land Army, foreign labour brought in from countries such as Portugal and, as in Knighton's shops and businesses, by an increased use of local female labour.

As elsewhere in Britain, the outbreak of war led to a surge in patriotism and a general desire to make as large a contribution to the war effort as possible, which manifested itself in a willingness to help refugees, to contribute to the welfare of those on active service and their families, and to care for the casualties of war. Occasionally, however, patriotism could be misdirected: thus in 1917 Knighton Town Council refused to send a representative to the Court of Governors of the

Plate 47: Wounded Belgian troops on their way from the station to the Red Cross Hospital in the former workhouse in October 1914. The postman gives the salute

University College, Aberystwyth, which was paying a pension to a former German professor, on the grounds that it did not believe in supporting Germans.[5]

The first chance to contribute to the war effort came in mid-October 1914 with the arrival of 10 wounded Belgian soldiers and the first of a number of Belgian refugees, with large crowds gathering at the station and in its vicinity to welcome them. The refugees were initially accommodated in the children's block of the workhouse, but already a group of Knighton women had independently rented and furnished Waterfall Cottage to house refugees from Belgium. The first occupants were a young married couple from Melines whose house had been destroyed by shelling, and who had loaded what they could find on a bicycle and fled. A week or so later two other Belgian families arrived in the town and were housed in two houses in Victoria Road by the relief committee, who in mid-November organised a tea and concert to celebrate the birthday of King Albert of the Belgians.[6]

The major wartime achievement of Knighton was the establishment and part-funding of the Red Cross hospitals in the town, in addition to helping to fund the Radnorshire hut at the Royal Victoria Military Hospital at Netley near Southampton. At the outbreak of war, Mrs C.C. Rogers suggested the setting up of three Red Cross hospitals in Radnorshire, at Knighton, Llandrindod Wells and

Presteigne. At first it was planned to use the National School as the hospital in Knighton, but in the end it was decided to use the children's block at the workhouse with Mrs Rogers as commandant. Towards the end of 1915 a second Red Cross hospital was established at The Cottage. Initially the two Knighton hospitals accommodated 33 convalescent soldiers, but capacity increased steadily and by the end of 1915 they housed 53.[7]

Early in 1917, with the 'Big Push' imminent on the Western Front, the authorities realised that additional hospital accommodation would be needed and at the end of February Mrs Rogers asked for the whole of the workhouse to be made available. This would give the hospital 100 beds, at a pinch 120, together with nurses' and officers' quarters, while the board room which the poor law guardians used for their meetings would be used as a recreation room. Once the Local Government Board had give permission, most of the workhouse inmates were moved to Rhayader workhouse, some to a house in Victoria Road and others boarded out so that work could start on conversion.[8]

Knighton Military Hospital, as the converted workhouse was called, was formally opened at the end of June 1917 with Mrs Rogers as commandant, Miss Covington as matron and Mrs Purdy, Mrs Price and Mrs Cockram in charge of the Voluntary Aid Detachment, volunteer nurses who had received a basic nursing training (VADs). Miss Covington had worked in military hospitals at Calais, Bolton and Exeter and such experience was invaluable since the hospital was now intended to treat a much wider range of casualties, while The Cottage continued to house convalescent soldiers. People rallied round to help: the Radnorshire Company supplied and cut up all the timber needed as fuel, while eggs and fruit and other goods flooded in from the neighbourhood.[9]

The authorities took it as given that the local community would part-fund such hospitals. As the initial cost of furnishing and equipping the hospitals in 1914 had already put the Knighton Red Cross society into debt, the area was soon involved in fundraising efforts such as concerts and dances. Mr Fred Hamer, the proprietor of the Border Counties Cinema, toured the locality giving shows at Knighton, Kington, Presteigne, Talgarth and Hay, donating proceeds to local Red Cross societies; by the end of 1915 he had donated £100 to the Knighton society.[10]

The need for fundraising events continued throughout the war since the authorities provided funds at the rate of 2 shillings per week for each soldier in the two hospitals, to cover heating, lighting, food, bedding and medical treatment – clearly an insufficient sum.[11] The fair proprietors donated half their takings on one evening at the May Fairs throughout the war, while the proceeds from comic football matches, dances, whist drives, concerts and garden parties all helped to swell the funds. Knighton Military Hospital continued to function until the summer of 1919, the premises not being vacated until August when the master and matron and 12 inmates returned. For her services as commandant Mrs Rogers was awarded the CBE.

The hospitals did not, however, absorb all the town's energies: the Soldiers' and Sailors' Wives and Families Association assisted the families of servicemen; money was raised for the Prisoners of War Relief Fund; while the Red Cross Working Party, led by Mrs J.H. Clee, produced hundreds of garments for refugees, and gloves hats and sweaters for servicemen. Mrs Bromfield, the wife of Radnorshire's chief constable, organised egg collections in the Knighton area for the use of military hospitals throughout the country.[12]

In the meantime everyday life in the town went on as best it could, though the normal pattern of the livestock trade had been disrupted, in part because train services were sharply cut and so reduced the volume of trade at the weekly market. Sport in the town virtually ceased, as the cricket, golf and football clubs, along with the Teme Valley Hunt were disbanded 'for the duration'. From reports in the local papers it would seem that there were only four football matches played in the town during the war, all for charity.

The first news of the signing of the Armistice to reach Knighton came when Mrs Bamford, the newsagent, received a telegram from the *Daily Mail* and displayed it in her shop window. The Post Office received a similar telegram, but at first the news was received with 'controlled excitement', since some doubted if it was true. By the afternoon the doubts had disappeared, the church bells were rung by a 'scratch' team of ringers, 'the streets were thronged with happy folk' and flags were flying from all the main buildings.[13]

The real celebrations however did not take place until after the peace treaties had been signed in July 1919. Peace Day was celebrated on 19 July when the town was decorated with flags – one of them, unwittingly, the flag of the Austrian merchant marine – and garlands, and the church bells were rung at intervals throughout the day. A cold lunch was provided for the returning soldiers and war widows, and in the afternoon a fancy dress parade took place, led by a 'scratch' band assembled by Mr Gough, starting from the National School and ending at Bryn-y-Castell where sports were held and children were presented with victory medals. Rain began at 5pm and continued all evening, bringing proceedings to an end, though there was dancing at the Drill Hall from 7pm until midnight. Not all the veterans were satisfied with the proceedings – a correspondent to the *Radnor Express* of 22 January 1920 contrasted the cold meal given the Knighton ex-servicemen with the silver medal the Llangunllo veterans had received. The Knighton authorities moved quickly to put matters right and approved the spending of £250 on a souvenir for each of the returning servicemen and for war widows.[14]

The British Legion

The Knighton Old Comrades Association had been formed towards the end of 1919 to help ex-servicemen who had fallen on hard times, and to ensure that those who had fought in the war should have some say in the town's affairs. On 30 June 1921 it was announced that the Comrades and similar organisations were to amalgamate to form the Knighton branch of the British Legion, one of the first branches to be formed in Wales, with the Revd D. Randall of Whitton as the first president and John Chadd as chairman. In 1925 a women's branch of the Legion was set up, with Mrs Rogers as president.[15]

The Legion continued the welfare work of the Old Comrades and to finance it, held a number of fundraising events such as concerts and later whist drives throughout the year. But their major fundraising event was the annual fête and sports held each summer, first at Bryn-y-Castell and later at Ystrad House. The Legion's most important social events were the annual entertainment for wives, war widows and children held early in the New Year which was attended by more than 400 in some years in the 1920s, and the annual dinner held a fortnight or so later.

The membership of the Knighton branch probably peaked in 1928, when it could claim 196 members, excluding the women's branch, and even in 1932 it had 176. The standing of the Knighton branch in Wales may be judged from the fact that the Legion sponsored the building of two houses for ex-servicemen on a site above Offa's Road in 1928, only the second pair to be built in Wales under the Legion's auspices. Initially the Legion's headquarters was their club room at the Norton Arms, which was provided rent-free, but in 1930 they moved to a wooden building on Station Road which had been used as an office by the Birmingham water works contractors, and later as a storeroom by George Parton. Volunteers thoroughly renovated and decorated the building, as well as installing electricity.[16]

The Cenotaph

An initial focal point for the commemoration of those who had been killed in the war was provided by the setting up and dedication of a 'War Shrine' on Broad Street early in 1917, where the death of a serviceman could be marked by the laying of a wreath, flowers or some other tribute.[17]

In May 1920, a public meeting was called to discuss what type of war memorial should be provided in the town. Most people favoured a monument of some type, though several other alternatives were suggested: a maternity home; a cottage hospital; a recreation and reading room; a library and museum; even a public lake for boating and swimming. The resulting War Memorial Committee favoured a memorial depicting a soldier in bronze, six feet in height on a plinth six foot high, resting on a base two feet in height. As such a memorial would cost between £600 and £700, however, it was finally decided to erect a cenotaph of grey granite at an

Plate 48: *The observance of the first Armistice Day, 1920, at Knighton.*
Lt Commander Bray can be seen towards the right at the rear, looking at
bandmaster Jack Evans playing the Last Post

Plate 49: *The British Legion parade marching down Broad Street to the dedication of*
the war memorial on 2 October 1921

Plate 50: The dedication of the war memorial or cenotaph on 2 October 1921

estimated cost of £450. A number of possible sites were discussed – near the church, in the cemetery, in front of the market hall, and on Station Road near Ystrad House and the junction with Church Lane, and the latter was finally chosen. The cenotaph, created by W.G. Stor Barber of Leominster, was erected at the end of September 1921 and included a plaque containing a list of 29 Knighton men killed during the war. Three names that had been omitted were added in October 1924, and the UDC subsequently took over the management of the cenotaph.[18] It was eventually moved to its present site following the demolition of the old police station and magistrates' room in 1976 and the creation of Brookside Square in 1979-80.

Knighton's Economy, 1918-39

Knighton was first and foremost a market town, and this is reflected by the large proportion of the town's labour force, rather more than 23%, engaged in the professions and commerce according to the census of 1921 and 1931. The second largest employment sector in the town, employing between 18 and 19% of the labour force, was personal service, overwhelmingly domestic service staffed by female labour.[19] Surprisingly, only 13% or so of the labour force was employed in agriculture, the third major employment sector in Knighton, a considerably smaller proportion than Presteigne's 23%.

Year	Population urban district	Occ. houses urban district	Unocc. houses urban district	Population rural district	Occ. houses rural district	Unocc. houses rural district
1901	2,139	448	9	4,856	987	62
1911	1,886	420	46	4,443	957	115
1921	1,701	433	24	4,190	982	67
1931	1,836	456	19	3,955	922	76
1939 (est)	1,809	-	-	3,244	-	-

Figure 21: Population and housing, Knighton urban and rural districts, 1901-39
(Source: Printed census data)

At first sight the census data of 1921 and 1931 relating to Knighton would seem to be encouraging, for the labour force grew from 728 to 763, an increase of nearly 5%, while the number employed in the three main sectors of the town's economy grew from 392 to 422, an increase of 7½%. However, the Knighton population figure for 1921 of 1,701, a 10% fall since 1911, seems surprisingly low and may indicate that a wartime migration of labour from the town to industrial areas, attracted by higher wages, had not yet been reversed. By 1939 the town's population

Plate 51: The Narrows between the wars

was falling once more. A more serious threat to Knighton's future as a market town was the sharp fall in the population of its hinterland, characterised by the sustained fall in the population of the Knighton Rural District of 33% since 1901, for this fall in population represented a fall in the size of the town's potential customer base.

This fall in the rural population may have been having some impact on Knighton retailers towards the end of the 1920s, for in 1928 the town's Chamber of Commerce, moribund for some years, was revived with no fewer than 30 members. It soon launched a drive to increase trade in the town, urging the UDC to build up the Michaelmas Fair by attracting a circus or some other entertainment and revitalising the

Plate 52: The Narrows between the wars

pleasure fair. It also promoted an advertising campaign under the banner 'Support Knighton Shops' in the *Radnor Express* in the pre-Christmas period, with a column and a half of small advertisements featuring Knighton retailers. The concern of the Chamber is understandable, for although the May Fairs of 1931 and 1932 attracted very large crowds, the town's shops did not do particularly well; in 1932 several retailers found their takings down compared with previous years. The decline in trade was probably behind the petition of 62 traders in 1933 asking the UDC to prevent travelling salesmen selling their wares around the clock tower on market days, something the UDC could not do since by charter Knighton was an open market. In 1936, by now with a membership of between 60 and 70, the Chamber backed the Knighton branch of the National Farmers' Union in its abortive attempt to establish a wool sale in the town. The Chamber could also adopt a defensive stance; in 1932 it strongly criticised the local bus services, claiming that with the exception of Thursdays their timetables were calculated to induce Knighton people to do their shopping in neighbouring towns, rather than to bring people into Knighton.[20]

The town's livestock trade was in a far healthier state; in terms of volume Knighton's throughput at its markets, not including the September sheep sales, had risen by nearly 19% between 1927 and 1937, though livestock prices fell sharply in the crisis years of 1921-23 and 1928-33. In the latter period sheep prices did not collapse until the second half of 1931 and soon recovered, the local press reporting a sharp recovery in ewe prices at the Knighton sheep sales in 1933. The strength of the livestock trade in Knighton can be judged from the presence in the town of two livestock markets, for in addition to the Sheep Market at the rear of the Norton Arms, run by the firm of Jackson and McCartney in the inter-war years, Messrs Morris, Marshall and Poole – later Morris, Barker and Poole – had purchased Pigeon Close, off Station Road, in 1915 where they opened a second auction market. Both firms held fortnightly sales on the same Thursday, sales of cattle followed by sheep beginning at 11.45am in both auction rings, making it difficult for farmers to keep an eye on both markets. The problem was solved when it was agreed that one firm was to sell cattle first and the other sheep, changing round each fortnight.[21]

The second part of Professor Ashley's report on sheep farming in Wales, published in the *Radnor Express* of 19 May 1938, estimated the throughput at both Knighton markets in 1937 as 8,012 cattle and 53,628 sheep (not including the September sheep sales). Both the cattle and the sheep were stores, the cattle mainly Herefords and the sheep Radnor Forest, Kerry Hill and Clun Forest crosses, the latter coming mainly from the Herefordshire and Shropshire areas of Knighton's hinterland. Ashley had a very poor opinion of the Knighton auction yards, rating neither as satisfactory on any of 18 criteria and regarding the facilities of both yards as 'abominably neglected'. Given the continuing fragility of the local and national economies, there was a reluctance to invest the large amounts of capital necessary to make substantial improvements, while the presence of two auction yards in the town presented another obstacle to a resolution of the problem.

In addition to the normal fortnightly store sales there were special lamb and wether sales, sometimes held in June but more usually in the later 1920s and the 1930s in July and August, as well as breeding ewe sales, largely of 2-year-old ewes, in September, held not in the auction yards but in a field near the railway station. As far as numbers are concerned, the lamb and wether sales usually involved between 3,000 and 4,000 animals, and in some years both firms held supplementary sales. The numbers of ewes sold in the sales in early September rose from between 10,000 and 12,000 at each sale to about 15,000 each in the late 1920s and early 1930s. The numbers disposed of at the supplementary sales of late September also increased, from about 8,000 to 10,000 in the 1920s to 12,000 or so in the later 1930s.

Of the progress of the town's industrial base in the period, relatively little is known. The Radnorshire Company, with Rowland Tench as managing director

Plate 53: The timber yard behind the Radnorshire Company's saw mills

since 1917, continued as one of the town's major employers of labour, widening its activities by establishing sawmills and going into the seed business. The Silurian Mills may have increased cloth production after the business was purchased by George Holroyd of Huddersfield in 1906. After Holroyd joined up in 1916 and was killed on active service, the business was managed by a J.A. Blackburn. There was no more talk of spinning wool and weaving small quantities of cloth for local people; instead, after carding, spinning and weaving, the cloth was sent to Huddersfield for finishing. During the war at least the labour force seems to have largely comprised women, for exemption from conscription was granted to only one man, a Mr Barber, a spinner. In 1925 a new firm was formed to take over the business, with a nominal capital of £3,000 in shares and a T.V. and F.S. Haighton as directors, but it seems unlikely that the company actually went into business, since the mills closed in 1926.[22]

Local wage levels for manual workers were closely related to those of farm-workers, usually a few shillings higher in recognition of farmworkers' payments in kind, and the sharp fall in farmworkers' pay from 44 shillings to 30 shillings per week in 1923 meant that most workers in the town found that their wages and standard of living fell markedly in the early 1920s. Not surprisingly, therefore, the first few years of peace saw a renewal of interest in trade unions and a short-lived interest in the Co-operative movement.[23] The re-introduction of a minimum wage for farmworkers halted the slide in 1924, and by 1930 an adult farmworker's wages were in the region of 31 shillings per week. However in 1932, at the height of the financial crisis, local farmworkers' pay had fallen to 29 shillings and 6 pence, not much more than the maximum transitional relief of 27 shillings and 3 pence a week for which an unemployed man with a wife and two young children was eligible. (Transitional relief was a weekly means-tested payment made to those who could not support themselves and their family as a result of unemployment, disability or illness and who had no other resources.) Not until 1938 did farmworkers' pay move beyond the 1930 level.

Unemployment

The extent to which unemployment posed a problem in the town in the inter-war years is difficult to determine. The healthy state of the livestock markets, the de-rating of agricultural land and buildings, later the introduction of subsidies on wheat and beef, combined with the development of marketing schemes for sugar beet, potatoes and livestock suggest that farm incomes in the town's hinterland may not have fallen as sharply as in some regions. This may well have assisted the town's businesses, compensating, to some extent, for the loss of population in the surrounding rural area. As far as farming in Knighton parish was concerned, the crop and livestock returns for 1924-25, 1934-35 and 1939 suggest that the inter-war years saw a reduction in the cereal acreage and an increase in the rotational grass acreage, making possible a steady increase in the number of sheep and cattle kept on the farms of the parish. The number of fulltime workers employed on the farms fell from 47-48 in 1924-25 to 39 in 1935 and 36 in 1939.

Local press reports and the UDC minutes suggest that there were three main periods when unemployment became an issue in the town, though the local economy was so fragile throughout the inter-war years that under-employment was common. Men tended to be taken on for a few weeks at a time, during lambing or hay harvest, or to undertake specific tasks such as hedging or ditching, while others were taken on as unskilled labour in order to finish off a building job. Even so, the possibility of unemployment loomed large in the minds of most working people, even though the local unemployed were counted in the tens rather than the hundreds.

The first of the three periods immediately followed the war, when the economy was adjusting to the new circumstances. In 1919 'Old Knightonian' complained that married women in the town were doing discharged soldiers out of a job, while in 1921 the UDC instructed its surveyor to find work for the unemployed, constructing paths in the allotments, breaking stone for roadwork and repairing a dangerous wall in the Cwm. The UDC clearly regarded unemployment as a temporary phenom-enon, but in the second half of the 1920s it became clear that it was not the case, for in 1925 'The Married Unemployed' petitioned the UDC asking for work, while

Plate 54: A quiet day in Broad Street between the wars

in August 1928 the UDC was asked to take action to relieve unemployment and to ensure that its surveyor took on unemployed men with a family rather than single men. The third period when unemployment became an urgent issue was in the early 1930s, and by early 1933 the number of unemployed men in Knighton was in the 40s. Early in 1934 the widening of the Knighton to Felindre road offered the chance of work and by late February ten local men were employed on the project.[24] Even so, unemployment may have been increasing in 1934 since occasional reports in the *Radnor Express* show applications for transitional relief in Radnorshire were running at a higher level in 1934 than in 1931-33 – although it should be noted that not all of those in receipt of transitional relief were unemployed.

Early in January 1935, working men called a special meeting at the Swan Hotel to discuss the question of unemployment and the measures that could be taken locally to provide work, to which they invited members of the UDC and county councillors. The meeting was attended by 50 working men, along with the local county councillors and five members of the UDC, including the chairman. A list of projects to provide work for the unemployed was drawn up, including improving the water supply, covering Wylcwm Brook, and providing a swimming pool and a physical training centre. Although a committee of working men was set up to discuss these projects with the UDC, nothing came of the proposals as central government held the purse strings and the Ministry of Health was not sanctioning public works other than those which could be justified on urgent health grounds.[25]

Public opinion was generally sympathetic to the plight of the unemployed, and not only those in the locality. In December 1928, the British Legion and the town's clergy gained the backing of the UDC to assist in relieving the distress in the south Wales coalfield. A committee was set up, and by May 1929 the Legion had dispatched a substantial amount of clothing to Merthyr Tydfil and made a donation of £50 to the Lord Lieutenant's Relief Fund.[26] However not everyone was sympathetic, even where local people were involved. The Knighton Committee of the Public Assistance Board, for example, seems to have prided itself that the transitional payments it made were on average markedly lower than elsewhere in the county.

In 1934 a prominent Knighton member of the Radnorshire Public Assistance Committee, which had replaced the old Poor Law Unions, reported that out-relief in Radnorshire was some 16% higher than the previous year, largely as a result of the large number of men unemployed. He mentioned that several farmers were ready to employ unemployed farmworkers if the transitional relief payments could be counted as wages, with the farmer paying an amount that made it up to the minimum wage level – an arrangement which would benefit the farmer much more than the unemployed labourer.[27]

By 1936 the unemployment situation was easing: the cost of out-relief in the second quarter had fallen by 9% and the number in receipt of relief had also fallen significantly – trends which were to continue in 1937 and 1938. With farm incomes recovering from the sharp fall in sheep prices in 1931-32 there was less resistance on the part of local farmers to paying the minimum rate of pay to their labourers, while the workmen employed by Knighton UDC not only found the sharp cut of 1931 in their wages restored, but their pay increased.[28]

Urban Amenities

The outbreak of war had put an end, for the duration, of any improvement in the town's facilities; indeed the period 1914-18 saw some deterioration in facilities as a result of tight restrictions upon local government expenditure which meant that only essential maintenance work was sanctioned.

The first attempt to bring electricity to Knighton came in 1912-13, but the war intervened before the scheme could be implemented. Another scheme came to nothing in 1920, but in 1922 the Knighton Electric Light Supply Company was set up with a nominal capital of £6,000 and five directors, four of whom, H.J. Clee, H.J. Brokensha, G.M. Perkins and Dr J.A.K. Griffiths, were local men.[29]

The UDC approved the erection of 'an electric power house' – a generating station – on George Street, and by the beginning of 1923 electric light was being installed in shops, offices and private houses, while a light installed at the junction of High Street and Russell Street – presumably for demonstration purposes – was 'doing excellent service'. The initial cost was a shilling a unit for lighting and 6 pence per unit for power. Take up was such that within a few months the company extended its supply to Stowe. In mid-July it tendered for the contract to light the streets from mid-August until mid-April from dusk until 10.30pm and their price of £125 – a pound less than that of the gas company – was accepted by the UDC. Knighton's streets were lit by electric light for the first time on the evening of Show Day 1923, the lights being switched on by a young boy, Richard Price of 2 Victoria Road.

Though the company was usually paying a dividend of 5% in the mid-1920s, it was only enjoying limited commercial success, for such a dividend was only possible because relatively few shares – 3,190 in all – had been sold. The problem was that its customer base was too small and no economies of scale were possible. In 1930 the company sold the business to the Shropshire, Worcestershire and Staffordshire Electric Company.[30]

The sewage scheme of the 1850s, whereby untreated sewage was discharged into the Teme, was severely criticised by the Medical Officer of Health for Radnorshire in 1914, but once again the outbreak of war meant that no action was taken. In 1919, after further complaints about the practice, the UDC commissioned a civil engineer to draw up a sewage treatment and disposal scheme, but the decision to implement it was not taken until 1930. Towards the end of 1932 a sewage disposal works was finally built at a cost of more than £7,500, which discharged the treated sewage into the Teme about a mile below the town.[31]

As for the water supply, an increase in leakages and frequent breakdowns of the pumping machinery thanks to only minimum maintenance during the war, coupled with a steadily growing demand for water, meant that in spells of dry weather the supply could not meet demand. The result was severe cuts in supply: in October 1919 the town received a supply for five hours a day, while in August 1920 the water supply was turned off from 9pm to 7am. During the 1920s the situation was helped by replacing the old leaking water main, enlarging the water storage capacity from 19,000 gallons to 65,000 gallons, and installing new water pumps. But with non-domestic water consumption increasing, cuts to supply continued in dry spells, even after an agreement in 1930 giving the town access to the Birmingham water supply.[32]

The town acquired two valuable social amenities after 1914: a cinema and a church hall, an additional venue for concerts, drama and other functions. The early history of the cinema in Knighton is very fragmentary. Cinema shows had been an important attraction at the May and October pleasure fairs since about 1900, but an attempt to open a cinema in 1913 was not supported by the UDC on the grounds that the population was insufficient to support such a venture. Nevertheless, an application for a licence was made in 1914, but to what effect is not known. By 1917 a cinema was functioning in the town and showing films nightly during the week at 8pm, with three shows on Saturdays: a matinee at 2.30pm and evening shows at 5.45pm and 8pm. During the 1920s and 1930s the 'Picture House,' as the Assembly Rooms were now called, functioned independently of the Norton Arms Hotel and was entered by a staircase leading directly from the street, with an emergency exit down stairs into the hotel. For much of the 1920s the lessee of the cinema was Lt Commander H.J. Bray, a piano teacher and the organist at the parish church. After his ship, the armed trawler *Searanger*, had sunk a U-boat in 1916, Lt Commander Bray had been awarded the Distinguished Service Cross.[33]

In May 1924, St Edward's church authorities had bought a house, outbuildings that had been used as a veterinary surgery, and a large garden at the corner of Church Street. After selling the house and converting the outbuildings into garages, a section of the garden was used as a site for a church hall. Designed by local architects Rogers and Shrimpton, the hall was built by Mr W. Cadwallader and opened in January 1927. It contained an entrance hall, toilets, a main hall which could seat 250, a stage, side room and a kitchen. With the Assembly Rooms in use as a cinema and the Market Hall well nigh derelict, it was much needed and took some pressure off the Drill Hall, the only other public hall available to the town.[34]

As a result of the sharp recovery in Knighton's population revealed in the 1931 census, it seemed likely that the town would soon acquire a purpose built secondary school – a highly desirable development for the town. In 1931 the UDC voted to ask the county council to provide such a school, in spite of reservations over the cost of the additional staff needed, but without immediate success. By 1937 the economic climate had improved and it was decided to build a senior school in Knighton – the first in the county – at an estimated cost of £26,000. The new school was to be built on Five Acre Field on the Ludlow Road and Mrs Coltman Rogers cut the first turf on 8 October 1938. It was due to be opened in September 1940, but the Second World War now intervened, and it was not until 1947 that Knighton Secondary School opened its doors.[35]

Housing

In the 1920s there was a shortage of housing in the town and the conversion of two houses into a schoolroom by the Norton Street Baptists in 1922 provoked some criticism and talk that the two houses 'could have been let a dozen times or more'. The housing stock had fallen from 466 houses in 1911 to 457 in 1921, but included 24 unoccupied houses. Many of the houses were however in a far from satisfactory condition, in 1926 the Medical Officer of Health reporting that 22 houses were 'not in all respects reasonably fit for habitation'.

Encouraged by talk of 'homes fit for heroes' expectations had risen, and people were no longer prepared to live in cramped, overcrowded accommodation.[36] In 1920 the UDC invited tenders for the erection of six council houses on part of the allotments adjoining Penybont Road, but in 1921 the scheme was deferred in view of the country's financial difficulties. Instead, the council chose to give an additional £10 subsidy, in addition to a government subsidy of £75, to encourage the building of private housing on former allotment land on the Penybont road (Offa's Road) near the junction with West Street and the Knucklas road. Presumably it was thought that this would free up housing for renting in the town.[37]

In 1932 the council revived the plan to build council houses on allotment land, increasing the proposed number of houses to 12, but the Ministry of Health refused to authorise the scheme on the grounds that in his last report the Medical Officer of Health had stated that there was no overcrowding in the town, and only one unfit house awaiting demolition. Yet the following year the 12 houses in Child's Alley were condemned (though not demolished until 1938), the UDC accepting the need to build housing for the displaced occupants as no suitable accommodation could be found for them. In 1936 a preliminary survey found that 8 houses in the town were definitely overcrowded, a further 26 possibly so, and another 13 likely to become so when a child occupant reached the age of 10. The UDC now had justification for its housing scheme and, despite protests from some residents on Offa's Road, 8 'working class, non-parlour' type houses were built on former

*Plate 55: The funeral procession for Francis Edwards in 1927,
with Lloyd George just right of centre*

allotment land on Penybont Road. The houses, known as Garth Terrace, were let to tenants at a rent of 4s 6d per week in 1937. After buying land on Frydd Road from the Church in 1936, the UDC was authorised by the Ministry of Health to build 12 houses on the site, to be known as Frydd Terrace.[38]

Social life in Knighton between the wars

In spite of the testing times social life in the town in the 1920s and 1930s appears to have been, across the generations, richer and more varied than in Victorian and Edwardian times. To some extent this may have been a reaction to the austerity and anxieties of the Great War, but technological developments, some of which were only fully appreciated, or began to approach their full potential in the 1930s, also played a part. This was certainly the case with the radio or the 'wireless' as it was known. Whilst Knighton had had a cinema since at least the later years of the war, 'talkies', which attracted larger audiences, were not shown in the town until the early 1930s. The attraction at the beginning of 1935 was a showing of 'Chu Chin Chow', a film made of a musical comedy first performed in 1916, described by the *Radnor Express* as 'one of the events of the season' with every available seat occupied.

As the price of motoring came down, general mobility increased. By the 1930s most farmers and many of the Knighton middle class possessed cars, while by 1932 bus services were running between Knighton and Newtown, Ludlow and Leominster, Presteigne and Hereford. Even as early as 1924 parking was causing problems: more than 100 cars were being parked, usually on the main streets, on market days, while West Street and Wylcwm Street were often completely blocked. In 1926 the UDC and the local police arranged for parking spaces, mainly on the side roads, for 54 vehicles on market day, alleviating the problem for a while, but in 1931 the UDC was considering the possibility of using a field or some other space in the town for additional parking on market or auction days. In 1931 a substantial proportion of the Chandos Arms was demolished in order to widen West Street.[39]

Most of the pre-war clubs and organisations continued to function during the inter-war years, with a few casualties such as the Gymnastic Club and the Church of England Men's Society. There were also a number of new organisations set up, notably the British Legion, the League of Nations Union and, in the sporting sphere, the Badminton Club, with the youth of the town the main beneficiaries. A Boy Scout group may have existed briefly in 1913, but it was in the post-war years that it flourished. In 1922, 23 Knighton Scouts along with three scoutmasters attended the jamboree at Alexandra Palace, and spent a day or so seeing the sights in London. Late in 1923 or early in 1924 a Girl Guide unit, which soon had a membership of 40, was set up in Knighton with Miss Coltman Rogers as district commissioner, and by 1928 a Ranger Company and a Brownie Pack were in existence.[40] The Guides seem to have been more successful in attracting and retaining members than the

Scouts, but the latter faced competition from junior football teams and from the cricket club which, in the 1930s, organised limited over knockout matches to give its junior members match practice.

In the sporting sphere the town's football club achieved its greatest successes in the early 1930s when playing in the North Herefordshire League, finishing as champions in the 1931-32 season and as runners-up in three of the next five seasons. The club also won many local cup competitions – three in 1929-30, four in 1930-31, two in 1931-32 and five in 1933-34. One of the club's players, T. Owen, played in a Welsh amateur international trial in 1929, while a former Knighton player, H. (Bert) Trentham, was a member of West Bromwich Albion's FA Cup-winning team of 1930 and won an English international cap against Ireland in 1933.[41]

Cricket continued to have a high profile in Knighton in the 1920s, thanks to the efforts of Sir Robert Green Price and Captain Lewis. The club was the only one in mid Wales to organise a cricket week in which, in addition to matches against the Gentlemen of Shropshire, Worcestershire, Montgomeryshire and Herefordshire, the Radnorshire Gentlemen played against the Free Foresters, a first class amateur side. The Foresters sometimes misjudged the quality of Radnorshire cricket and during the 1925 Cricket Week, after the Radnorshire Gentlemen had made 463 in their first innings, the Foresters made only 135 and 277. The press report suggested acidly that the Foresters' bowling and fielding 'were not up to the expected standard'.[42] After 1929, however, the Radnorshire side played only a few matches at the County Ground at Bryn-y-Castell, and in the 1930s the only noteworthy innovation was the introduction of knock-out cricket, which served to widen local interest in the game.

Other sports also flourished in the town, notably golf, badminton, tennis and bowls, the two latter receiving a boost when the Liberal Club, which had bought Ystrad House and its extensive grounds in 1932, opened the latter as a sports ground and laid out a new bowling green and two hard tennis courts.[43] The only sport failing to make an impact was hockey, for the club was wound up in 1932.

Drama and music, both instrumental and choral, had featured in the social life of the town since at least Victorian times. A dramatic society had existed since at least 1872 and functioned fitfully in the 1880s and 1890s, but if in existence in the 1900s it kept a very low profile. The society re-formed after the war, and from 1923 produced a play annually, often light comedies such as *Tons of Money*, *The Ghost Train* and *Charley's Aunt*. The society did not have a monopoly on drama, however, since St Edward's Sunday School produced a pantomime each year at the church hall, whilst the Women's Institute also took an interest in drama as did the two Methodist churches. In 1934, in the course of a fundraising event, the schoolroom of the Broad Street Methodist Church was transformed into a circus ring, with the men of the church as ringmaster, clowns, and the singers and dancers of 'The Broadway Chorus', and the boys as acrobats.[44]

Knighton had had a band since that formed in 1850 by Henry Lote the architect and William Archibald the bank manager. It functioned intermittently until the outbreak of war in 1914, and in 1919 it was decided to revive the band and after a number of fundraising events for instruments and uniforms, the band was functioning again by 1925, though it gave no public performances for a while. It ceased to function briefly in the early 1930s but by 1935 it was giving concerts at the clock tower on Saturdays, and it became customary for it to play in various parts of the town each Christmas Eve.

During the war the Ladies Choral Society had ceased to function, but with the Armistice Knighton's old strength in depth in choral singing soon became apparent. In the 1920s there were no fewer than four choirs in the town: the Knighton Male Voice Choir conducted by T.L. James; the Knighton Ladies Choir conducted by W.E. Hughes; the Knighton Mixed Choir; and the old established choir of the Knighton Ladies' Choral Society, then known as the St Cecilian Ladies' Choir conducted by Mrs A.M. Graves. The exact relationship between the choirs is difficult to fathom, but it seems that the first three choirs operated under the auspices of the Knighton Choral Society, while the St Cecilian Choir operated independently.[45] Given that each choir practiced at least each week, that some women were members of both the Ladies' Choir and the St Cecilian Choir, and that most members of the choirs were also members of a church or chapel choir, the commitment of choir members is impressive.

Until the early 1930s the choirs operated in a highly competitive environment, taking part in eisteddfodau far and wide, and with a reasonable degree of success. After one such concert in 1926 by the St Cecilian Choir, the *Radnor Express* commented that it was 'questionable if the quality of the singing will ever be matched in Knighton'. In 1931 the emphasis of the choirs changed; the competitive environment of the eisteddfod was replaced by one of being part of a mass choir singing extracts of such works as *The Messiah* and Brahms' *Requiem* at Newtown musical festival. The only exception came in 1935 when instead of taking part in the Newtown musical festival the Society joined with six other Radnorshire choirs in *The Messiah* at Llandrindod Wells. Though the opinion of the *Radnor Express* was 'Never before has *The Messiah* been so well performed in Radnorshire', the event was not a financial success and was never repeated.[46] In the 1930s the driving forces were Alun Thomas, the conductor between 1931-37 and his successor, Mrs Walker of Stanage Park, the daughter of Mrs Coltman Rogers, together with Mrs A.M. Graves the accompanist, while the three outstanding soloists from the town were Miss Belle Cartwright, Mrs T. Owen and Mrs Polkinghorn.

Perhaps the most eminent Knighton singer of the period was Alexander T. (Alec) Jones who, in 1910, secured a 20-week engagement at Covent Garden as a bass vocalist, being selected out of 4,000 applicants, and did well enough to secure a further 14-week engagement there in 1911. He subsequently sang with several other grand opera companies, including Moody Manners and the Carla Rosa Company. Educated at the National School in Knighton, he had worked as a carpenter whilst developing a powerful bass voice, featuring in local concerts and frequently winning at many local eisteddfodau. He subsequently formed the Neapolitan Grand Opera Company which he brought to Knighton in 1922 and 1923, on the last occasion performing six popular operas in the town. He died in Nottingham in 1932.[47]

The majority of the members of the choral societies were women, and one of the features of Knighton life in the inter-war years was the increasingly prominent role played by women. Prior to 1914, apart from the Mothers' Union and the women's groups in the local churches, there were no organisations in the town catering specifically for women, a situation that soon changed in the post-war years. In 1919 Miss Rogers set up the Victory Club, a social club for women which met in the old premises of the North and South Wales Bank on Broad Street. The club had a large library which was open to the public for an hour on Wednesday and Saturday evenings. When the club disbanded in 1928, its funds were donated to the Knighton District Nursing Association.[48]

The Knighton, or rather, the Tref-y-Clawdd Women's Institute, was set up in 1934, surprisingly late given that the Radnorshire Federation had been set up in 1923 and that Whitton WI was functioning in 1927. As the WI was essentially a rural organisation catering for relatively isolated country women, perhaps initially it may have been thought irrelevant in Knighton's urban environment. Between 60 and 70 women attended the inaugural meeting at the Church Hall at the beginning of October, and 50 enrolled as members.[49] The Women's Institute movement was dominated by the women of the county elite in the inter-war years, and in Knighton Mrs Townshend, the wife of Admiral Townshend who had taken The Lee, was elected president in 1935. The WI widened women's horizons and gave them a collective voice in the local community which a local council could not ignore with impunity – and the Knighton Urban District Council had its first women councillor, in the person of Mrs Gwendoline Pugh, in 1927.

It should be remembered that all the local organisations and clubs were self-financing and were almost invariably in need of funds. The most popular method of funding was a dance or a whist drive – the Women's Section of the British Legion held a whist drive every fortnight – and to appeal to the old and young and maximise attendance, local organisations tended to put on joint whist drives and dances. The May Fair and Knighton Show at the end of August remained the premier events in the social calendar of the inter-war years, but with the regular weekly or monthly meetings of local organisations and all their fundraising events, the Knighton socialite could have a very busy life.

The Approach of War

With the possibility of a second world war looming, the chief threat to Knighton was thought to be that of air raids, given the strategic importance of the railway carrying anthracite from south Wales to the industrial Midlands and with the nearby Knucklas viaduct, and the water pipeline to Birmingham. As early as July 1938 steps were being taken to develop an effective civil defence force. An Auxiliary Fire Service of 12 men was set up, with Mr C.H. Fowler as officer in charge, to cover not only Knighton itself, but all the parishes in the Knighton Rural District. A recruiting drive for Special Constables was launched and Lt Commander H.J. Bray, the commander of the Knighton Section of Special Constables, organised First Aid classes for his men, the instructors being Dr Brook, Police Sergeant Morris, Mr D.J. Taylor and Mr Price.[50]

In October 1938 there seemed to be a brief possibility that war might be averted, and Knighton UDC sent a letter to Neville Chamberlain, the prime minister, thanking him for his success at Munich which had enabled him to promise 'Peace in our time'. The decision to send a message of thanks to Chamberlain was not unanimous, but was carried by 4 votes to 3.[51]

In the meantime, the rush to prepare for the possibility of war went on. The clerk to the UDC, Mr Philip Parker, was appointed as the local food executive officer and later as the fuel executive officer. First Aid and ambulance classes for the townspeople were held in the Magistrates' Room next to the police station in Broad Street, and all households had gas masks supplied. To ensure that the authorities would be able to have detailed information on the local population, a National Registration Scheme was launched with Philip Parker as the local chief officer. All households were visited to gather information on accommodation available for evacuees, much of this work being done by the local Women's Voluntary Service led by Mrs E.P Rogers. In the Knighton Rural District, the WVS was similarly busy under Mrs James of Cantal School. Strenuous efforts were also being made to bring Civil Defence up to strength for it was not only ARP (Air Raid Precautions) wardens that were needed, First Aiders, ambulance drivers and attendants, rescue services, and staff for report centres and for the respirator service were also in great demand.[52]

❧ 10 ❧

KNIGHTON IN THE MID 20TH CENTURY

Whereas the war years 1939-45 were perhaps the most difficult time the town has faced in the last couple of centuries, the 1960s and 1970s were possibly the most prosperous decades that it has experienced.

Knighton at War

Since UDC minutes for the period 1939-45 are missing, being either destroyed or in private hands, the main source for this section has been the *Radnor Express*.

With the outbreak of war in September 1939 every aspect of life in Britain became more closely regulated than it ever had been before, and was to remain so for some years after peace returned in 1945. The principal agent of regulation was Knighton UDC, which exercised control though food and fuel committees with the clerk to the council, Mr Philip Parker, acting as food and fuel executive officer. As registration officer he was also responsible for the issue of identity cards. In mid-September fuel rationing was introduced, with consumers limited to 75% of their previous consumption. Food rationing started in October 1939, along with price controls, in order to prevent hoarding and racketeering. Rationing was soon extended to clothing, while strict control was exercised over all raw materials. Black-out regulations were enforced strictly, and householders who failed to prevent light showing through windows or doors initially faced a fine of 7s 6d, later raised to 10s, with £1 for a second offence. Even after the immediate crisis of 1940-41 had passed, regulations were enforced rigorously. One man was fined 10 shillings (50p), with 21 shillings special costs, for being consistently late for work at Hobson's aircraft components factory in December 1943 and early January 1944, while another Knighton man, a driver in a rescue party, was fined 5 shillings for failing to present himself for ARP duties.[1]

Food production was also closely regulated. The War Agricultural Executive Committee supervised farmers' production and ensured that the UDC arranged for the cultivation of the gardens of unoccupied houses, and for vacant allotments to be ploughed up and planted with potatoes – subsequently giving the 1½ tons so produced to the Public Assistance Institution, as the workhouse had been called since 1929.[2] The livestock trade was strictly controlled, as was the small-scale keeping of pigs and poultry. However, in all probability rationing and controls never had the impact in Knighton that they did in larger urban conurbations since, as in the First World War, most residents had close links extending back over many generations with country folk of the surrounding area, who could produce a few 'extras' to supplement rationed foodstuffs.

In the second half of 1940 the Knighton area had its first direct taste of warfare in the form of air raids. That of 1 July on Gwernaffel may have been directed at the pipeline carrying water to Birmingham from the Elan Valley, while that of 31 July near Llangunllo could have been aimed at the pipeline or possibly at Knucklas viaduct, a vulnerable point on the Central Wales line. Another raid came on 25 September when six bombs fell near the junction of the Knighton-Presteigne and Whitton roads, three of them falling on Jenkin Allis Farm. This attack seems to have been random, possibly the result of damaged enemy aircraft jettisoning their bomb loads before heading back to base.[3]

The raids certainly seem to have alerted the public to the threat. At the beginning of July 1940 the clerk of Knighton Rural District Council wrote to the chief constable, who was in charge of Civil Defence for the county, asking whether, in view of recent enemy action, a series of lectures could be arranged on how to deal with incendiary bombs. In Knighton, Mr Prince, the chief air raid warden, raised the question of the audibility of the siren which had been placed at the police station, and as a result Mr Davies loaned a more powerful siren which he had used in his timber business. The householders of the Ffrydd Terrace council houses were given permission to build an air raid shelter on the waste ground in front of their houses.

There was some concern expressed over the safety of the 40 or so country children who attended the National School in the event of an air raid, and it was decided that they could use the cellars under the Market Hall as a shelter. Preparing for the worst, firewatchers had been, first aid stretcher parties and nurses had been trained, and first aid posts set up. Once the crisis of 1940-41 had passed, in order to maintain morale and momentum and gain a higher public profile, the Civil Defence authorities organised competitions and parades.[4]

The first enrolments in the LDV, the Local Defence Volunteers – the initials were sometimes unkindly taken to mean 'Look, Duck and Vanish' – took place on 15-16 May 1940 at Knighton police station, and by the beginning of June 80 men had enrolled in the Knighton area. Mr P. Edwards was in charge and divided his men into four sections. According to the *Radnor Express* of 6 June 'strong points and observation posts had been selected and prepared'. The initial aim of the LDV was for it to be a force drawn from local people who could respond quickly to the tactics employed by the Germans when invading Holland and France should they be applied to Britain. These involved the use of parachutists and fifth columnists behind allied lines to disrupt supply lines and divert front-line troops from countering the main assault. The intention was that the LDV, with knowledge of both local people and the ground, would be able to counter such tactics wherever they might be employed in the country, leaving regular forces to counter any invasion by sea.

In July the LDV became the Home Guard, the Knighton group forming 'A' Company of the 1st Radnor Battalion, with the veterans Major C.A. Masters as Company Commander and Captain W.C.J. Richards as second-in-command. 'A' Company consisted of 11 officers and 332 other ranks and was divided into seven platoons: Knighton, Beguildy, Llangunllo-Llanbister Road, Knucklas-Llanfair, Stowe-Stanage, H.M. Hobson Components Ltd, Knighton, and a mobile platoon on horses. Initially uniform consisted of denims with a forage cap, but by the end of 1940 battledress had been issued to all the local Home Guard units, with one flash on the shoulder stating 'Home Guard' and a second on the arm with 'RR' signifying 'Radnor Rifles'.

In October 1942 the Radnor Home Guard was reorganised into two battalions, with the Knighton, Presteigne and New Radnor forming the 1st Battalion, under the command of Lt Col H.B. Watkins, MC, DCM, with Major C.A. Masters as second-in-command. In April 1944 came another innovation, the acceptance into the Knighton Home Guard of seven 'nominated women' in their capacity as members of the Women's Home Guard Auxiliary Signals.[5]

Much of the time was spent on training and exercises, often with regular troops. On one Sunday morning in early June 1942, the Llandrindod and Rhayader units of the Home Guard, supported by regular troops, carried out a mock invasion of Knighton which was defended by the local Home Guard reinforced by the Presteigne unit. The *Radnor Express* of 11 June reported that the defence was effective and that the 'invaders' were held back until the end of the exercise with several casualties, 'some of them real'.

The Knighton platoon carried out a wide range of duties: manning observation posts, operating a nightly road patrol which stopped all road users and checked their credentials, and investigating any suspicious occurrences. The platoon also liaised closely with other branches of Civil Defence, tracking aircraft with the Observer Corps and assisting the ARP (Air Raid Precautions) wardens in enforcing blackout regulations. Other platoons in the company patrolled their area on a daily basis, sometimes on horseback and operating road blocks. The Knucklas and Llangunllo platoons had the additional responsibility, in conjunction with regular troops, of guarding the Knucklas viaduct, looking out for parachutists and saboteurs and making preparations to resist, should an invasion occur.

Once the immediate threat of invasion had passed, the Knighton Home Guard felt the need to show its potential to the general public and in both 1943 and 1944, to celebrate its formation, organised a parade at Knighton followed by a demonstration at Bryn-y-Castell.[6] The Home Guard was not always taken seriously during the war, and certainly has not been since. However, with the regular forces overstretched, it proved to be invaluable, supplementing regular troops stationed locally, thus freeing some for more strategically significant duties both at home and abroad.

Once war had become likely, the area received a flow of evacuees from London, and the industrial towns of the Midlands and the North, as safety was sought from bombing raids. Many were 'voluntary' evacuees who had roots in the area and brought their children with them, others were children sent from areas of Liverpool such as Bootle who were accompanied by their teachers, but the majority were workers at H.M. Hobson (Aircraft and Motor) Components Ltd of Acton, London, which had migrated to Knighton in order that production, mainly of aircraft carburettors, would not be disrupted by bombing raids. By the beginning of August 1941 there had been an influx of about 1,200 people into the area administered by the Knighton Rural District Council, while Knighton itself had accommodated many more than the additional 650 persons which had earlier been considered the maximum.[7]

H.M. Hobson Ltd arrived in December 1940 and took over the newly built school on Ludlow Road, while 40 bungalows were built on Fronhir to accommodate workers and relieve the pressure on accommodation in the town. Even so there was still overcrowding, and in some cases day- and night-workers used the same beds, while it was common to find families living and sleeping in a single room. The situation was eased somewhat towards the end of 1941 when the UDC found a further 69 householders willing to take in a worker as a lodger and a further 11 householders each willing to take in a family, while a marked reduction in the intensity of air raids from the end of 1941/beginning of 1942 led some of the 'voluntary' evacuees to leave Knighton and return home.[8]

The lifestyle of many of the factory workers was less staid than that of many residents, who were scandalised by the factory organising football matches on Bryn-y-Castell on Sundays; this caused some friction between the town and the firm. The UDC did not allow Hobson's to use the Market Hall for recreational purposes and refused to allow Hobson's Musical and Dramatic Society to borrow the town band's instruments, on the grounds that they did not belong to the UDC. The British Legion, meanwhile, only allowed Hobson's to rent their premises for the summer months for use as a social club on condition that no alcoholic drinks were to be consumed on the premises and that it was not to be used on Sundays.[9]

How many children were evacuated to the Knighton area is difficult to determine, since many were unofficial evacuees who came and returned home as they saw fit and over whom the authorities had no jurisdiction. Most were the children of residents who had moved away from the town and settled in London or in other major conurbations. Some were accompanied by a parent but others had been sent to the area to live with grandparents or other relatives. As far as the official evacuee scheme was concerned, at the start of the war plans had been made to evacuate 800 children to east Radnorshire, to be divided proportionately between Knighton UDC, Knighton RDC and Presteigne UDC. The greatest number, 350, were to be found billets in the Rural District. In Knighton an appeal had been made for blankets and camp beds and the Conservative Club had been taken over and converted into a hostel/hospital for evacuees. Billeting officers were appointed for the town with authority to decide which official evacuee was placed in which home, and a billeting tribunal established to adjudicate in cases where a householder disputed a billeting officer's decision.

Similar arrangements were made in Knighton Rural District and they received their first official evacuees – 69 children and 3 teachers, all of whom were billeted in the Llanbister and Dolau areas – in December 1940, with further parties arriving in May, June and November 1941. According to the *Radnor Express* the first official evacuees to arrive in Knighton itself – 33 children accompanied by a number of teachers – arrived in January 1941, with further groups arriving later in spring and early summer. By far the greatest number of these evacuees were from Bootle. By July 1941, 124 evacuees had been billeted in the Urban District and 376 in the Rural District, the two districts hosting almost 25% of 2,063 evacuees billeted in the county. Supplies of clothing were issued to the more needy cases, and in the rural area the WVS (Women's Voluntary Service) distributed Wellington boots provided by the American Red Cross. There must have been concern at the state of the children when they first arrived, for in May 1944 the Mayor of Bootle visited Radnorshire and explained that they had been in air raid shelters day and night for eight days immediately prior to evacuation. [11]

Home area	Number	Host area	Number
Bootle	1,046	Knighton UDC	124
Litherland	349	Llandrindod UDC	361
Crosby	214	Presteigne UDC	134
Other local authorities	142	Colwyn RDC	188
Private evacuees	312	Knighton RDC	376
		New Radnor RDC	244
		Painscastle RDC	147
Total	**2,063**	Rhayader RDC	547

Figure 22: Evacuees in Radnorshire, July 1941
(Source: *Radnor Express*, 10 July 1941)

Initially the Bootle children in Knighton were taught in the Baptist School-rooms at the Norton Street and Victoria Road chapels using stock and stationery from Knighton School. But in May 1943, most of the evacuees having returned home, those remaining were absorbed into the Knighton School, with a Bootle teacher attached to the Knighton staff temporarily.[12]

The billeting officers and Bootle authorities kept a close eye upon the treatment of the children, but even so there were a few problems. In 1941, after a case of overcrowding in the Llanbister area was discovered, the Ministry of Health launched an inquiry, while in 1942 two evacuees in the Rural District were hastily transferred from a farm where they had been made to work long hours and eat their meals in a barn. In general, however, the evacuees appear to have flourished in what must have been very alien conditions, and in January 1945 the Mayor of Bootle wrote to express his appreciation and thanks for the care the evacuee children had received in Radnorshire.[13]

Starting with Christmas 1941 and for the following two Chrtismases, Mr L. Lewis, the assistant billeting officer, organised entertainment for the evacuees and the other children of the two districts. With the help of local bus companies, the children from the Rural District were brought into Knighton, where they joined with the town's children for a free film show provided by Mr Brown, a party at the Church Hall provided by the WVS, community singing and presents, before being bussed home.[14]

The evacuation from Dunkirk in early summer 1940 and the Battle of Britain between July and October 1940 seem to have brought the whole of Knighton firmly behind the war effort, partly as a result of the involvement of local men in both actions. Lt P.A.S. Lane RN, later killed in action, was in charge of a rowing boat ferrying troops from the Dunkirk beaches to 'the little ships' lying offshore. Pilot Officer Jack Hamar, DFC, was killed in July 1940 when his engine stalled as he prepared to land after a sortie to identify an aircraft in the Felixstowe area. His funeral at Knighton on 28 July was attended by representatives from every organisation in the town and clearly had a profound effect upon the townspeople.[15] Another factor which may have helped the town identify with the war effort was the presence of local men with distinguished war records, such as Lt Commander Bray and Lt Col Watkins, in the command structure. Virtually every family in the town had at least one family member on active service, and in a few, someone had been killed, wounded or been made a POW, while others had family members in the industrial towns, with first-hand experience of air raids. Thus nearly everyone in the town had an incentive to 'do their bit'.

One of the ways in which civilians could assist was through National Savings, which helped the government finance the war effort, and Knighton responded enthusiastically, saving in the region of between £1,500 and £2,000 monthly and

Year	Effort	Target	Raised
1941	War Weapons Week	£50,000	£52,000
1941	Warship Week	-	£42,000
1942	Tanks for Attack	£10,000	£13,000
1943	Wings for Victory	£40,000	£52,000
1944	Salute the Soldier	£42,000	£46,000

Figure 23: Special Savings Drives 1941-44
in the Knighton Area
(Source: *Radnor Express*)

over half a million pounds in total. The urban and rural areas also contributed generously to the special savings schemes as is shown in Figure 23. These figures are impressive, but it should be remembered that there was little in the shops to buy.[16]

Both in the town and the surrounding countryside determined attempts were made to increase food production. In the town the Garden and Allotment Society ensured that all allotments and gardens were cultivated in such a way to maximise fruit and vegetable production. The school also joined in: in September 1940 they picked 672lbs (304kg) of whinberries, while in October 1941 they picked blackberries for 'the jam centre'. This was run by the Tref-y-Clawdd WI who in 1940 produced 1700lbs (770kg) of jam. However, attempts by the Ministry of Food to set up a British Restaurant to provide a nourishing meal at a set price of 9d (3½p) – which would have eked out the meagre rations of at least some in the town – was given short shrift by the UDC, urged on by the town's café proprietors.[17]

In the rural districts the farmers, spurred on by the War Agricultural Executive, increased the acreage under the plough, and in Radnorshire as a whole between 1939 and 1943, the acreage under cereals more than doubled, while the acreage under potatoes increased by more than 500%. In some instances open moorland was brought into cultivation, including 195 acres on Litton Hill on which were grown potatoes in 1943, oats in 1944, and 145 acres of oats and 50 acres of barley in 1945. The change in farming patterns in Knighton parish is shown in Figure 24. The early war years, when overseas supply of foodstuffs was greatly restricted, saw a marked rise in the acreages devoted to cereals and potatoes, but in 1944-45, with overseas food supplies more secure, cereal acreages in the parish were reduced.

This expansion of arable in the county was done without cutting back more than marginally on livestock, for although the area under grass had fallen by 10% between 1939 and 1943, the number of livestock kept had hardly been affected:

Year	Sheep	Cattle	Wheat (acres)	Barley (acres)	Potatoes (acres)	Oats (acres)
1939	4,775	692	7	4	7¼	317½
1943	4,185	709	104½	90½	27½	426¼
1945	3,847	649	41½	75	37	406¾

Figure 24: War-time production, Knighton parish
(Source: TNA PRO MAF 68/3931, /4079, /4153)

the number of sheep in the county had fallen by 6½% while cattle numbers had increased by nearly 4%. As far as Knighton parish was concerned, the area under grass fell by 12½%, the number of sheep fell by 12½% and the number of cattle increased by 2½% over the same period. The large increase in the arable acreage without too major an impact upon livestock stemmed from a variety of factors, not least that increased mechanization reduced the need for horses and released land for other uses. There was also additional labour in the form of the Women's Land Army from the hostel at Whitton and from prisoners of war. Meanwhile, there was government direction through the 'quota' system, subsidies and other incentives, as well as fixed prices for farm products.[18]

Another communal effort in aid of the war effort was a drive to collect salvage. In addition to the collection of waste paper, tin cans, aluminium and bones, the iron railings in the town were dismantled and collected for the war effort early in 1942. In an attempt to bring home to the public the importance of the salvage drive, the Ministry of Information published posters which demonstrated the contribution that salvage could make to the war effort: 8 books made a mortar shell carrier; 16lbs of paper made two cases for 40mm shells; 2lbs of iron made 4 rifle barrels and 4lbs of bones made sufficient cordite for 8 bullets for the gun of a Hurricane. In 1943, when the town's salvage target was 1 ton of iron, 2 tons of paper, 2 hundredweight (99.6kg) of bones and 2 books per head of the population, Knighton's Salvage Officer was the UDC surveyor, C.H. Fowler, .[19]

Unlike in the First World War, apart from the sports clubs, most of the town's organisations kept going throughout the war, with their activities directed towards fundraising for the Nursing Association, the Shrewsbury hospitals, the British Legion and newcomers such as the Services Welfare Fund and later its Welcome Home Fund, together with the Radnorshire YMCA Van that was used to provide refreshments for servicemen. The cinema, together with fundraising events such as concerts by the Choral Society, the Male Voice Choir and the town band, whist drives and dances, all provided a welcome respite from the tensions of wartime life. Care was taken to provide amenities and entertainment for the British, American and Canadian troops who were stationed at Stanage Park at various times in the course of the war, and the WVS provided a canteen in the British Legion premises on Station Road, while the hostel on Broad Street provided facilities for servicemen for reading and for writing letters home.

The Coming of Peace
VE Day, 8 May 1945, marking the end of war in Europe, saw hastily arranged celebrations. The town was rapidly decorated with flags and banners, the clock tower was floodlit, and the town band was called into action. Early in June, six Knighton prisoners of war returned from Germany and were welcomed home at a

dinner held for them. VJ celebrations to mark the Japanese surrender started on 15 August with a bonfire on the Garth and dancing at the clock tower with the town band providing the music. On the following day the UDC organised a tea party for the schoolchildren, followed by sports when ice cream and ginger beer were provided by the town's retailers. Over the next month or so there were street parties for the children in all parts of the town organised by the residents. As the *Radnor Express* of 30 August explained:

> … there was no scarcity of jellies, jams, blancmanges cakes, ice creams and trifles. These events were made possible by the generosity and industry of the people in the various districts.

The official Victory celebration on 8 June 1946 was in some ways an anti-climax since it was very much a repetition of VE and VJ Day celebrations – a tea for the children, followed by sports and then a bonfire.[20]

When the Services Welfare Association had set up the Welcome Home Fund it had been hoped to raise £2,000, but the sum raised was rather less. After giving grants to a fund in memory of the fallen, to the Distress Fund of the local British Legion, and £10 to the next of kin (mother or wife) of each of the fallen, the balance was to be divided equally between the estimated 240 ex-servicemen and women. In July 1946 each received a bank credit note for £7 and a card of thanks bearing the town's coat of arms.

There remained the question of a permanent tribute to the 19 servicemen who had been killed in the Second World War, and it was decided to attach a plaque bearing their names to the cenotaph. This was unveiled on Sunday 24 August 1947.

Post-War Reconstruction

In March 1944, when an eventual Allied victory seemed assured, a UDC committee had met to consider priorities as far as post-war development was concerned. Four priorities were duly identified, of which additional housing was clearly the most important; the others were additional parking to increase market day business; the modernisation of one of the auction markets to safeguard the town's future as a livestock centre; and a hospital. The 'wish list' was, of course, much longer: a public library, an agricultural college, a double railway line, a 'through' bus service, a youth hostel, more hotel accommodation and an extension of electricity to the outlying areas of the town.[21]

It had been assumed that with the coming of peace the close regulation of every aspect of life would cease, controls and rationing of food, fuel and materials would end and normal life would resume. However Knighton Food Control Committee was still functioning in early 1948, the salvage drive continued, rationing of some foods continued until 1954, and building materials were strictly controlled, with licences required even for the small quantities needed for house repairs.

The Welsh Board of Health strictly controlled the number of houses permitted to be built in any area and despite the obvious housing shortage in the town, between 1946 and 1948 Knighton was permitted to build no more than ten houses in a year, nearly all to be built by the UDC. Even in 1950 only one of the ten houses allocated to Knighton for construction was reserved for private building. In such circumstances competition for tenancies of the new houses was intense, and arguments over the allocation of the new houses on Ffrydd Road in 1946 led to a protest bearing 293 signatures. Rather reluctantly the UDC introduced a points system for the future allocation of tenancies, rather than the existing system of relying upon councillors' personal knowledge of the applicants. [22]

The 1940s saw a number of developments which sought to safeguard Knighton's future as a livestock centre and market town and enhance the town's amenities and place them on a more secure footing. The most important step was the purchase and subsequent development of the auction yard off Station Road and Bowling Green Lane. Although the UDC owned the old Sheep Market, access and exit were difficult and room for expansion very limited, and the Morris, Barker and Poole yard had much greater potential. With the help of Tudor Watkins, Radnorshire's MP, the Welsh Board of Health sanctioned the development and the UDC borrowed £15,000 to carry it out: £4,000 to purchase the existing yard and Swan Meadow for its extension, £1,000 for the installation of a weighbridge, and £10,000 for the reconstruction of the yard. The new auction yard, constructed by J. McColville & Son of Ludlow, had a covered sales ring and could accommodate 900 cattle and 2,000 sheep. It was formally opened in October 1949, with Jackson and McCartney and Morris, Barker and Poole as joint tenants. [23]

The old Sheep Market behind the Norton Arms Hotel was then converted into a car park holding 120 cars and came into use in 1950, greatly reducing the congestion on Knighton streets, particularly on market day. In the early 1960s another car park was opened at the rear of the auction yard, on Swan Close off Bowling Green Lane, previously part of Bryn-y-Castell, and in the early 1970s a third car park was opened on Market Street following the demolition of Hill Crest and several houses. [24]

The Recreation Ground and Bryn-y-Castell were rented from private owners, and the UDC and its lessees, the football and cricket clubs, were reluctant to embark on expensive improvement. The purchase of the Recreation Ground for £1,000 and of Bryn-y-Castell for £2,226, both in 1946 by the UDC, removed this obstacle. Another significant UDC purchase was that of the vicarage and its extensive grounds in 1946 for £3,000. Part of the ground floor of the vicarage was used as the Town Hall and the remainder of the buildings and the garden was ultimately used to provide living accommodation for the elderly.[25]

In 1947, on the suggestion of Mrs Coltman Rogers, a branch library was opened in the old offices of the Radnorshire Company in Broad Street, next to the present HSBC Bank. Knighton also acquired a purpose-built cinema. At the end of 1946 the lessee of the cinema in the Norton Arms, Mr J.R. Brown, submitted plans to build a cinema on Brookside which were approved by the UDC and the county planning officer, but turned down by the Ministry of Works. Only after it had proved impossible to negotiate a new lease on the Norton Arms premises and an attempt to buy the disused Wesleyan Church on West Street had failed, was approval given to the Brown brothers for the cinema which opened in 1950. The British Legion, now with a membership of more than 200, larger than ever before, moved from its Station Road premises to Plough Road, converting two Army huts from Stanage Park into a new clubroom in 1947-48. [26]

The expansion of Knighton

The few houses built in the later 1940s had hardly made an inroad on the demand in the town for housing, for in 1947 Dr Booth, the Medical Officer of Health estimated that 52 more houses were required. By 1964 it had built six estates comprising some 120 houses: Garth Terrace (pre-war), Ffrydd Terrace (part pre-war) on both sides of Ffrydd Road, Offa's Road, Ffrydd Close, Fronhir (some factory bungalows remaining) and Pontfaen. Three other estates were also under consideration or in the planning stage: Under Ffrydd Wood, The Laurels and sheltered accommodation near the Town Hall, later named St Edward's Close, subsequently augmented by the building of additional flats on Offa's Way. In the early 1970s preliminary planning work was being done on the Radnor Drive estate. Not all the houses built were allocated to those on the UDC housing list, as some were allocated to businesses in the town for essential workers and others used to attract new firms to the town by providing accommodation for key workers. Pre-war local authority housing in the town was updated, and substandard housing in the town on Market Street, Plough Road and the Cwm was demolished, some of the space created on Market Street being used to create a car park.[27]

	UDC Population	UDC Houses	RDC Population	RDC Houses
1931	1,836	456	3,955	922
1939	1,809	-	3,499	-
1951	1,871	559	3,244	904
1961	1,824	605	2,782	868
1971	2,008	695	2,597	835

Figure 25: Knighton Urban and Rural District populations and housing 1931-71
(Source: Printed census data)

In the 1950s private house building had been confined to building single houses on the roads leading out from the town centre, essentially ribbon development, most notably along the Presteigne road. With the removal of restrictions on house building at the end of 1955, though still subject to planning consent, the scale of private building increased and in the 1960s began to equal and sometimes to exceed the public building programme. The first steps in the development of the Farrington Lane estate, subsequently known as The Dingle and Rocke's Meadow, were taken in 1962, and for an estate on Ffrydd Road in 1967, while in 1969 plans for the development of the residential estate on the Garth were submitted. The real surge, however, came in the early 1970s with the continued development of the Farrington Lane estates and of new private housing estates at Millfield Close on Frydd Road, at the Cwm, Underhill Crescent and George Close.[28]

The increase in the town's housing stock placed a growing strain on the town's sewage system, and in the later 1960s the sewage treatment and disposal works off Ludlow Road were improved and extended at a cost of nearly £50,000. The expansion of the town also meant that many of the residents found themselves too far away from the shops of the town centre to use them on a daily basis, so provision was made for a shop on the Fronhir and Radnor Drive estates.[29]

Expanding the Town's Economy

The auction yard of 1949 had been built to satisfy the minimum acceptable standards and it soon became clear that if competition from rival livestock centres such as Ludlow and Craven Arms was to be beaten off and the livestock trade was to remain at the heart of the town's prosperity, the auction yard needed to be expanded and its facilities greatly improved. Throughout the 1950s and 1960s improvements were carried out, including housing for cows and calves in 1954, additional parking and

	1961	1962	1963	1967	1968	1969	1970	1971
Store cattle	13,948	10,690	10,945	6,981	9,200	10,896	11,577	12,715
Other cattle	929	468	534	253	428	477	481	545
Total cattle	14,877	11,158	11,479	7,234	9,628	11,373	2,058	13,260
Fat sheep and lambs	13,690	16,826	17,454	14,317	18,616	18,127	24,156	33,800
Store sheep and lambs	4,721	11,545	16,487	35,673	41,188	39,154	35,817	39,550
Total sheep	18,411	28,371	33,941	49,990	59,804	57,281	60,973	76,350

Figure 26: Annual throughputs of cattle and sheep, Knighton Livestock Market 1961-71. (The sharp reduction in the throughput of cattle in 1967-68 was the result of a foot and mouth outbreak)
(Source: Knighton UDC Minutes, 29.1.1964, 26.1.1972)

washing facilities for livestock transport lorries in 1959, and additional cattle and sheep pens in 1964 and again in 1971.

As Figure 26 demonstrates, in terms of throughput, the investment in improved auction yard facilities seems to have been slow to pay off, for it was not until 1969 that the 1937 throughput figures of 53,628 sheep and 8,012 cattle were surpassed. However the sheep trade had changed considerably since the 1930s and 1940s when the emphasis had been upon store ewes and wethers, for by the 1960s the emphasis was on the production of store lambs to sell on and increasingly on fat lambs for slaughter. Initially there was some disappointment at the slow rate of growth, but with the newly merged auctioneering firm of McCartney, Morris and Barker setting out clear plans for the development of Knighton market in 1968, local sentiment changed and by 1972 satisfaction was being expressed at the 'most pleasing upward trend' in the volume of trade.[30]

	1931		1951	
	Number employed	%	Number employed	%
Farming	102	13.4	76	10.4
Metal manufacturing	30	4	49	6.8
Building and decorating	64	8.4	84	11.5
Transport	60	7.9	86	11.8
Professions and commerce	181	23.8	170	23
Personal service	130.9	18.9	81	11.1

Figure 27: Occupational categories in Knighton in 1931 and 1951
(Source: J. Owen Pryce *et al, A Review of Populations in Mid-Wales, 1901-51*, 1959, p.126)

The town's retail sector may not have enjoyed the same measure of prosperity, for the number engaged in the professions and commerce had fallen slightly between 1931 and 1951, though still employing 23% of the town's labour force. Over the next couple of decades the number of shops, cafés and banks fell from 70+ in the early 1960s, to 65 in 1967 and 59 in 1968 and 1971.[31] The reason for the fall was undoubtedly the sharp decline in the population of Knighton Rural District, which fell by a third between 1931 and 1971. However a similarly sharp increase in farm incomes went some way in compensating for this fall in the town's potential customer base, as did the rise of 13% in the town's population by 1971.

Several trends in occupational patterns in the town present in 1951 were to continue over the next couple of decades. The increased employment in metal manufacture apparent in 1951 was probably the result of the establishment and expansion of several agricultural engineering businesses in the town in response to the increased mechanisation of agriculture.[32] Since mechanisation of agriculture had barely taken off in the locality by 1951, employment in agricultural engineering in the town was to increase markedly over the next few decades. Another factor making for growth in this sector was the rapid increase in the use of cars and lorries, which encouraged the establishment of service and repair businesses, though not all on the scale of S.W. Brisbane's garage at Whitehall, which dealt with both sales and maintenance.

The relatively modest post-war building programme embarked upon in Knighton had seen a modest increase in employment in this sector by 1951, but the ambitious house-building programmes embarked upon in both the private and public sectors in the following decades meant that employment in construction increased markedly as much of the work went to local firms. Another growing area of the local economy in 1951 was the transport and communications sector, and growth was to continue over the next few decades, the closure of the freight service at Knighton Station in the mid-1960s offering local road haulage firms such as Roberts Transport additional opportunities.

The number employed in farming in Knighton – essentially in the Farrington and Cwmgilla ward – fell by some 25% between 1931 and 1951, rather more than the 19% fall experienced in Knighton Rural District, but largely as a result of the same causes: increasing mechanisation and the amalgamation of holdings. The parish crop and livestock returns suggest that the same factors produced a similar outcome over the next few decades: thus the number of farm workers in Knighton fell from 36 in 1939 to 27 in 1955 and 25 in 1965, while the number of holdings fell from 48 in 1939 to 39 in 1955 and 35 in 1965. However, the agricultural sector of the local economy was buoyant, for under the guaranteed minimum price regime of the post-war decades output increased rapidly: the number of cattle on Knighton farms increased by 92% between 1945 and 1965 and the number of sheep rose by some 80%.[33]

The sector showing the sharpest fall in the number of workers in both the Urban and Rural Districts between 1931 and 1951 was personal service – domestic servants, gardeners and hotel and catering staff – predominantly a female labour force.

Combining these trends, the town's industrial base expanded rapidly over the next decades to improve local employment prospects, particularly in the later 1960s and early 1970s. One of the larger employers was S.W. Brisbane's tyre business at Mill Green. Known initially as Radnor Tyre Services Ltd and later as Brisbane's Motorway Group, it employed 140 workers by the mid-1960s and a further 80, mainly women, were taken on in 1968.

The Radnorshire Company – the official name of the business from 1946 – also extended the scale of its activities in the town. In 1959 it began to manufacture animal feedstuffs and opened a larger plant for this in 1961. The company was taken over by Rank, Hovis McDougall in 1966, though it retained its separate identity and its trade name, Radco. In 1969 it extended its activities again, opening a new cereal processing plant.[34]

With the aid of the Mid Wales Development Association new industries were attracted to the town. In the early 1960s Messrs E. Walters (Ludlow) Ltd built their clothing factory on West Street, expanding it substantially in 1967, significantly increasing its largely female labour force. In the later 1960s, the west Midlands engineering firm F.W. McConnell Ltd and its subsidiary, Benson Nu-Way, set up works on the Ludlow Road and obtained local authority housing for their key workers. In 1972, after closing a factory at West Bromwich, McConnell's increased the scale of their operations in Knighton significantly, estimating that over the next two years they would require another 50 local authority houses for their employees. By this time Knighton was no longer just a market town with a flourishing livestock trade, but was developing a promising industrial base.[35]

Not everything was going Knighton's way, however. Many in the town had hoped that its new school on Ludlow Road would become the secondary school serving east Radnorshire, but the County Education Committee's decision in the 1950s to enlarge the County School at Presteigne dashed these hopes. Then, in 1965, the same body decided, despite heated local protests, to establish the new comprehensive school for east Radnorshire at Presteigne rather than Knighton. Nor did the town get the agricultural college it had once hoped for, and the young people of Knighton, after travelling to Presteigne for their secondary education, found it necessary to travel to Llandrindod or Newtown Colleges of Further Education for post-16 technical and vocational education.[36]

Knighton also experienced difficulties in retaining its hospital which developed from the old workhouse hospital after the setting up of the National Health Service and the reorganisation of the welfare system. Initially the hospital catered for the aged infirm former inmates of the workhouse, but in the mid-1950s the Brecon and Radnor Hospital Management Committee approved the provision of additional facilities and by 1963 the hospital had 30 beds available for the geriatric and the chronically sick, two maternity beds and a small physiotherapy department. The hospital was also developing post-operative care of acute surgical cases after the patient had been operated on at Hereford or Shrewsbury. However, neither the local general practitioner, Dr Brian Davies, nor the UDC was able to secure from the Welsh Hospital Board any definite assurances as to the future of the hospital.[37]

In August 1964 the Welsh Hospital Board announced that the structural condition of Knighton Hospital necessitated its demolition and that alternative accommodation would be provided at Llandrindod Wells. The chairmen of Knighton UDC and RDC, Mrs Catherine Medlicott and Mr C.E. Watkins, launched a campaign to reverse the decision, but to no avail as in February 1967 Tudor

Watkins, the local MP, informed the UDC that the decision to close the hospital had been confirmed.[38]

This only served to stiffen local opposition. Dr Davies marshalled the main arguments against closure: that the additional facilities required at Llandrindod would cost at least as much as would be required and that the closure of the maternity beds would mean that mothers would have to choose between home delivery or going to Llandrindod where there were no support services such a surgeon, anaesthetist or blood bank. Stowe, Leominster and Wigmore RDCs gave their support to Knighton. In March 1971 the Knighton Hospital Closure Protest Committee organised a delegation to the Regional Hospital Board at Cardiff. In March 1972, after a face-saving reappraisal, the Board advised the Secretary of State for Wales that Knighton Hospital should be retained, though on a reduced scale, with 13 geriatric beds and 5 GP medical beds. For the time being the hospital was safe, though the question of maternity beds was left unresolved.[39]

The Post-War Social Scene
At first glance, with the ending of the war the town seems to have returned to the social environment of pre-war days. By 1946 the football, cricket and golf clubs were back in action, and with all the local organisations in need of funds, there was soon a regular almost weekly round of dances, whist drives and, later, bingo sessions to lighten the post-war austerity. The town band, by 1949 resplendent in new uniforms and with new instruments, was giving frequent concerts in the summer months and agitating for a bandstand to be built on the recreation ground. However, it took a few years to revive the traditional Carnival and Show at the end of August on the scale that local public opinion expected and in 1945 and 1946, in place of the show, successful meetings were held on the old racecourse of the 1870s.[40]

The town's recreational and social amenities were considerably extended. Bryn-y-Castell was developed into Knighton's main recreational centre complete with sports facilities and a children's playground. Play areas were set up at Fronhir and Pontfaen, while the recreation ground on West Street, which had been intended for industrial development, was refurbished to serve the growing number of families living on the outlying housing estates on Offa's Road and Penybont Road. Sporting facilities were enhanced when the UDC purchased the old Ystrad House bowling green on Church Road and built two hard tennis courts on Bowling Green Lane.

The UDC also increased the number of public halls available for use by local organisations. In 1953 it purchased the Victoria Road Baptist chapel, no longer used for worship, and with the aid of county council grants converted it into a two-storey community centre with offices and a club room on the ground floor and a public hall on the first floor, handing its management over to a committee of representatives of local organisations. In 1970 the Education Committee decided that the hall on the first floor of the Market Hall was no longer needed for school meals for the primary school – the ground floor was let as an egg packing centre – and the UDC decided to refurbish the hall which, renamed the Russell Room, was made available from 1972 for letting as a function room. There was thus no shortage of public halls in the town, rather the reverse, but each venue had its own loyal customers. When the UDC decided in 1973 to close the Victoria Road Hall, the Women's Institute and the Football Club protested so vigorously that the decision was overturned.[41]

Not all the great institutions of pre-war Knighton survived long after 1945. One of the first casualties was the Choral Society, which had continued to function throughout the war. By 1947 the number of members had fallen sharply, the decline being most marked among the tenors and basses, and although the society carried on for a while, it soon went out of existence. Thus the old choral tradition which had existed in the town for nearly a century had vanished, largely as a result of the disappearance of the local chapel choirs, the reservoir on which the society had depended.[42] The Male Voice Choir carried on for a number of years, however, and for a while another choir, the Silurian Singers, was active in the town.

Another eventual casualty was the cinema, where the dilemma faced by W.H. and R.J. Brown was familiar to all proprietors of small cinemas – audience receipts were too small to warrant the hiring of modern popular films, and there was thus a tendency for audience figures to spiral downwards, with competition from television becoming more intense as the 1950s progressed. In an attempt to boost attendance the Browns backed the UDC scheme to expand the nearby car park and in 1963 sought to increase the size of the cinema. However, the plans were rejected and eventually the cinema was converted into what became known as Brown's Club, but this met with little success. In 1973 an application was made to change the use of the premises to a discount store.

Perhaps the most effective social organisation in the town in the early post-war years was the Knighton and District Arts and Crafts Club, founded in 1930 and better known as the Knighton Arts Club. The club seems to have been a federation of three autonomous sections – arts and crafts, music, and drama – which in the early post-war years organised exhibitions, concerts and dramatic productions, some by local people and others by professionals. The club also organised short courses in art and music appreciation, drama and elocution. The driving force behind the club, despite her increasing years, was Mrs Ada M. Graves (c.1878-1962), formerly headmistress of the Girls' National School and the widow of C.W. Graves, a gifted musician. During the inter-war years she had played a major role in the town's cultural life, conducting the St Cecilian Choir, acting as accompanist for the Choral

Society and producing plays for the Tref-y-Clawdd WI, in addition to serving as Ranger Guider for a time.

One change that was noticeable in the post-war decades was that social provision was increasingly geared towards the younger generation. In addition to the improving sports facilities, a growing number of youth organisations came into being, notably the Young Farmers Club – the fourth in the county – formed in May 1944, units of the Army and Air Force Cadets, the Scouts and the Youth Club and, after the closing of the cinema, the short-lived Brown's nightclub. The growing social influence of the younger generation is perhaps best illustrated by the Knighton Pop Festival held on Saturday 23 August 1970. It was organised by the Knighton Contemporary Arts Society – in effect by Christopher Plant and Elwyn Powell, helped by David Moore, Gareth Kell, David Owen and others. It was scheduled to run from 12 noon until midnight, though it overran by about an hour. The Move featured as the headline band and another distinguished performer was Alexis Korner, but the other artists were relatively unknown. The festival attracted an audience of about 2,000 and passed off without trouble. In retrospect an attractive feature of the festival was the support it received from the town establishment: local firms and bodies provided the temporary platform, the scaffolding and the backcloth, while the UDC gave cautious support and cleared the litter from the site (now occupied by the Community Hall) afterwards.[43]

↝ 11 ↜

TOWARDS THE 21ST CENTURY

This chapter covers the last quarter or so of the 20th century, but only with a very broad brush because it is too soon for the long-term significance of recent developments to be identified with any degree of certainty.

The urban economy

Between 1971 and 2001 Knighton's population increased by 51% and its housing stock by at least 57%, both unprecedented rates of growth. The greater part of the increase in both cases came in the period 1971-1981 as a result of the expansion of the town's industrial base and the implementation of housing programmes drawn up in the 1960s in both the public and private sectors. During the 1980s and 1990s the rate of growth in both the town's population and housing stock slowed down, but still amounted to a healthy 13%.

Year	Population	Housing stock
1971	2,010	695
1981	2,687	964
2001	3,043	1,090

Figure 28: Knighton's population and housing stock 1971-2001. (N.b. The housing data refers to houses and does not include flats)
(Source: Printed census data)

While some of the post-war housing was infilling within the existing built-up area, most of it was built along the western and southern fringes of Knighton and represented a considerable extension of the town. To the west, along the western edge of Offa's Road and Penybont Road, lay the Radnor Drive and the Garth developments, while along the eastern edge of those roads lay the Laurels Meadow, Hatfield Close and the Millfield developments. To the south, on the northern side of Ffrydd Road lay the extended Ffrydd Terrace and Ffrydd Close, while on the southern side of road lay the Underhill Crescent, the other part of Ffrydd Terrace, Under Ffrydd Wood and the development near Jackets Well. To the east of Ffrydd Road lay Ludlow Road, to the north of which lay the Fronhir and Pontfaen estates, while the triangle of land between the school on the south side of Ludlow Road, Presteigne Road to the north of the new cemetery (consecrated in

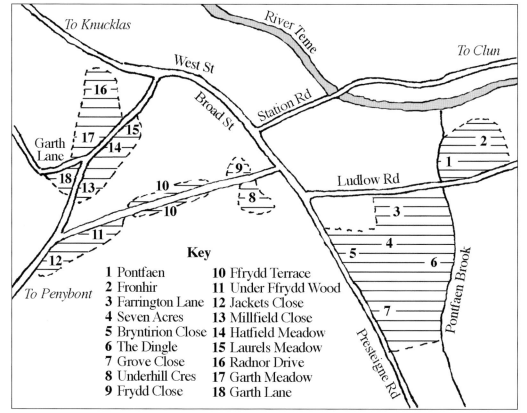

Figure 29: Map showing the main post-war housing developments in Knighton

1992), and Pontfaen Brook began to be developed from both Presteigne Road and Farrington Lane.

The marked growth in the town's population and housing stock might seem to suggest that through the last quarter of the 20th century Knighton's economy, unlike that of Britain as a whole, enjoyed a sustained period of prosperity, untouched by the downturns of the late 1970s and early 1980s, and the opening years of the 1990s. But this was far from the case, for the 1980s and 1990s saw Knighton's industrial base shrink. By the late 1970s the scale of the Radnorshire Company's activities in the town had begun to decline – the builders' supplies business was discontinued, and the seed processing business was sold off, as was the coal supply business. In 1982 the name, 'The Radnorshire Company' disappeared and in the following year Rank, Hovis, McDougall sold its agricultural division to Dalgetty who continued to operate the Teme Mill.[1]

As early as 1981 F.W. McConnell Ltd. was beginning to reconsider its position in Knighton, and by the later 1990s only the heating division of its subsidiary Nu-Way Benson was operating in the town and part of the works on Ludlow Road lay empty. Roberts Transport had gone out of business in 1993. The clothing factory on West Street was also experiencing difficulties: in 1994 E. Walters (Ludlow) had sold it to Messrs Dewhirsts, who in turn had sold it to Peter Christian at the end of 1998, the number of workers employed falling after each sale. By the later 1990s the tyre business on Mill Green, now known as Motorway Retreads, was also shedding workers. Radnor Hills Mineral Water Co. Ltd., incorporated in 1996, was the only major new business established in the area.[2]

The area of the town devoted to the retail trade was also shrinking, retreating down the High Street towards Broad Street, down Station Road towards Bridge Street, and down Bridge Street towards Broad Street, and the trend continued in the first decade of the new century. In employment terms, the fall in this sector, from 23% of the working population in 1951 to 18% in 2001 is smaller than one might expect, possibly because the fall in the number of small retail businesses was in part balanced by increased employment in Harry Tuffin's supermarket, which opened on its present site in 1983.[3] However, the 2001 census data may well understate the fall in employment in the retail sector in Knighton, for some may have found employment in nearby towns rather than in Knighton itself.

However, other sectors of the economy, notably construction, personal services and agriculture appear to have been more resilient and continued to flourish throughout the period.

The Ageing of Knighton

The proportion of the town's population aged 60 or more rose steadily over the 20th century, from 9.9% in 1901, to 16.6 % in 1951, to 20% in 1971 and 46.3% in 2001, and in all probability will continue to rise as life expectancy increases.[4] This was not a new development, for the percentage of the population over 60 had been growing steadily since at least 1851, but the rate of growth accelerated markedly during the last quarter or so of the 20th century.

The central cause had always been out-migration of younger age groups from Radnorshire in general and Knighton in particular in search of more favourable employment opportunities elsewhere, but in the last two or three decades of the century there was also an inflow of older age groups from the conurbations, notably from the west Midlands, attracted by cheaper housing and a more attractive environment, but with easy access by rail and road to their former home region. Some indication of the inflow can be obtained from the 2001 census data which showed 38% of the population born in Wales and 58% born in England, whereas, given Knighton's position just on the Welsh side of the border, one might expect the proportions to have been at least broadly equal, if not more in favour of Welsh-born.[5]

The question of providing suitable care and/or accommodation for the elderly had been considered by the authorities long before the surge of the last quarter of the century. In 1955 the county council bought The Cottage and subsequently converted it into an old people's home, initially catering for the elderly previously living at the former workhouse. In the early 1960s a Knighton Old People's Welfare Club was functioning, with a membership of 120 and an average of between 70 and 80 attending the weekly meetings. By 1967, 20 old people's flats had been built on the garden of the former vicarage, to be called St Edward's Close, in four blocks: Frydd House, Teme House, Kinsley House and Garth House. By 1970 a further eight flats were built on part of the vicarage garden, the development being named Offa's Way, while in 1976 further sheltered housing, Jubilee House, was opened in that area of the town.[6] In the meantime care was taken to ensure that the public house-building programme catered for a wide range of housing needs and included four, three and two bedroom accommodation, including, as on Frydd Close, small bungalows suited to the needs of the elderly. In the later 1990s, another old people's home, with accommodation for 10 people, opened at the newly extended hospital, but as this was balanced by the closure of The Cottage, it was not taken kindly by some in the town. The site of The Cottage was then developed into sheltered housing for the elderly.

The ageing of the town's population has not been without social costs in the form of an increased demand upon local medical and social services. In this respect it should be noted that in 2001, 389 of Knighton's 1,325 households, nearly 30%, consisted of pensioner households.[7] However, not all the consequences are negative. In the first place people in their 60s and early 70s increasingly regard themselves – and are regarded – as 'middle aged' rather than 'old', and, if retired and still socially active, provide many of the volunteers upon whom local social and community organisations depend. Secondly, the elderly provide a significant source of employment, since many in this age group require at least part-time assistance with domestic cleaning, gardening, property repairs, painting and decorating. Again, the elderly provided a significant proportion of the clientele of the 150 of the Knighton workforce employed in the health and social welfare sectors, according to the 2001 census.

The Growth of Tourism

Since at least the beginning of the 20th century some people had been lobbying for the exploitation of Knighton's potential as a touring base, citing the fresh air, beautiful unspoilt scenery, the many historical monuments and the opportunity to engage in a range of country pursuits and sports. However beyond paying lip service to the Knighton Development Association, little of significance was done until the formation of the Tref-y-Clawdd 1970 Society. The Offa's Dyke Association had had its inaugural meeting the previous year, in March 1969.

These groups were very much the creation of Frank Noble, whose interest in Offa's Dyke and enthusiasm for the historical and cultural development of Knighton

Plate 56: The commemorative stone at Pinner's Hole erected to record the opening of the Offa's Dyke footpath by Lord Hunt and the opening of the Offa's Dyke Park

and its hinterland attracted wide support. Relations with the UDC were sometimes strained, but work on the proposed Offa's Dyke Park went ahead and Lady Green Price and Lord Hunt respectively opened it and the long distance path on 10 July 1971. The Society received a Prince of Wales Award for its efforts in the autumn of 1971 and pressed ahead with the purchase of the old National School, which ultimately became the first Offa's Dyke Centre, complete with a picnic area and car park.[8]

From its base in the Offa's Dyke Centre, the Association provided information on the Dyke, promoted it and sought to safeguard it, provided detailed guides and maps, and encouraged archaeological and historical research. In the later 1990s a purpose-built centre, just above the old National School, was provided by Powys County Council and leased to the Offa's Dyke Association. This now also serves as the Knighton Tourist Information Centre, providing a wide range of information for visitors to the town and the surrounding area.

There seems to have been a growing awareness of Knighton's historical heritage on the part of local public opinion in the later 1960s and 1970s, but beyond the designation of the High Street, Church Road as far as Wylcwm Street, Wylcwm Street, Wylcwm Place, Broad Street and Bridge Street as far as the Swan as a conservation area – later extended to include the Cwm, little was done.

However, in the later 1990s, with the aid of European Union and other grants, a major programme of street refurbishment was embarked upon in the town centre. The first area to be refurbished was Brookside Square, created in 1978-79 after the old police station and the magistrates' room had been demolished in 1976. After this had been completed, attention turned to the High Street, where the drainage was improved, steps and paving were laid, a handrail was provided, and the street lighting was modernised.

Not all the attempts to conserve the town's heritage succeeded. In 1987 the Russell Room was demolished and attempts to use the site to provide a new market hall or a restored Butter Cross or a town museum came to nothing. Similar attempts to acquire the Cottage and the Old School for community use also failed. Even so, the private development of an astronomical observatory on Reeves Hill and the decision to make Knighton the starting point of Glyndwr's Way, a 126-mile trail through mid Wales, undoubtedly enhanced the town's potential to attract tourists.[9]

Knighton's amenities were greatly enhanced in the closing decades of the century. First the long discussed swimming pool was built adjacent to the primary school on Ludlow Road and this was later developed into a modern sports centre, while in 1984 the community centre was built off the car park adjacent to the auction yard. Administered by a committee of volunteers on behalf of the community, it provides an attractive modern setting for many of the town's social activities. In addition the facilities of the hospital were enhanced: in 1981 a physiotherapy unit was added, while the provision of a new wing providing residential care for the elderly to replace The Cottage has probably strengthened the long term prospects of the hospital.[10]

Public capital investment in Knighton projects in the closing decades of the century amounted to more than £1 million. This undoubtedly enhanced the town's facilities and confirmed its standing as the social and commercial centre for the surrounding countryside. In particular it has provided a sound base from which visitors can explore the surrounding countryside, and by 2001 76 people, 5.5% of the town's working population, were employed in hotels and catering.[11]

Farming in the Knighton area

Over the last few decades of the century the pattern of farming in the Knighton area has changed substantially. In the first place, stocking levels more than doubled, the number of sheep and lambs kept in the parish more than doubling and the number of cattle increasing by 95%. To some extent this was at the expense of the acreages under cereals and roots, which fell sharply from 510 acres in 1965 to rather less than 200 acres in 1984. But this was not the main cause, for there had been a steady and substantial improvement in the quality of grassland in Radnorshire over the post-war decades as a result of the reclamation of rough grazing, and a substantial improvement in the quality of sown pasture in particular.[12]

Two other changes have been happening in the farming community – the growing use of contract services rather than reliance upon permanently employed

186

labour for major routine tasks such as ploughing, mowing or harvesting, and the growing reliance upon grass silage production. The latter has largely replaced the need for growing special forage crops such as oats and root crops and has greatly reduced, although not eliminated, the need for haymaking, an uncertain undertaking always at the mercy of the weather.[13]

As in the county at large, the nature of sheep farming in the Knighton area has changed substantially in recent decades, for the emphasis is now on the production of either fat lambs ready for slaughter or store lambs to sell on for finishing. Relatively few two-year-old ewes are now offered for sale, and the large sheep sales of September are a thing of the past. Nor are the indigenous breeds of sheep – the Kerry Hill, Radnor Forest and Clun Forest – the dominant local breeds. Other breeds have been introduced to improve carcass quality, including – once the ban on imported breeds had been lifted in the later 1960s – foreign breeds such as the Texel. In the cattle sector the previously dominant Hereford breed have made way for early maturing continental breeds such as the Limousin.[14]

Knighton in 2001[15]

As we have seen, Knighton's infrastructure improved significantly during the last three or four decades of the 20th century and an analysis of the 2001 census data by the Office of National Statistics suggested that the town's economy was in good shape. Only 2.88% of the economically active in the town were unemployed and it was not over-dependent on any one sector of employment. The manufacturing and the retail sectors each employed 18% or so of those in employment, construction and health and social work each accounted for more than 10%, and education, hotel and catering, transport, property and farming each accounted for more than 5% of those in employment.

Even so, there is some cause for concern. It is clear that a significant proportion of those in Knighton in employment in 2001 worked outside the town since the average distance travelled to their place of work was 18.5 kilometres. This would suggest that to some extent Knighton was becoming a dormitory town, with some travelling each day to work in neighbouring towns such as Presteigne, Llandrindod Wells and Ludlow. However, the outflow from Knighton was almost matched by the inflow of those travelling to the town for work, and not only from its rural hinterland but from also from neighbouring towns such as Presteigne. Even so, with 52% of Knighton's working population travelling to work in their own car, the employment opportunities of those in the 21% of Knighton households without a car were clearly reduced, given the poor public transport available in the early morning and early evening.

The establishment of the Knighton Business Enterprise Park in the late 1990s aimed at increasing employment opportunities in Knighton, by no means an easy task. Conventional manufacturing undertakings require substantial economies of scale to be competitive and these are not likely to be available in Knighton. Moreover, the town is some distance from the motorway network, which would add to transport costs. Not surprisingly the Development Board for Rural Wales and its successor the Welsh Development Association, with the support of local opinion, sought to establish small specialised industrial units in the town, each employing a workforce of 10 or 12. However, with about one-third of those in Knighton between the ages of 16 and 74 having no formal qualifications, and many young people leaving the town on the completion of their secondary education, it may be difficult to attract to the town 'high tech', high value-added businesses requiring a relatively small but highly skilled labour force.[16] Faster broad band speed would help in this respect.

The problems faced by Knighton are by no means unique; they are shared to a greater or lesser extent by neighbouring communities on both sides of the border. In some ways Knighton is better equipped to deal with them, since it retains one of its core functions, that of a centre for the livestock trade, while its tourism industry is growing, and its townscape and facilities have been transformed in the closing decade of the 20th century. Nor should the traditional enterprise and initiative of its people, so frequently shown in the past centuries, be underestimated.

Bibliography

Primary Sources – Manuscript

Bodleian Library
Walker Ms C.13

British Library
Additional MSS 70106
Additional MSS 70007

The Estate Office, Brampton Bryan
Harley Papers, Bundles 24, 25, 53

Cambridge University Library
Particulars of Crown lands sold between March 1649 and September 1656

Herefordshire County Record Office
Bishop's Transcripts, Knighton parish
Calendar of Harley Papers at Brampton Bryan
HD/5/14/86 1716 Knighton Triennial Visitation
HD/5.15/17 1719 Knighton Triennial Visitation

Knighton Town Council
Town Council Minutes 1974-2000

Lambeth Palace Library
COMM III/4 Admissions 1655-56

The National Archives
SP19 Papers of the Committee for the Advance of Money
SP23 Papers of the Committee for Compounding with Delinquents
CRES 49/4919-4929 Cantre Mellenith General Correspondence
CRES 49/4953 Knighton Market Hall
CRES 49/4954 Application for the purchase of Knighton Market Hall 1852-54
CRES 49/4646 The sale of Farrington and Cwmgilla to Edward Rogers
CRES 49/4955 Knighton Tolls and Market Hall
CRES 49/5027 Correspondence relating to Knighton enclosure
CRES 15/9/10 /13,/14/95 Woods and Forests Correspondence relating to Knighton tolls etc
CRES 5/220-221 Knighton Manor and Borough court rolls
MH 12 Includes Knighton Poor Law Union papers
MAF 68 Includes Knighton parish crop and livestock returns

National Library of Wales
Knighton parish registers
Harpton Court Collection
Norton Deeds
Ormathwaite Papers

Price of Norton Deeds
Walter Davies (Gwalter Mechain) MSS
Great Sessions 4/496/7

Northamptonshire Record Office
Finch Hatton MS 133

Powys County Archives Office
The Lewis Lloyd Collection
R/QS/S 3653 Poor relief expenditure, Knighton parish 1800-16
Order books of the Radnorshire Turnpike Trust
Knighton Board of Health Minutes
Knighton Rural District Council Minutes
Knighton Urban District Council Minutes
Farrington and Cwmgilla enclosure award
Knighton enclosure award
Knighton Tithe Commutation Schedule, 1539
Green and Nixson Deposit, Box 16 Lt. Commander Bray
      Box 18 Documents relating to Knighton Electric Light Supply Company
      Box 19 Documents relating to Knighton cinema
R/DX/57/1 Lt Commander H.J. Bray's Scrapbook
R/DB/RAD/M/1 Radnorshire Coal, Lime and General Supply Company, Directors' Minute Book
R/DB/RAD/ SH/1 Radnorshire Coal, Lime and General Supply Company. Share register
R/DB/RAD/X/7 The Radco Centenary booklet
R/DX/125/4 William Hatfield MSS
R/D/PHP/13, 14
W.C. Maddox, *History of the Radnorshire Civil Defence Scheme 1935-46*, unpublished typescript

Radnorshire Society Library
W.H. Howse MSS Notebook W

Primary Sources – Manuscript
Place of publication London unless stated otherwise

Official Publications
Acts and Ordinances of the Interregnum, (ed) C.H. Firth and C.S. Rait, 1911
Calendar of the Proceedings of the Committee for the Advance of Money, (ed) M.A.E. Green, 1888
Calendar of the Proceedings of the Committee for Compounding with Delinquents, (ed) M.A.E.
      Green, 1892
Calendar of the State Papers Domestic, 1651-52
House of Commons Papers, George III 1717-1788, Vol. 46
House of Commons Papers, George II, Reports and Papers 1775-86, Vol.31
Second Report of the Poor Law Commission, 1836
Third Report of the Poor Law Commission, 1857
Report of the Commission of Inquiry for South Wales, 1844
Report of the Commission on the State of Education in Wales, 1847
Inventory of Ancient Monuments in Radnorshire, Royal Commission on Ancient Monuments in
      Wales And Monmouthshire, 1911
Office of National Statistics, Neighbourhood Statistics, (http//www.neighbourhood statistics.gov.uk)

Other calendars and collections of documents

Calendar of State Papers Domestic, 1650-52

Exchequer proceedings concerning Wales in tempore James I, (ed) T.I. Jeffreys Jones, Cardiff, 1955

Lewys Dwnn: Heraldic Visitation of Wales and part of the Marches between 1586 and 1613, (ed) S.R. Meyrick, Llandovery 1846

Portland MSS, vol iii, HMC, 1894

Radnorshire: a collection of miscellaneous papers relating to the history of the county, (ed) J. Lloyd, 1900

The Religious Census of 1851. A Calendar of the Returns relating to Wales, Vol. 1 South Wales, (ed) Ieuan Gwynedd Jones and David Williams, Cardiff, 1976

Contemporary Printed Sources

A General View of the Agriculture of Radnorshire, John Clark, 1794

A General View of the Agriculture of South Wales, Walter Davies, 1815

The State of the Poor, Sir Frederick Eden, London, 1797

Report .... On a Public inquiry into the Sanitary Condition of Knighton, William Lee, 1849

Royal National and Commercial Directory of Gloucestershire and North and South Wales, 1858-59, Isaac Slater

Slater's Directory of South Wales, 1880

Kelly's Directory of South Wales, 1891

The History of Radnorshire, Jonathan Williams, 1859 and 1905 editions

The Parliamentary History of the Principality of Wales, W.R. Williams, Brecon 1995

Newspapers

Brecon and Radnor Express

Hereford Times

London Gazette (www.london-gazette.co.uk)

Radnorshire Echo

Radnorshire Standard

Hereford Journal

Kington Gazette

Mid Wales Journal

Radnorshire Express

The Times

Thesis

D. Roy Ll. Adams, The Parliamentary Representation of Radnorshire, 1536-1832, MA thesis, University of Wales, 1970

Secondary Sources

O.R. Ashton, '18th Century Radnorshire. A Population Study', *TRS xl*, 1970

A.R. Blain, *Monaughty, a brief history*, privately published, 1984

Alice Blackburn, *Alice's Knighton*, n.d.

Sir Joseph Bradney, 'Pilleth, Nantygroes and Monaughty', *TRS xxi*, 1951

Mary Cadwallader, *Knighton*, Cascob, 1996

Clwyd Powys Archaeological Trust, *Historic Settlement Survey – Radnorshire – Knighton*, www.cpat.org.uk

E.J.L. Cole, 'Account of the Keeper of Radnor Castle', *TRS, xxxiii*, 1963
        'Early High Sheriffs of Radnorshire; *TRS xxxvii*, 1967, *xli*, 1971

C.H. Collins Baker, *The Life and Circumstances of James Brydges, Duke of Chandos*, Oxford, 1949

D.S. Davies 'Knighton', *TRS xii*, 1942

R.M. Deakins, 'Agriculture in Radnorshire in World War II and After', *TRS lxxv*, 2005

C.J. Delaney and I.M. Soulsby, *The Archaeological Implications of Development on the Historic Towns of Radnor District*, Cardiff, 1973

Elizabeth Dunn, Owen Glyndwr and Radnorshire', *TRS, xxxvii*, 1967

Jacqueline Eales, *Puritans and Roundheads*, Cambridge, 1990

M.A. Faraday, 'The Assessment for the Fifteenth of 1293', *TRS, xliii*, 1973

      'Mortality in the diocese of Hereford 1442-1551', *TWFNC, xlii, Pt II*, 1977

      ' The Radnor Hearth Tax Returns of 1670', *TRS, lix*, 1989

Sir Cyril Fox, *Offa's Dyke*, 1935

Franzden, T. www.jamesboswell.info/biography/chase-price-mp-leominster-and-radnor

M. Gelling, (ed) *Offa's Dyke Reviewed by Frank Noble*, 1983

W. Hatfield, *Knighton*, 1947

Tony Hobbs, *The Pubs of Radnorshire*, Logaston, 2006

W.H. Howse, *Radnorshire*, Hereford, 1949

      Knighton Town Guide, 1951

Charles Hopkinson and Martin Speight, *The Mortimers*, Logaston, 2002

Colin P.F. Hughes, 'A History of Schools in Radnorshire: The Knighton Area', *TRS lxv*, 1895

D. Hutchinson, 'Charles I in Breconshire and Radnorshire', *TWFNC*, 1913

Brian Jones, *The Churches of the Knighton Deanery*

J. Jones, *History of the Baptists in Radnorshire*, 1895

R. Tudur Jones, *Vavasor Powell*, Leominster, 1975

Knighton Rotary Club (ed), *Knighton 1800-1950*

W.C. Maddox, *A History of the Radnorshire Constabulary*, Llandrindod Wells, 1959

R.J. Moore Colyer, 'Gentlemen, Horses and the Turf', *WHR Vol.16, No 1*, 1992

Sir Lewis Namier and John Brook, (ed), *The History of the House of Commons, 1759-90*

C.W. Newman, 'Charles Price and Rousseau', *TRS xliii*, 1973

Frank Noble 'Archaeological Finds in the Knighton Area', *TRS, xxvii*, 1957

      'Further Excavations at Bleddfa Church', *TRS, xxxiii*, 1963

R.C.B. Oliver, *The Squires of Penybont Hall*, 1971

Leonard Owen, 'The Population of Wales in the 16th and 17th Centuries', *Hon Soc Cymm*, 1959

G. Archer Parfitt, *Radnorshire Volunteers. A Regimental History of Radnorshire, 1539-1968*, Hay-on-Wye, 1968

Keith Parker, (ed) *Mid-Victorian Knighton*, Knighton, 1983

      Radnorshire from Civil War to Restoration, Logaston, 2000

      Parties, Polls and Riots, Logaston, 2009

      'Radnorshire and the New Poor Law to c1850', *TRS, lxxiv*, 2004

      'The Sale of Crown Lands in Radnorshire in the 19th Century', *TRS, lxxv*, 2005

J. Owen Pryce *et al*, *A Review of Population Changes in Mid Wales, 1901-1951*, typescript, n.d.

William Rees, *South Wales and the March, 1284-1415*, 1967 reprint

Paul Remfry, *Castles of Radnorshire*, Logaston, 1996

Gwynfryn Richards, 'Royal Briefs from the Restoration of the Church in Wales', *JHSCW vii*, 1957

Geoffrey Ridyard, The Silurian Mills, Knighton', *Melin 20*, 2004

www.ukrockfestivals.com/knighton-festival-1970.html

Ian Soulsby, *Towns of Medieval Wales*, 1983

M.A. Toynbee, 'A Royal Journey through Breconshire and Radnorshire', *TRS xx*, 1950

      'A Royal Journey through Herefordshire and Radnorshire', *TRS xxi*, 1951

Frank and Caroline Thorn (ed), *Domesday Book; 25 Shropshire*, Chichester, 1986

Wales Rural Observatory, Research Report 13, *Small and Market Towns in Rural Wales*, 2007

Paul Woodfield, 'Town Houses of Knighton', *TRS xliii*, 1973

References

Abbreviations

A & O	*Acts and Ordinances of the Interregnum*
BL	British Library
Bod Lib	Bodleian Library
BRE	*Brecon and Radnor Express*
CCAM	*Calendar of the Committee for the Advance of Money*
CCC	*Calendar of the Committee for Compounding with Delinquents*
CSPD	*Calendar of State Papers Domestic*
CUL	Cambridge University Library
HCRO	Herefordshire County Records Office
Hon Soc Cymm	*Transactions of the Honourable Society of Cymmrodorion*
HJ	*Hereford Journal*
HMC	Historical Manuscripts Commission
HT	*Hereford Times*
JHSCW	*Journal of the Historical Society of the Church in Wales*
KG	*Kington Gazette*
Lamb PL	Lambeth Palace Library
PCAO	Powys County Archives Office
RE	*Radnor Express*
RS	*Radnorshire Standard*
RDC	Rural District Council
TNA	The National Archives
TRS	*Transactions of the Radnorshire Society*
TWFNC	*Transactions of the Woolhope Field Naturalists Society*
UDC	Urban District Council

Chapter 1

1. F. Noble 'Archaeological Finds in the Knighton Area, 1954-57, *TRS xxvii*, 1957, p.62
2. Sir Cyril Fox, *Offa's Dyke*, p.40; M. Gelling (ed) *Offa's Dyke Reviewed by Franck Noble*, p.47
3. Gelling, p.41 and 94 Note 27
4. Roy Millward and Adrian Robinson, *The Welsh Borders*, p.109-10
5. Fox, p.170, 279
6. Gelling, p.50-53
7. Gelling, p.58-59
8. This paragraph summarises Gelling, p.45-47

Chapter 2

1. C.J. Delaney and I.N. Soulsby, *The Archaeological Implications of Development in the Historic Towns of Radnor District,* 4.3.1

2. Frank and Caroline Thorn, *Domesday Book 25 Shropshire*, 8.1
3. This section relies heavily on Paul Remfry, *Castles of Radnorshire*, and Charles Hopkinson and Martin Speight, *The Mortimers*
4. RCAM, *Inventory of Ancient Monuments in Radnorshire*, p.53
5. RCAM p.55-56, Remfry p.114
6. W. Hatfield, *Knighton*, p.8; W.H. Howse, *Knighton Town Guide*, p.9, I. Soulsby, *Towns of Medieval Wales*, p.155, Paul Woodfield, Town Houses of Knighton', *TRS xlviii*, 1973, p.50
7. Remfry, p.114, Woodfield, p.50
8. Remfry, p.112, Woodfield, p.60
9. Maurice Beresford, *New Towns of the Middle Ages* p.571, Woodfield, p.51. Soulsby 1983, p.155
10. Woodfield, p.53 Note 5, *HJ* 5.6.1861, UDC Minutes 13.3.1933

11. Hatfield, p.20-21, Howse 'Radnor Miscellany' *TRS xxiii*, 1953 p.69

12. Brian Jones, *The Churches of Knighton Deanery*, p.21; Bod. Lib, MS Gough, Wales 6, cited by Hatfield, p.29-21

13. Hatfield, p.15-16, Woodfield, p.52

14. M.A. Faraday, 'The assessment for the Fifteenth of 1293 in Radnor and other Marcher Lordships', *TRS xliii*, 1973, p.83-84

15. Faraday, 1973, p.79

16. Woodfield p.51; Leonard Owen. 'The Population of Wales in the 16th and 17th centuries', *Hon Soc Cwmm*, 1959, p.112

17. A.W. Langford 'The Plague in Herefordshire', *TWHFNC xxv Pt ii*, p.147; William Rees, *South Wales and the March 1284-1438*, p.255

18. Rees, p.256, 261 Note 2

19. Hatfield, p.15-16; Frank Noble, 'Further Excavations at Bleddfa Church', *TRS xxxiii*, 1963, p.61

20. Sir Joseph Bradney, 'Pilleth, Nantygroes and Monaughty, *TRS xxi*, 1951, p.40-41; Elizabeth Dunn, 'Owen Glyndwr and Radnorshire', *TRS xxxvii*, 1967, p.32-33

21. Noble 1963, p.60-61, Dunn, p.32-33, Remfry, p.63-64

22. Woodfield p.52-54, E.J.L. Cole 'Account of the Keeper of Radnor Castle', *TRS xxxiii*, 1983, p.37, M.A. Faraday, 'Mortality in the Diocese of Hereford, 1442-1551',*TWFNC xlii Pt ii*, 1977, p.165-168

23. J.L. Lloyd, *Radnorshire: A Collection of Miscellaneous Papers*, p.37

Chapter 3

1. This section is based on J.L. Lloyd, *Radnorshire: A Collection of Miscellaneous Documents*, p.9-16

2. T.I. Jeffreys Jones, *Exchequer Proceedings Concerning Wales*, p.319

3. Lloyd, p.214

4. Brampton Bryan, Harley Papers, Bundle 53, Jonathan Williams, *Radnorshire*, p.91-93

5. S.R. Meyrick, *Lewys Dwnn. Heraldic Visitation of Wales and Part of the Marches between 1586 and 1613*, Vol 1, p.252, A.R. Blain, *Monaughty, a brief history*,

6. Meyrick, Volume 1, p.257, E.J.L. Cole, 'Early High Sheriffs of Radnorshire', *TRS xxxvii*,

1967, p.42, *TRS xli,* 1971 ,p.70

7. Leonard Owen, 'The Population of Wales in the 16th and 17th centuries', Hon Soc Cwmm, 1957, p.112

8. *Exchequer Proceedings*, p.319

9. PCAO, R/D/LEW/2/387

10. HCRO, Calendar of Harley Papers, Bundles 14, 34, 63

11. Jacqueline Eales, *Puritans and Roundheads*, p.42

12. The account of the sieges of Brampton Bryan and Hopton castles is based on Keith Parker, *Radnorshire from Civil War to Restoration*, p.71-84

13. The account of Charles' journeys through Radnorshire is based on M.A. Toynbee, 'A Royal Journey through Breconshire and Radnorshire', *TRS xx*, 1950 and 'A Royal Journey through Herefordshire and Radnorshire', *TRS xxi*, 1951

14. D. Hutchinson, 'Charles I in Breconshire and Radnorshire', *TWFNC*, 1911, p.219

15. Hatfield, p.19-20

16. Gelling, p.46, Parker 2000, p.106-09

17. *CCC* Pt 3, p.991

18. BL Additional MSS 70106, 24.6.1642 Tombes to Sir R. Harley, Northamptonshire Record Office, Finch Hatton MS 133

19. *CCC* Pt 3, p.219, 991, TNA PRO SP19/73 p.143, SP 23/213 p.247-248

20. Radnorshire Society Library, Howse MSS Notebook W, p.34

21. *CCAM*, p.1123, TNA PRO SP/22, p.1925, 203, 286-287, SP 19/134, p.24-25

22. *CSPD* 1651-52, p.445-446

23. *A&O*, Vol I p.1097, Vol 2 p.1448

24. Hatfield, p.30-31

25. Bod Lib, Walker MS C13

26. Lamb. PL Comm/4, p.196, *Portland MSS*, Vol 3, p.207, BL Add MSS 70007 p.71, 97, 221

27. This account of the life of Vavasor Powell is based on R. Tudur Jones, *Vavasor Powell*

28. NLW Great Sessions 4/496/7, HCRO HD 5/14/88, HD 7/7/423

29. Woodfield, p.56-63

30. M.A. Faraday, 'The Radnorshire Hearth Tax Returns of 1670', *TRS lix*, 1989, p.33 and *TRS lx*, 1990, p.74-75

31. Parker 2000, p.67

Chapter 4

1. NLW The Norton Deeds, Nos 14,15, HCRO Calendar of Harley Papers, Bundle 59
2. Ruth Bidgood, 'Families of Llanddewi Hall, Radnorshire', *TRS xlviii*, 1993, p.48-49, HCRO Calendar of Harley Papers, Bundle 59, D.R.Ll. Adams, MA thesis, University of Wales, 1971, *The Parliamentary Representation of Radnorshire 1536-1832*, p.230-239, C.H. Collins Baker, *The Life and Circumstances of James Brydges, Duke of Chandos*, p.456-457
3. NLW, Price of Norton Deeds, Nos 34,35
4. Bidgood, p.48-49
5. Adams, p.281
6. Collins Baker, p.427, Adams, p.268-269, 281, 304; www.jamesboswell.info/biography/chase-price-mp-leominster-and-radnor
7. Sir Lewis Namier and John Brook (ed, *History of the House of Commons, 1759-90*, Vol 3, p.326-331, C.W. Newman, 'Charles Price and Rousseau', *TRS xliii*, 1973, p.86
8. Namier and Brook, Vol 3 p.330, HCRO, Calendar of Harley Papers, Bundle 59, Norton Manorial Roll, 6.9.1766
9. Bod Lib MS Gough Wales 6, cited by Hatfield, p.20-21
10. HCRO HD'5/14/88, HD 5/15/17, Gwynfryn T. Richards, 'Royal Briefs from the Restoration of the Church in Wales', *JHSCW viii*, 1959, p.42-43
11. The description of the old church is based on D.S. Davies, 'Knighton', *TRS xii* 1942, p.45-46
12. Sir Frederick Eden, *The State of the Poor*, Vol 3, p.900
13. *HT* 2.12.1882
14. PCAO R/D/PHP/13-14
15. *HT* 8.11.1862
16. *HJ* 20.8.1794
17. This section is based on D.S. Davies, 'Knighton', *TRS xii*, 1942, p.41-47
18. Eden, p.900-901, *HJ* 27.4.1796
19. *House of Commons Papers, George III, Reports and Papers 1775-1786*, Vol 31, *House of Commons Papers, George III, Reports and Papers 1717-1788*, Vol 46, Eden, p.901

Chapter 5

1. *HJ* 25.11.1807
2. *HJ* 1.7.1795
3. John Clark, *A General View of the Agriculture of the County of Radnor*, p.22
4. W.H. Howse, *Radnorshire*, p.90
5. Clark 22, Walter Davies, *A General View of the Agriculture of South Wales*, Vol 2, p.288
6. O.R. Ashton, '18th Century Radnorshire. A Population Survey', *TRS xl*, 1975, p.45, 54
7. *HJ* 17.3.1802, 1.4.1807
8. *HJ* 9.3.1826
9. *HJ* 10.10.1821, 1.5.1822, NLW Great Sessions Minute and Imparlance Book, Wales 14.47
10. *HJ* 8.7.1829
11. PCAO, R/UD/KN/A/299 Knighton Tithe Commutation Schedule, 1837
12. NLW, Ormathwaite Papers, FG 1/7, p.371
13. R.C.B. Oliver, *The Squires of Penybont Hall*, p.31-34
14. *HJ* 14.3.1792, 29.7.1818, 22.3.1826
15. *HT* 11.8.1849
16. *HJ* 13.1.1836, *HT* 24.11.1849
17. TNA, PRO, CRES 49/4953
18. *Second Annual Report of the Poor Law Commission*, 1836, p.586, *Third Annual report of the Poor Law Commission*, 1837 p.295-296, 308-309
19. TNA, PRO, MH12/16690, Knighton Union Papers 1836-45, Head to Chadwick
20. MH12/16690, 26.4.1837 Green to Poor Law Commission, 16.2.1840 Mason to Poor Law Commission
21. TNA, PRO, CRES 49/4923, Schedule of Presentments
22. *HJ* 22.7.1803, 8.7.1818

Chapter 6

1. *HT* 14.10.1840
2. *HT* 11.9.1849, 21.11.1849, Tony Hobbs, *The Pubs of Radnorshire*, p.28-49
3. *HT* 1.12.1849,
4. *HT* 1.12.1849, 20.4.1850, 19.2.1853
5. *HT* 10.1.1852, *HJ* 21.2.1853
6. *HJ* 9.7.1853, 4.2.1854
7. *HT* 12.2.1861, *HJ* 27.8.1864
8. *HJ* 5.6.1861, *HT* 22.8.1863, 10.10.1863
9. *HT* 22.4.1837, 12.2.1852, NLW, Walter Davies MSS, Notebook AAB

10. *HJ* 22.4.1837, 26.9.1838
11. *HT* 21.4.1855
12. This section is based on PCAO, R/UD/KN/Q/990/01-03, The Minutes of Knighton Board of Health, 1853-93
13. *HT* 20.7.1878
14. *HT* 27.9.1851, 26.6.1852, 2.10.1852, *HJ* 15.8.1863
15. Except where indicated to the contrary, this section is based on 'The Coming of the Railway' in *Mid-Victorian Knighton*
16. *HT* 22.12.1849, *HJ* 26.12.1849
17. W.C. Maddox, *A History of the Radnorshire Constabulary*, p10
18. *HT* 23.3.1861
19. *HJ* 7.11.1860
20. The main sources for this section: *HT* 26.5.1855, 18.4.1863, *HJ* 10.7.1861, 18.4.1863, 20.2.1864, 2.4.1864, 27.4.1865, *RE* 17.10.1901, 14.5.1914
21. The main sources for this section: *HT* 23.7.1864, 16.3.1867, 26.5.1871, 23.9.1871, *HJ* 18.6.1864, 16.7.1864, 23.7.1864, 30.9.1865
22. TNA PRO CRES 49/4955, 9.1.1883 Gough to Woods and Forests, *HT* 12.8.1880, 19.8.1882
23. *HT* 29.10.1853, 30.5.1857, 24.10.1857
24. *KG* 14.5.1872, *HT* 4.1.1873, *HJ* 11.5.1872
25. www.measuringworth.com/ppoweruk
26. AO R/QS/DE/28, R/QS/DE/TNA, TNA PRO MAF68/567
27. *HJ* 5.9.1859, 23.8.1862
28. *HJ* 26.9.1849, 24.4.1850, 1862
29. *HT* 8.10.1853, *HJ* 6.10.1858
30. Isaac Slater, *Royal National and Commercial Directory of Gloucestershire... and North and South Wales 1858-59*, p64, *HT* 21.7.1855, 25.7.1857, 28.6.1862, *BRE* 11.3.1897
31. This account of the Silurian Mills is based, mainly, on Geoff Ridyard's 'The Silurian Mills, Knighton' in *Melin 20*, 2004
32. Ridyard does not mention this reference to the Mills
33. *KG* 9.3.1875
34. PCAO R/DB/RAD/19/1, The Radnorshire Coal, Lime, and General Supply Company, Director's Minute Book
35. See 'The Radnorshire Company', by 'Observer' in Knighton Rotary Club, *Knighton 1800-1850*

36. TNA PRO CRES 49/4955, 10.11.1882 Woods and Forests to HM Treasury, PCAO R/QS/7E/25 Farrington and Cwmgilla Enclosure Award, PCAO R/QS/DE/19 Knighton Manor Enclosure Award

Chapter 7
1. *HT* 17.8.1872, 2.10.1875
2. PCAO Knighton Local Board Minutes 4.9.1883
3. TNA PRO MAF 68, Knighton parish crop and livestock returns for 1875 1877, 1885-86, 1894-1894-95, 1904-05
4. *HT* 27.4.1872, 31.12.1872
5. *RE* 18.11.1909, 1.5.1913, 23.7.1914, *RS*, 21.12.1913 26.4.1914, 11.7.1914
6. *Slater's Directory of South Wales*, 1880, *Kelly's Directory of South Wales*, 1891
7. TNA PRO MH12 Knighton Union Papers, 1883-84, 17.3.1883 Dr Covernton's Report of 1882 on Knighton Rural Sanitary Area
8. *RE* 15.6.1911, 11.7.1981
9. *BRE* 9.10.1891, 11.2.1897
10. *RS* 1.10.1902
11. *HT* 31.3.1883
12. *HT* 25.3.1905, 1.6.1905, *RE* 20.6.1912
13. *RE* 20.4.1897, 10.4.1902
14. Cadwallader p.112, *HT* 30.5.1857, PCAO Knighton Local Board Minutes, 9.10.1877, 9.7.1878, 10.9.1878, 26.11.1878
15. *HT* 22.6.1878, 17.8.1878, 26.10.1878, 20..9.1879, HJ 29.9.1878
16. *RE* 18.5.1905, 18.5.1911, PCAO R/QS/DE/9 Knighton Enclosure Award
17. *HT* 24.1.1891, 2.5.1891
18. NLW Harpton Court Collection, c/1765
19. *HT* 8.5.1880
20. *RE* 4.5.1899
21. *RE* 7.7.1898, TNA PRO MH 12 Knighton Union Papers 1887-88, 3.5.187 Ricketts to Local Government Board
22. *RE* 16.7.1903, 17.3.1904, 31.3.1904, 14.77.1904, *RS* 16.3.1904
23. *RE* 16.7.1903, 30.7.1903, *RS* 18.2.1904
24. *The Times* 2.9.1892
25. *RS* 24.10.1908
26. Ieuan G. Jones & David Williams, *The Religious Census of 1851*, Vol 1, *South Wales*, p.65
27. *RS* 13.7.1912
28. *RS* 13.7.1912

29. *HT* 26.4.1890
30. TNA PRO MH 12 Knighton Union Papers, 1871-74, 4.1.1874 Deacon to Local Government Board, 1876-76,15.3.1876 Deacon to Local Government Board
31. *HT* 6.5.1882
32. *HT* 2.2.1878
33. *BRE* 15.4.1892
34. This brief biography is based on *RE* 25.3.1929 and www.accessgenealogy.com
35. PCAO W. Hatfield MSS, *Towns and Villages of the Knighton Area*
36. *HT*13.5.1882, *RE* 22.4.19, 22.5.1886, 7.8.1886, 22.4.1943
37. *RE* 28.2.1901,7.9.1905, 30.12.1911, 17.5.1917, 14.2.1924
38. *HT* 25.2.1888, 24.3.1888, *RE* 22.3.1923
39. *RE* 18.5.1905, 8.6.1905, *RS* 12.4.1905, 16.8.1905

Chapter 8
1. *HJ* 3.10.1860
2. Roy Palmer, *The Folklore of Radnorshire*, p31
3. TNA PRO CRES 49/4955, 'Knighton Tolls and Market Hall, 1837-1883, *HT* 25.11.1882
4. *HT* 30.12.1854, *HJ* 29.5.1861
5. *HJ* 3.7.1886, *RE* 31.101907
6. TNA PRO MH 12, Knighton Union Papers, 1834-1845, 21.6.1841 Jones to Poor Law Commission, *HJ* 9.4.1864, *HT* 21.1.1875
7. MH 12 Knighton Union Papers, 1846-1853, 11.8.1847 Mason to Poor Law Commission
8. MH 12 Knighton Union Papers, 1879-80, 22.1.1879 Local Government Board to Knighton Union, Knighton Union Papers, 1884-85, 18.11.1884 Deacon to Local Government Board
9. MH 12 Knighton Union Papers, 1889-90, 12.1.1889 Deacon to Local Government Board
10. MH 12 Knighton Union Papers, 1875-76, Report dated 19.11.1875
11. *HT* 6.3.1886, 3.4.1886, *Rads Echo* 3.12.1886, 4.1.1887
12. *RE* 10.9.1908, 9.12.1909, 9.5.12, 14.11.1912
13. *HT* 28.9.1844, 19.10.1844, 24.10.1857, 28.12.1861, 30.1.1869, *HJ* 20.9.1862
14. The Religious Census, 1851, Vol 1, p.653
15. *HT* 17.7.1875, 17.6.1876, 21.7.1877

16. *BRE* 28.2.1896, *HT* 29.8.1896
17. *BRE* 18.2.1897, 22.4.1897, *RE* 13.7.1899, *RS* 26.4.1899
18. *HJ* 22.11.1862, 6.12.1862
19. *HJ* 22.11.1879
20. *HT* 19.3.1870
21. *A History of Primitive Methodism in the Knighton Circuit*
22. *HT* 9.8.1851, 29.9.1860
23. J. Jones, *History of the Baptists in Radnorshire*, p.86-89, *RE* 19.4.1923
24. *Norton Street Baptist Church. In Commemoration of One Hundred Years of Worship*, *RE* 11.7.1901, 20.4 1905, 28.10.1915
25. *Report of the Commission of Inquiry For South Wales 1844, Minutes of Evidence*, Questions 7243, 7246, 7249-50
26. *HT* 17 November 1848, 1.4.1848, 13.7.1848, 13 July 1850, *HJ* 29.3.1848
27. *HT* 23.5.1840, 15.8.1840
28. *HT* 13.8.1858
29. *RE* 4.5.1899
30. *HT* 23.10.1847, 22.10.1887, *RE* 18.12.1932
31. *HT* 19.3.1864, *HJ* 16.3.1867
32. *HJ* 26.3.1864, 15.2.1873
33. *HJ* 1.12.1855, 23 3.1859, *HT* 5.12.1857
34. *HT* 13.5.1882, *RE* 22.4.1943
35. *HT* 4.2.1860, 3.3.1860
36. *HT* 10.3.1860, 21.7.1883
37. *HJ* 27.6.1860, 14.7.1860
38. *HT* 9.4.1882, G. Archer Parfitt (ed) *Radnorshire Volunteers. A Regimental History of Radnorshire, 1539-1968*, p42
39. *KG* 28.9.1869, *HT* 2.9.1871, *BRE* 21.8.1891, 26.8.1897
40. R.J. Moore Colyer, 'Gentlemen, Horses and the Turf', *WHR*, Vol 16, No 1, 1992, Howse, *Radnorshire*, p.187-88, *HJ* 15.3.1862
41. *HJ* 15.3.1862, 19.4.1862, 26.4.1862, 11.43.1863, *HT* 27.4.1862
42. *HT* 7.4.1883
43. *HJ* 23.4.1864, *HT* 26.1.1878
44. *RS* 17.12.1902, *RE* 5.6.1918
45. *HJ* 1.8.1860, 11.3.1863, and 19.8.1865. I gratefully acknowledge the assistance of Jim Morris on this section. His knowledge of Knighton cricket is second to none
46. *HT* 13.5.1876, *RS* 6.2.1901
47. *HT* 28.10.1882, 9.8.1883

48. *HT* 18.1.1887, *RE* 26.2.2899, 15.9.1904, 9.7.1908
49. *HT*, 6.10.1883, 2.9.1884
50. *HT* 25.2.1888
51. *RE* 8.10.1899, 21.12.1905, 6.9.1908, 31.3.1910, *RE* 4.4.1914
52. *RE* 7.11.1901, 24.4.1913, 8.5.1913, 28.6.1913

Chapter 9
1. Parfitt, p.99
2. *RE* 27.5.1915, 7.10.1915
3. *RE* 27.5.1915, 26.4.1917 27.9.1917, 11.7.1918, 16.12.1918
4. *RE* 7.8.1919 mentions 'the 200 or so' who had returned home
5. *RE* 22.6.1916
6. *RE* 29.10.1914, 12.11.1914, 19.11.1914, 26.11.1914
7. *RE* 12.8.1914, 27.8.1914, 22.10.1914, 24.12.1914, 25.11.1915, 3.12.1915
8. *RE* 8.3.1917, 22.3.1917
9. *RE* 5.7.1917
10. *RE* 18.2.1915, 25.2.1915, 11.11.1915
11. *RE* 1.8.1918
12. *RE* 10.4.1915, 13.1.1916, 25.4.1918
13. *RE* 14.11.1918
14. *RE* 24.7.1919
15. *RE* 30.6.1921, 7.7.1921, 26.11.1925
16. *RE* 26.2.1928, 2.8.1928, 22.10.1931
17. *RE* 15.2.1917
18. *RE* 10.7.1919, 6.10.1921
19. J. Owen Pryce *et al*, *A Review of Population Changes in Mid-Wales, 1901-1951*, p.126
20. *RE* 28.6.1928, 6.12.1928, 1.12.1932, 21.9.1933, 12.3.1936
21. PCAO, R/D/GNX/Box 19, Deeds deposited by Green and Nixson, *RE* 14.12.1922
22. *RE* 25.1.1917, 22.10.1925, Alice Blackburn, *Alice's Knighton*, p.43
23. *RE* 22.8.1918, 23.1919, 22.1.1920, 7.9.1922, 17.5.1923
24. *RE* 24.7.1919, 16.8.1929, Knighton UDC Minutes, 4.12.1921, 14.10.1925, 14.2.1934, 14.3.1934
25. *RE* 24.1.1935
26. *RE* 20.2.1928, 16.3..1928
27. *RE* 9.3.1933
28. *RE* 10.9.1936, UDC Minutes 12.12.1934
29. *RE* 17.8.1922, PCAO R/D/GNX/Box 18, Documents relating to the Knighton Electric Supply Company

30. *RE* 4.1.1923, 1.3.1923, 3.9.1923
31. *RE* 16.10.1930, 25.8.1932, UDC Minutes 9.10.1919, 12.11.1919, 8.8.1928, 10.6.1931
32. *RE* 6.11.1919, 7.7.1920, 19.8.1920, 7.10.1920
33. *RE* 7.7.1913, 15.1.1920, 16.5.1933, PCRO R/D/GNX/ Box 16
34. *RE* 3.2.1927
35. *RE* 30.4.1931, 16.9.1937, 29.2.1940, Colin P.F. Hughes, 'A History of Schools in Radnorshire: The Knighton Area', *TRS lxv*, 1995, p.55
36. *RE* 23.2.1922, 29.1.1926
37. *RE* 17.2.1921, UDC Minutes 17.2.1921, 19.3.1925, 9.4.1925
38. *RE* 21.7.1932, 25.8.1932, 17.11.1932, 19.3.1936, 28.5.1936, UDC Minutes 11.6.1935, 10.7.1935, 12.2.1936, 11.11.1936, 13.1.1937, 9.6.1931
39. *RE* 20.11.1924, 23.12.1926, 14.7.1932, 25.7.1932
40. *RE* 12.10.1923, 28.8.1924, 12.2.1925, 5.3.1928
41. *RE* 31.1.1929, 14.5.1931, 5.10.1933
42. *RE* 13.8.1935
43. *RE* 8.12.1932
44. *RE* 15.2.1934
45. *RE* 5.3.1925, 18.6.1926
46. *RE* 21.5.1931, 12.5 1932, 27.6.1935
47. *RE* 15.9.1910, 26.4.1922, 27.10.1932
48. *RE* 30.10.1919, 10.3.1921, 3.5.1928
49. *RE* 11.10.1934
50. *RE* 31.3.1938, UDC Minutes 18.7.1938, 31.10.1938
51. *RE* 20.10.1938
52. *RE* 2.6.1938, 29.9.1938, 16.2.1939, 13.4.1939, 14.5.1939, 22.6.1939

Chapter 10
1. *RE* 23.3.1944
2. *RE* 21.11.1940, 2.5.1941, 20.11.1941
3. PCAO W.C. Maddox, *History of the Radnorshire Civil Defence Scheme, 1935-46*, unpublished typescript, p.4
4. *RE* 25.7.1940, 22.8.1940, 29.6.1944, PCAO, Knighton Rural District Council Minutes, 4.7.1940
5. Parfitt, p.127-28, *RE* 4.5.1944
6. *RE* 20.5.1943, 4.5.1944
7. *RE* 7.8.1941, 21.8.1941
8. *RE* 21.8.1941, 23.10.1941
9. *RE* 20.2.1941, 22.5.1941, 25.8.1941

10. *RE* 7.9.1939, 25.7.1940, Knighton RDC Minutes 1.9.1939
11. *RE* 10.7.1941, 27.7.1944, RDC Minutes 13.2.1941, 10.4.1941
12. C.P.F. Hughes, p.54
13. RDC Minutes 3.7.1941, 11.1.1945
14. RDC Minutes 17.12.1942, 14.1.1943, *RE* 21.1.1943
15. *RE* 1.8.1940, 9.9.1943, *Mid Wales Journal* 17.6.2011
16. *RE* 18.10.1945
17. PDF Hughes, p.57, *RE* 28.11.1940, 26.2.1942, 6.8.1942
18. TNA PRO MAF 68 Knighton parish crop and livestock returns, 1939,1943,1945, R.M. Deakins, 'Agriculture in Radnorshire in World War II and After' *TRS lxxv*, 2005, p.124-28
19. *RE* 8.4.1943, 6.5.1943
20. *RE* 17.5.1945, 4.6.1945, 30.8.1945, 13.6.1946
21. *RE* 30.3.1944
22. *RE* 12.12.1946, 19.12.1946, 13.2.1947, 20.2.1947, UDC Minutes, 4.12.1946
23. *RE* 2.5.1946, 23.12.1948, 20.10.1949, UDC Minutes, 26.4.1946, 10.7.1946, 12.2.1947, 14.5.1947, 3.11.1948, 10.8.1949
24. UDC Minutes, 10.5.1950, 26.5.1950, 29.7.1959, May 1964, 15.3.1972, 12.4.1972
25. *RE* 18.4.1946, 16.1.1947
26. *RE* 31.7.1947, 4.11.1948, UDC Minutes 12.2.1947
27. *RE* 21.8.1947, UDC Minutes MOH Report May 1964, 21.10.1964, 25.1.1965, 12.4.1967, 30.4.1969, 28.1 1970
28. UDC Minutes 13.6.1962, 22.2.1967, 19.2.1969, 16.12.1970, 8.3.1972, 22.3.1972, 14.6.1972, 11.4.1973
29. UDC Minutes 24.4.1963, 10.9.1969
30. UDC Minutes 26.1.1972
31. UDC Minutes MOH Report 1961, 1962, 1967, 1968, 1971
32. J. Owen Pryce, p.118
33. TNA PRO MAF 68 Knighton parish crop and livestock returns 1945, 1955, 1965
34. See 'Observer's article on 'The Radnorshire Society' in Knighton Rotary Club, (ed), *Knighton 1800-1950*
35. UDC Minutes 14.6.1967, 2.10.1968, 20.8.1969, 10.9.1969, 9.9.1972
36. UDC Minutes 15.5.1946, 12.2.1947, 10.2.1965
37. UDC Minutes 9.9.1953, 8.5.1963, 12.6.1963, MOH Report for 1963
38. UDC Minutes 21.8.1964, 8.2.1967
39. UDC Minutes 7.3.1967, 12.4.1967, 13.1.1971, 15.3.1971, 29.3.1971
40. *RE* 26.7.1945, 24.2.1949
41. UDC Minutes 14.10.1953, 24.9.1955, 19.8.1970, 10.5.1972
42. *RE* 30.7.1947
43. *RE* 18.5.1944, 1.6.1944, www. ukrockfestivals.com/knighton-festival-1970. html

Chapter 11
1. See 'The Radnorshire Company' by 'Observer' in Knighton Rotary Club (ed), *Knighton 1800-1950*
2. Town Council Minutes, 16.12.1981, 16.11.1984, 26.6.1998, 18.1.1999, 19.1.2000
3. J. Owen Pryce, p.126, Office of National Statistics, www.neighbourhoodstatistics.gov. uk, www.harrytuffin.co.uk
4. J. Owen Pryce, p.126, www. neighbourhoodstatistics.gov.uk
5. www.neighbourhoodstatistics.gov.uk
6. UDC Minutes, 24.1.1955, MOH Report for 1960, 12.4.1967, 9.4.1969, 25.11.1971, 15.12.1976
7. www.neighbourhoodstatistics.gov.uk
8. UDC Minutes, 26.3.26.3.1969, 13.5.1970, 28.6.1972
9. Town Council Minutes, 15.5.1991, 16.7.1997, 15.9.1999
10. Town Council Minutes, 21.10.1981, 15.5.1991
11. www.neighbourhoodstatistics.gov.uk
12. R.M. Deakins, p.128-29, 131
13. TNA PRO MAF 68/4523, /4961,/5460,/5986
14. R.M. Deakins, p.129, 131
15. The data in this section is derived from www. neighbourhoodstatistics.gov.uk
16. Wales Rural Observatory, *Small and Market Towns in Rural Wales*, p.107, 109

Index

Wainwright, Mr A.C. 101
Walker, Mrs 160
Walsh, Arthur H.J. (third Lord Ormathwaite)
    99, 105
  Lady Jane 71
  Sir John Benn 51, 72
Walsh and Co. 79
Walsingham, Thomas 14
Walters, E. 177, 182-3
Walton 3
Warren, Henry 71
Wars of the Roses, the 15
Watkin, Morgan 33
Watkins, Mr C.E. 177
  George 75
  Lt Col H.B. 165, 168
  Tudor 172, 178
Weale, William 101
Weale and Lloyd 123
Webb, Samuel 58
Wellington, duke of 38
Welsh, Dr 99
Welsh Church, disestablishment 98, 99-100,
    102-3

West of England Agricultural Labourers'
    Association 89
Weston 3
Weyman, Edward 71
Whitehead, Ralph 136
Whitton 29, 58, 170
Wigmore Castle 6, 25
Willey Court 28
  Hall 30
Williams, Mr 66
  Revd W. 101
Williams and Jones, Messrs 97
Wills, Thomas F. 85
Wilson, John 85, 122, 123
wives, sale of 124
Womaston 3
Woodburn, W.S. 74
Woodfield, Paul 4, 9, 10
Woolley, John 33
Woosnam family 41
Worcester 55
Workers' Union 89
Wright, Dr 25-6, 27